Information Fantasies

Information Fantasies

Precarious Mediation in Postsocialist China

XIAO LIU

UNIVERSITY OF MINNESOTA PRESS
MINNEAPOLIS LONDON

The University of Minnesota Press gratefully acknowledges financial support for the publication of this book from the Chiang Ching-kuo Foundation for International Scholarly Exchange.

A different version of chapter 1 was previously published as "Magic Waves, Extrasensory Powers, and Nonstop Instantaneity: Imagining the Digital beyond Digits," *Grey Room*, no. 63 (Spring 2016): 42–69. A different version of chapter 2 was previously published as "The Curious Case of a Robot Doctor: 'Human,' Labor, and Expert Systems," *Frontiers of Literary Studies in China* 10, no. 4 (2016): 646–73; reprinted by permission from Higher Education Press, copyright 2016.

Every effort was made to obtain permission to reproduce material in this book. If any proper acknowledgment has not been included here, we encourage copyright holders to notify the publisher.

Copyright 2019 by the Regents of the University of Minnesota

All rights reserved. No part of this publication may be reproduced, stored in a retrieval system, or transmitted, in any form or by any means, electronic, mechanical, photocopying, recording, or otherwise, without the prior written permission of the publisher.

Published by the University of Minnesota Press
111 Third Avenue South, Suite 290
Minneapolis, MN 55401-2520
http://www.upress.umn.edu

Printed in the United States of America on acid-free paper

The University of Minnesota is an equal-opportunity educator and employer.

Library of Congress Cataloging-in-Publication Data
Names: Liu, Xiao, author.
Title: Information fantasies : precarious mediation in postsocialist China / Xiao Liu.
Description: Minneapolis : University of Minnesota Press, [2019] | Includes bibliographical references and index. |
Identifiers: LCCN 2018026856 (print) | ISBN 978-1-5179-0273-5 (hc) | ISBN 978-1-5179-0274-2 (pb)
Subjects: LCSH: Information society—China. | China—Intellectual life—1976—Technological forecasting—China. | Future, The, in popular culture.
Classification: LCC HN740.Z9 I5678 2019 (print) | DDC 303.48/330951—dc23
LC record available at https://lccn.loc.gov/2018026856

UMP BmB 2019

Contents

Introduction "Information Pot" and Postsocialist
Politics of Mediation　　1

1　Extrasensory Powers, Magic Waves, and Information
　 Explosion: Imagining the Digital　　39
2　The Curious Case of a Robot Doctor: Rethinking Labor,
　 Expert Systems, and the Interface　　83
3　The "Ultrastable System" and the New Cinema　　119
4　Affective Form: Advertising, Information Aesthetics,
　 and Experimental Writing in the Market Economy　　159
5　Liminal Mediation and the Cinema Redefined　　195

Epilogue The Virtual Past(s) of the Future(s)　　255

Acknowledgments　　263

Notes　　267

Index　　301

INTRODUCTION

"Information Pot" and Postsocialist Politics of Mediation

The photo in Figure 1 was taken in 1993 at a gathering of *qigong* practitioners in west suburban Beijing. Since the late 1970s, a *"qigong* fever" had swept across post-Mao China, attracting more than 60 million regular practitioners. This *"qigong* fever" involved many high-level Party officials and research institutes and universities across the country, as well as leading scientists, such as Qian Xuesen, a most renowned and politically influential scientist, whose name is associated with China's missile and space projects. In the photo, the practitioners, obviously in a meditative trance, each was wearing a cooking pot on their heads. Dubbed "information pots," they were expected to receive information from the outer space so that a "resonance between heaven and mankind" (天人感应) could be formed.

A cosmological view that was formed and developed around the last three centuries BC, when a unified and centralized political order arose for the first time in the history of China, "resonance between heaven and mankind" provided legitimacy and guidance to the imperial power and its rulership. In this cosmic world, the macrocosm of the heaven and the microcosms of the state and the body became a single manifold set of resonant systems.[1] Yet this view of resonance between cosmos and body gained new meaning in this contemporary context, not only because the cosmological view was now transformed for new "worlding" practices, but the resonance, considered as revealing of an ideal "human and heaven"

1

relationship (tianren guan 天人观), was also embraced by Chinese scientists and intellectuals as the philosophical foundation for a more holistic understanding of the human body. The keyword that bound both top-level scientists and ordinary people, official concerns and popular appeal around qigong, was "information." Qian Xuesen, for example, was enthusiastically promoting the study of qigong as a shortcut to find out a secret mechanism of more direct and immediate communication between the human body and the information environment. The CCP and the government, having recently officially announced the end of the Cultural Revolution and reorganized themselves around Deng Xiaoping's economic development plans, were eager to catch up with the Western developed countries and ride on the wave of the "information revolution." In 1978, Deng Xiaoping, the architect of China's post-Mao reforms, called for the rapid development in electronic computing, cybernetics, and automation technology at the National Conference of Science. Various predictions of an incoming "information society" gained wide circulation and attention in China, especially with the translation of Alvin Toffler's book *The Third Wave* into Chinese and his visits to China in person in 1983 and 1988. (The Chinese translation of *The Third Wave* first appeared in Hong Kong in 1981, and a full translation of the book in mainland China was published in 1983.) In both official and intellectual discourses and in the scientific and popular imagination, "information"

Figure 1. "Information Pot."

was fantasized as the magic force that would bring post-Mao China into a new era. Tied to what I call "information fantasies" in the post-Mao late 1970s and 1980s, the scenario in the photo crystallizes the anxieties and aspirations, as well as the confluences and contradictions, of various social forces and ideologies in a drastically changing society.

This scenario of "information pots" is also a fascinating case of media and mediation. I should note several points about the photo:

First, the fact that people were collecting information from the air suggests that the space without was here understood as an active space full of information.[2] The pots used for information collection expressed the desire to embrace an uninterrupted connectivity disregarding the boundaries of the terra. This connectivity through the air and the outer space was facilitated by other media technologies new to 1980s China, such as wireless broadcasts and satellite technology. China successfully launched the first man-made satellite in the 1970s. The use of synchronous orbiting satellite technology for communication and television broadcasts started around the mid-1980s. Figure 3 is a photo submitted to a photography competition organized by the Chinese Institute of Electronics in 1984. In this photo, a set of satellite antennas sticks out from an ordinary residential courtyard. The enclosed structure of the yard appears to set boundaries to a seemingly autonomous space, but the antennas reach into the sky, bringing a virtual mobility to the courtyard by connecting it to an invisible network of information circulation. This scenario became increasingly common across the country. Shu Ting, the famous female "misty" poet living in Fujian province, once described the skyscape of her city as: "This is my city / and I long for your arrival / Chimneys, cables, fishbone antenna / Knit a net across the interrupted sky."[3] Since the late 1970s, such antennas had densely occupied the rooftops in Guangdong, a south China province adjacent to Hong Kong. Nicknamed "fishbone antennas" because of their shape, most of them were set up illegally by local residents for the purpose of stealing television signals from Hong Kong.[4] Throughout the 1980s, these antennas had constantly been the object of controversy, speaking to the contradictions between the liberal desire of opening up and the persistence of control, between new consumer desires stimulated by the

Figure 2. Book covers of the Chinese translations of *The Third Wave*.

第三次浪潮

〔美〕阿尔温·托夫勒 著

朱志焱 潘琪 张焱 译

new media environment and a late socialist system that was still wary of the corruption from the "sugar-coated bullets" of Western capitalism. It was not until 1992, when the programs of four television channels in Hong Kong were officially included into the television networks of Guangdong, that the history of illegal fishbone antennas ended. Incidentally, another more conspicuous-looking big cooking pot-shaped type of satellite receiver that became popular around this time was nicknamed "satellite pot" (卫星锅) in Chinese. "Information pots," "fishbone antennas," and "satellite pots" all reached into the sky and generated new fantasies of mobility and connectivity transcending the boundaries of the terra and conjoined humans and information environments.

Half mythical, this new vision of an enveloping information environment was spurred by rapid developments in wireless communication in 1980s China, which turned airwaves into a most powerful medium in both the scientific and popular imagination. Airwaves are about ubiquitous connectivity. The imaginary of mysterious "waves" as the premium media of connectivity appeared precisely at a moment of China's Opening, when the boundaries formed during the Cold War seemed to soften and dissolve. However, in retrospect, this vision of a boundary-free

Figure 3. Antenna. Originally titled "*Xiaoyuan shenchu*" [Deep in the courtyard], photographed by Qiao Jian. From *Electronics World*, no. 10 (1984).

globe turned out to be too idealistic or even liberal-minded. Today as China boasts the world's second-largest economy and the world factory for various sleek-surfaced e-products, the deteriorated labor conditions at Foxconn and other contract manufacturers of transnational corporations continue to make headlines. If "waves" as a magic medium promised ubiquitous connectivity, the connections were always uneven and precarious when the negotiations of and conflicts between the local and the global, between socialist sentiments and capitalist logic, constantly inflected the fluctuations of the waves. As I shall argue throughout the book, though "information fantasies" took over in post-Mao China, there were always ambiguities and discontents toward the advent of the purported "information society." In this sense, the setting of late 1970s and 1980s China provides a tension-ridden site for a critique of the ineluctable connectivity and for reflections on how the futuristic discourses of "information society" appropriated and competed with socialist imaginations.

Second, striking in the photo is a belief in the necessity of a seamless incorporation of the human body into information environments. The human body is conceived simultaneously as a medium with immense potentiality and as an inadequate medium that always requires some facilitation, such as that of the "information pot," to strengthen its connectivity. It is precisely this precarious nature of mediation that gives rise to various politics and technocratic visions in manipulating the body and making it the locus for the competition of powers and economic interests. Although the "information pot" scenario appeared as a revival of an ancient philosophical idea, the human body in this scenario was more of a black box for information input and output. The body not only received information from outer space, but it also exchanged information, and thus formed feedback loops between the body and the environment. This had to do with the dissemination of cybernetics, information theory, and systems theory in China, which Qian Xuesen and other enthusiasts adopted as a new frontier of scientific research, but, more important, as a method for analyzing human society, economic structure, Chinese history, and even literature and the arts.

The human body as a medium is not a new phenomenon. Traditional Chinese philosophy and religious practices, as well as spiritualism in the nineteenth century, had featured different versions of the body-as-a-medium within different epistemological modes.[5] The increasingly pervasive computational environments bring the human body to the center of current media studies, especially in the new media scholarship on digitization and networks.[6] But the emergence of an "information body"—the body as a medium for information processing—in China in the 1980s, on the one hand, registered the ways in which contemporary media technologies transform the perceptions and interactions of the human body with the world, and, on the other hand, was a discursive construction deeply entrenched in the politics of the postsocialist world, accompanying the production and unleashing of consumer desire in the process of marketization and concurrent with the privilege of "information workers" over factory workers and peasants, who were once valorized as socialist subjects.[7] This "information body," however, is not merely a passive receiver or transmitter of information. Mark Hansen in his *New Philosophy for New Media* highlights the role of the human body in "enframing" information and the process through which the body, in conjunction with various apparatuses, renders information perceptible and gives forms to digital images. He argues that because digital data "explodes" the framed image that is the basic unit of photography and film, the human body is empowered as a "convertor" of polymorphous digital data, able to actualize singular experience.[8] According to Hansen, this process demonstrates the human body as a final site to resist the universalizing and homogenizing power of capitalism epitomized in the unlimited interconvertibility of digital data. Because of its "sensorimotor power to create the unpredictable, the experimental, the new," the body becomes a site that can resist the capitalist imposition of universal exchangeability as manifested in digital convergence.[9] An insightful intervention as it is, this idealized notion of the human body nonetheless is ahistorical, abstracted from any specific socioeconomic conditions. Hansen assumes that the body itself is automatically capable of the resistance.[10] My task here is to historicize the ways in which the informationization of the body in post-Mao China concurred with the process of depoliticizing political subjects and with the transformation of revolutionary "people" into postsocialist subjects. This process was exhilarating because it stimulated utopian and techno-futuristic imaginations and unleashed desires, senses of freedom, and aspirations for multiple possibilities, but it also turned out to be depressing and dystopian. As socialist subjects were emptied out and marginalized, the human body turned into a ceaseless information-processing machine for value extraction and was increasingly subject to various ideological and marketing "information bombs."

Finally, but no less significant, in the photo is a cooking pot, usually not used for communication, turned into what we may call a medium, which produces and facilitates new relations between the human body and the information environment. This transformation of a pot into a medium destabilizes a fixed, conventional conception of medium and raises the question of what media do. Alexander Galloway, Eugene Thacker, and McKenzie Wark have recently expressed dissatisfaction with the general understanding of media as devices and apparatuses in current media studies because this understanding obstructs broader discussions of the modes of mediation. Instead of asking what media are, they call for probing more into the question of "what is mediation?"[11] Moving away from the fixed, narrow notion of media as merely devices, we may ask: How is mediation generated and what is generated from the process of mediation? In this instance of the information pot, the becoming of medium provokes us to rethink mediation as the production of relations and the redrawing of boundaries. The reconfiguration of boundaries in both social and technical realms, as Katherine Hayles remarks, is a most salient feature of cybernetics.[12] Cybernetics provides a vision of information flowing across humans and machines, life forms and nonlife forms, which is also a vision of ubiquitous mediation. Yet the seemingly obstruction-free information flows are never a politically neutral process but, as Hayles insightfully points out, are imbricated in imperial powers and the expansion of capitalism in its drastic removal of and redrawing of boundaries. I would argue that, in the context of 1980s China, the seemingly free information flows have to be considered as an effect of mediation that involves constant negotiation of contradictions and reconfiguration of relations and boundaries. It is therefore crucial to examine the conditions that make the information flows possible—

the redistribution of powers, the eliding and reconstruction of regional and class differences.

Such a critique of cybernetics is yet to be done, especially beyond the context of Western developed countries, which are often assumed as the "origin" and the main ground for the development of information science and technology.[13] Moving away from the one-directional influence mode, this project contextualizes the circulation of cybernetics and informatics in post–Cold War geopolitics and examines the "information fantasies" in post-Mao China as inseparable from the boundary-destroying and boundary-redrawing processes in various social arenas, the reshuffling of Cold War powers, and the emergence of new sorts of connectivity that were generated during socioeconomic changes. The sense of liberation and excitement accompanied by these processes inspired imaginations of information technologically advanced futures, but the boundary-breaking forces of the market also engendered a postsocialist precariousness that put social values, morality, and human identities in constant crises. It is precisely such rich contradictions of post-Mao China that provide me with a pivotal point to launch a critique of the postwar discourses of cybernetics in explicating its complex entanglement with postsocialist politics.

Not long after the "information pot" photo was taken, the CCP changed its tolerating and endorsing policy in 1994, denouncing *qigong* as a "pseudo-science," which eventually ended the decade-long "*qigong* fever." In the same year, full internet connectivity was achieved in mainland China. Although there had been burgeoning local networks and restricted access to the internet among research universities in Beijing, Chengdu, Shanghai, and other big cities since the late 1980s, it was not until 1994 that a full access to the World Wide Web was realized. The decade of the 1980s before the arrival of the internet witnessed dramatic social changes in Deng Xiaoping's China. While the violent suppression of nationwide demonstrations mainly led by college students on June 4, 1989, put an end to speculations about varied possibilities of the future, the overnight color-changing in Eastern Europe and the dissolution of the Soviet Union in 1989 and 1990 were assumed to signify the end of the Cold

War. In 1992, Deng accelerated market reforms and China's integration into the global market. Today China is never more deeply enmeshed in the global information capitalism. According to Yuezhi Zhao and Dan Schiller, with an average growth rate of more than 25 percent, the China-based information technology industry had already become the world's fourth-largest by 2000. Many enterprises in the information industry are joint ventures or are operated with influence from foreign shareholders, and the enormous Chinese market has been seen as having irresistible appeal by transnational corporations.[14] In other words, China's transformations into postsocialism and its integration into the global information systems took place simultaneously as two intertwined processes.

I will examine these intertwined processes by focusing on the information fantasies in post-Mao China from the late 1970s to the end of the 1980s. I will also unearth a neglected history of China's participation in the global production and flows of information technology and imaginations before the advent of the internet in China in the 1990s. Providing a site-specific, historically situated case, I question the often overgeneralized media history and media theory that limit the discussion on the transition from analogue to digital within the context of North America and Western Europe. By bringing in the postsocialist specificities of a non-Western country, I hope to shed new light on issues such as digitization, cybernetic control, the relation between human body and image, the imbrication of affect and the interface, and the transformations of cinema in new media environments, all of which are of great concern in current media studies. Methodologically, by focusing on information and media practices before the general popularization of digital media and the internet in China, I will shift from the fetish with the digital to a historical account of imagining and repositioning the digital in a society undergoing drastic changes. Moving beyond the ossified division between the analogue versus the digital, I will delineate a historically specific account of the emergence of new media, which I argue is not determined by the technology of digitization alone but is shaped by a set of technocultural imaginations and practices with the advent of the global conditions of postsocialism at the turn of the 1980s.

Media and Mediation

Consider Galloway, Thacker, and Ward's recent proposal of shifting the focus from the study of media to the question of mediation. Criticizing Friedrich Kittler and Marshall McLuhan for their fixation on the "media-centric nature of media," Galloway argues that their elevation of substrate and media objects over the modes of mediation often risks agglomerating difference into reified objects, whereas a philosophy of mediation tends to "proliferate multiplicity."[15] This substitution of reified media objects for mediation, according to Galloway, induces a dichotomy that posits "the dead junk of the hypomnemata" against the "good and balanced human specimen."[16] In other words, the narrow understanding of media as a discrete and institutionalized substrate such as radio, film, and television ignores the specific histories and local logics of technologies and their imbrication with social forces, reducing multiple, complex forces of mediation into "one" form of media object, which consequently obscures the competitive "origins" and heterogeneous histories of media technologies. Moreover, the false dichotomy between reified media objects and human beings fails to acknowledge the constant reconfiguration of human-technical entanglement and their boundary in the processes of mediation. As Jussi Parikka remarks, it would be more productive to take media studies as "less a unified field than a discursive, institutional and theoretical strategy to carve out a specific angle within existing disciplines and ideas," with the focus on "the creative processuality and ontology of this existence that comes out in slightly differing ways that are able to reflect on its own conditions of material existence."[17]

Tracing the genesis of the media concept, John Guillory tells us that the concept of a medium of communication was absent in the English language until the nineteenth century, its emergence more a response to the proliferation of new technical media such as the telegraph and phonograph.[18] Yet the notion of mediation followed a different path, referring less to the operation of technical media and more to a broader and more universal process to govern relations among different terms of thought or domains of reality. In the Continental philosophical tradition, for Hegel, for instance, mediation is a key term that involves a dialectic of relations such as between subject and object, mind and world, which point toward, as Guillory accounts, the "reconciliatory moments" along the trajectory of one's "peculiar self-generating dialectic."[19] This understanding of mediation as a dialectic of relations and a process becomes fundamental to sociological theory and especially to the Marxist tradition, which dwells on notions such as social totality and mediatory agencies. "Mediation" in philosophical and social theory thus deals with broader scopes of contacts, conflicts, negotiations between different realms, and agents and objects, rather than with the narrow sense of communication that is dependent upon technical media. Guillory thus comments that the misleading "extrapolation of a process of mediation from the fact of a particular communicative medium (speech, writing, print) depended not on the incorporation of the concept of medium into a more general conceptual framework, but the reverse, a reduction of the social totality to communication as its representative instance."[20] Guillory holds Charles Sanders Peirce responsible for this reduction, whose semiotics, according to him, reduces "notions of totality—the world or human society—to the instance of symbolic exchange," and whose generalization of social theory from the instance of communication, language, or writing, consequently, also propelled the formation and the methods of structuralism, communication studies, and information theory.[21] Guillory's insight resonates with Galloway's critique of "media-centric" media studies for the fixation on the "dead junk" of media objects that leads to the neglect of the processes of mediation, which also in turn obscures the constant redefinition of "medium" per se in shifting social relations and epistemological realms beyond its technical definition alone.

Indeed, a move toward mediation necessarily entails a reassessment of the role of media in relation to society. Often considered as the vehicle for message transmission, media presumably reflect social reality. This view of reflection is dominant among certain traditions of cultural and media studies, which assumes that media contents are the representation of social issues, whether truthful or distorted. Derived from the base-superstructure formula that separates the material production and reproduction from the political, juridical aspects and especially from art works and ideas, this objectivist mode of reflection assumes that art and media passively represent social reality, which reifies "reality" and social life into static objects rather than taking them as a material social process. In contrast, mediation is intended to describe an active process, as Raymond Williams ingeniously puts it, "an act of intercession, reconciliation, or interpretation between adversaries and strangers."[22] This mode of mediation avoids the direct causal or determinist relations between the assumedly separated realms of the base and the superstructure; nor is the mediation necessarily seen as distortion or disguise. In his explication of mediation, Williams also cautions against the assumption of "separate and pre-existent areas or orders of reality."[23] In other words, the mediating process is not determined by prior natures of autonomous areas or actants, nor do any actants remain unchanged in the mediating process. In this sense, Williams in fact proposes a theory of mediation without medium, as he argues: "All active relations between different kinds of being and consciousness are inevitably mediated, and this process is not a separable agency—a 'medium'—but intrinsic to the properties of the related kinds."[24] If mediation is inevitable and ubiquitous, and all beings are simultaneously mediating and being mediated, nothing can be alienated from this mediation process as a static object called medium: there are no media.

A special issue of the *Grey Room* on "new German media theory" shares a similar vision. In the editor's introduction, Eva Horn begins with the impossibility of finding a common ground for defining media, as the field of media studies expands to include "doors and mirrors, computers and gramophones, electricity and newspapers, television and telescopes, archives and automobiles, water and air, information and noise, numbers and calendars, images, writing, and voice," all of which fall into the purview of media studies.[25] Such an expansion is a significant step beyond the conventional notions of mass media and technical media that appear as discrete substrate highly unified under the names such as radio and film. Some of the most ambitious media studies scholarship in recent years moves beyond the narrow definition of media as message-bearing institutions to environments, infrastructures, and technics of affordance.[26] This shifting understanding of media not only reorients media studies from its narrow concentration on representation contents, but it also questions the base-superstructure dichotomy by emphasizing the material effects of media.

Rather than simply including any given objects in the rapidly expanding purview of media studies, this shift in fact raises the methodological question as to whether the expansion leads to merely a reconceptualization of media on the ontological level or an investigation into the processes of mediation around which material, social forces are mobilized and reassembled for the production and reconfiguration of relations. A shift in emphasis onto the processes of mediation means to forgo any transhistorical concept of media but instead looks into the "becoming" (and disappearance) of medium in historically specific circumstances. Once "medium" is no longer taken for granted as a given object, the notion of "medium," in Eva Horn's words, "reduces to a fragile and even ephemeral state of 'in-between-ness,' as much a moment (let alone an object) of separation as of mediation, a moment taken by a virtuality becoming an actuality, a moment of structuring and encoding and thus of the creation of order, but also the source of disruption and 'noise.'"[27] These moments highlight the ever-shifting terms of mediation that take the form of temporal and spatial reorganization, a "worlding" process that generates new relations, conflicts, and negotiations.

Indeed, the shift in focus to the processes of mediation countervails the fetish of "new media" and their technological forms. Computers, the internet, the iCloud—all these digital media and network communication technologies have been invested with game-changing powers that are expected to bring human beings to a brand-new world with promises of unprecedented wealth, democracy, and freedom. Today, legends of Silicon Valley miracles and icons of tech-gurus such as Steve Jobs and Mark Zuckerberg again and again reinforce the idea that revolutions will come from "garage inventions" of tech geeks. Devices such as "smart" phones and touchpads are fetishized as the objects of desire and new fashions, while the iCloud and pervasive Wi-Fi connections invoke simultaneously uncanny intimacy and mysterious awe of the "digital sublime," as dubbed by Vincent Mosco.[28] The myth surrounding digital technology, as Mosco demonstrates, can find its corresponding formations of mythic pronouncements around past technological advances such as from the telephone to the radio.[29] The enshrining of the digital, as it happens, can be found in the long history of capitalist reification of social relations as alienated objects for commodity fetish and the fabrication of ideological myths. In this sense, it is necessary to echo Guillory's insight here that mediation should not be reduced to technical media and communication.

This, however, is not to deny the social transformations that occurred with the ubiquity of microprocessors and communication networks, nor is it to ignore the materiality and material effects of technologies. In fact, the enormous weight and prominence that digital media have accumulated should be taken seriously as revealing the changes in ways in which our so-called information society is organized and operating. James Beniger sees the ascendance of computation and communication technology as the natural extensions of what he calls the "Control Revolution," already in process since the late nineteenth century. The arrival of the "information society," according to Beniger, should be seen as a response to the control crisis unleashed by the Industry Revolution when "the continuous extraction, reorganization, and distribution of environmental inputs into final consumption" increased to an unprecedented degree.[30] This crisis was tackled by the rise of bureaucratic organizations and rationalization, with fast developments in information-processing and communication technologies, leading to distinct areas of information management. The proliferation of microprocessors since the 1970s, as Beniger points out, introduced a new stage that witnessed the convergence of mass media, telecommunication, and computing in "a single infrastructure of control at the most macro level."[31] This convergence of media and communication in the "control revolution" recently has been discussed extensively in the context of digital media and has generated historical, archeological, and theoretical investigations into the question of intermediality even before the advent of the digital.[32] The key point here is that, Beniger, writing in the 1980s, at a time when the discourses of "information society" popularized by best sellers such as *The Third Wave* seized the imaginations about information technology and digital media, astutely detects media as the infrastructure of control. To be sure, Beniger's "control" has less to do with the Orwellian vision of totalitarian surveillance than with the broader sense of managerial organization and coordination in socioeconomic activities through technical and bureaucratic means, or, in his words, control in the broadest sense means "any purposive influence on behavior."[33]

While Beniger's "control revolution" situates the ascending visibility of media and communication technology in relation to the long history of industrialization and economic development, missing in his account are the ways in which media and technology intervene in and intersect with the realms of politics and social relations, as his discussion of "industrialization" is simplified as technical and managerial aspects of economic activities. In contrast to Beniger's neutral rendering of "control," Gilles Deleuze sees the rise of "society of control" in the postwar world as indicating the modes of governance shifting from the concentration on institutions and sites of confinement, such as school, factory, and hospital, as outlined by Foucault, to more distributed forms of networks and modulations. While the shift from disciplinary society to the society of control should not be taken as abrupt, absolute, or linear and exclusive to each other, Deleuze's notion of "control" suggests transformations in the modes of and sites for governance and labor deployment. As the notion of "social factory" raised by autonomous Marxists indicates, capitalist labor exploitation and value extraction has expanded, with ubiquitous communication technology, beyond the traditional settings of factories and work places to social media, networks, and other sites of communication.[34] Data collection, information tracking, and other forms of "information work" and surveillance all further place communication and computational technology at the forefront of political and economic contests. Yet instead of aggrandizing technology per se, a shift to mediation foregrounds the myriad agents and forms of labor and forces that come into contact, conflicts, and negotiations with one another, without reducing the mediation processes into merely the functions of communication technology.

The Interface

The emphasis on the interactions of different agents and forces in the mediation process brings us to the human–machine interface, which has garnered much attention and investment in the current tides of informationization and computization. According to the *Oxford English Dictionary*, the interface refers to "a surface lying between two portions of matter or space, and forming their common boundary." This definition indicates the hybrid nature of the interface as it is always predicated on two or more disparate units or substrates, as well as the connecting function of the interface and its liminality of sitting at the boundary. As Branden Hookway tells us, the word "interface" was coined in the nineteenth century by the engineer James Thomas, who worked in the field of fluid dynamics.[35] "Interface" was used to describe the dynamic boundary condition between two distinct fluid bodies that are held in a state of contestation. At once separating the two bodies and putting them in contact, the interface thus governs the changes and the balancing of forces that press against it from all sides. The interface is, as Hookway remarks, "not a form so much as a tendency toward a forming, which proceeds through a seeking of difference and its counterpoise in equilibrium."[36] The interface, never fixed or static, is always in the dynamic process of forming and dissolving. In this sense, rather than an inherent feature of a particular body alone, the interface points to the process for two or more entities to act upon one another, which in turn redefines and transforms the acting bodies.

The recent surge of interest in the interface has to do with what Katherine Hayles sees as the fourth phase of the evolution of cybernetics in history, which focuses on the coupling of human bodies with other technologies. Cybernetics, from the day of its birth, is imbued with the ambition to transcend the boundaries of humans, animals, and machines. This most recent development Hayles identifies comes with Graphical User Interface (GUI) of microcomputers and ubiquitous media such as mobile phones, GPS technology, embedded sensors, and actuators that "overlay virtual information and functionalities onto physical locations and actual objects," and thus "have created environments in which physical and virtual realms merge in fluid and seamless ways."[37] In other words, the recent phase of cybernetic development is characterized by both the pervasiveness of the interface between humans and machines and the "dissolving" of the interface into the information environments. It is everywhere, almost mundane and invisible.

Behind the immediacy created by the "dissolving" of the interface is the mediation and configuration process of integrating the body into the information environments. In fact, immediacy is always disrupted as the inevitable frictions between different agents and forces bring to the foreground the problematic of mediation. As a result, the "user-friendly interface" is called upon to smooth out friction and conflicts. Yet the interface in this formula is reified as "a thing, an entity, a fixed or determined structure that supports certain activities," in Johanna Drucker's words.[38] Such an understanding of the interface relies on technological solutions to problems and conflicts in order to create an effect of transparency and immediacy. Alexander Galloway has confronted this reductionist approach and proclaims that the interface is not a thing, but a translation, and in the end, an effect of mediation.[39] If the fantasy of total mediation or the disappearance of mediation has been haunting contemporary cybernetic and media imaginations, Galloway uses the term "interface" to preserve the differences and frictions that resist total absorption and the appearance of immediacy. Frictions not only can be found between the representational surface and the medium that frames the representation, and thus suggests the existence of an unrepresentable outside, but also persist between machines and its logical simulation, between modules and layers, and, most important, between humans and the world formalized through computers according to human actions. The interface is filled with agitation from the unrepresentable social and unworkable relations.

Yet if the interface is not a thing but a process of dynamics that leads to its own formation and dissolution, why does the interface attract so much attention from designers and engineers, especially in IT and game industries, to media and cultural scholars, and play such an important role in contemporary culture? If the interface inevitably points to the notion of mediation, and remains irreducible to an entity independent from the acting bodies, why do we need this specific term to refer to the interactions between humans and computational devices?

The objectification and fixation of the interface as a thing first of all paves the way for commodification. The slogan "user-friendly interface" appears frequently in the market promotion of new digital and computational devices. By reducing the interface to the built-in features of machines, the complex configuration and coevolution between humans and machines can be simplified as a conviction of technological superiority for any conflict resolution. The word "interface" also implies an interactive aspect, which is often elevated as the core value of the information society, and a feature that distinguishes digital and social media networks from mass media by encouraging participation and thus, presumably, leading to democracy. This interactive ideology has been debunked in various ways in the critical scholarship of new media.[40] Undoubtedly, the hyperattention to the interface attests to Hyles's observation about the penetration of the cybernetic logic into all areas of social life with the proliferation of sensors and microprocessors. This technical condition concurred with the expansion of value extraction beyond the walls of factories and conventional workspaces, and beyond the regular work schedule, to blur the boundary between work and play.

What does the interface do? I argue that the prominence of the interface should be seen as the symptom of a segmented society, in which increasing labor is demanded to bridge the gaps that result from the alienation of labor distribution and knowledge production that appear as superficially autonomous zones and layers. That is, the "interfacing" and "bridging" function becomes prominent today precisely because of the increasing atomization and segmentation of society—despite the fast developments in communication technology. This segmentation manifests in various forms of gated and ghettoized communities and in the imagination of atomized individual life, but foremost in the mode of labor deployment and knowledge production that makes knowledge of any highly specialized areas inaccessible to laypersons. For instance, the notion of the "user-friendly interface" inadvertently reveals the gap between zones of specialized knowledge and any user without "inside" information. This maintenance of division informs the design of the interface from the very beginning. John Harwood, in his study of IBM's corporate design, tells us that the division between the invisible back station and the highlighted I/O unit of computer interfaces evolved from a deliberate industrial design that is built on the ergonomic logic of integrating the human into a man–machine system. While the internal operations of the computer are located away from the I/O unit and kept concealed from its user, points of interaction, such as consoles and keyboards, "should in some way translate and amplify the electronic activity within for the 'user' outside."[41] Such an arrangement of what its designers referred as the "parlor-coal cellar" division ensures that the operator concentrates on his or her own work on the I/O unit, leaving the internal working of the computer to technical experts, and thus cements the division of labor for optimizing corporate productivity.

The "user-friendly interface," therefore, while it relentlessly ties humans to the system of information production and control, also limits every user to the status of a layperson deprived of knowledge about the operations of the system. The interface is simultaneously relentless connectivity and systematic segmentation. The ubiquity of the interface suggests that these two interconnected aspects are key to the interface effects of information capitalism. Critical reflections on the interface should fundamentally address the issues of labor distribution and knowledge production. The discourses and imaginations around an early artificial intelligence called the "expert system" in China provides such an entry point for me to develop a critique of the interface by bringing in the politics of knowledge production at a time when the systems dependent upon expert consultation and specialized labor division started to replace the "mass-line" of knowledge production and dissemination of the Mao era. The interface, far from the built-in features of machines, points to the interfacing and affective labor in connecting layers and bridging gaps in a society increasingly divided by hierarchies of labor and the compartmentalization of knowledge production as well as emergent social barriers. The haunting of socialist experience nonetheless persisted as the historical and ethical horizon for imagining alternatives to information capitalism.

The interface is thus positioned at the confluence of unresolved social conflicts and forces from past and present, when Chinese society was ridden with contradictions and frictions arising from its socialist history and the new enterprise of rejoining the global capitalist market, from the governance of a party that still claimed its socialist commitments but often prioritized economy development at the price of fairness and equality, and from a new sense of individual desire and fantasies of possibilities unleashed in this process and the palpable anxieties of the looming precariousness brought about by marketization. In this sense, the interface is a mediating process that involves not only the renegotiations of human–machine boundaries but also the intersections and confrontations of variant social agents.

The mediation practices that I will examine thus are not limited to the representation function of traditional media; instead, they focus more on the production of subjectivity and the shift of power relations in mediation processes. Media are not treated as a set of pregiven, observable substrates but as the product of an unfolding process that accompanies and in turn conditions new epistemic and political possibilities. From this perspective, the interface effects I examine are not limited to the interactions between intelligent machines and human beings but rather invoke mediation as social practices that continuously produce and reconfigure social relations and postsocialist subjectivities.

Precarious Mediation and the Cinema of Liminality

The "information fantasies," which are manifested in the scenario of "information pot," and in the fascination with artificial intelligence and a transparent, friction-free interface, as well as in the imaginations of magic devices that promise instant, nonstop information transmission, reflect the dream of all-inclusive mediation that integrates human beings into seamless, real-time information circuits. Yet I shall demonstrate throughout the book that mediation is always precarious, not only because media technologies are always prone to dysfunction and failure. The precariousness of mediation that I examine is more importantly tied to the unsettling social changes in post-Mao 1980s China, when everything seemed about to melt into the air yet also was forever locked in the "ultrastable structure" of history, and people seemed eager to embrace a new era yet could not agree or answer the perplexing questions in evaluating the socialist past and its relation to the future. At this time of aspirations and anxieties, creation and deterioration, liberalization and suppression, the "high-culture" fever coexisted with the proliferation of popular cultural forms; highly experimental modernist writing and filmmaking flourished along with enthusiastic discussions about "entertainment films." Chinese intellectuals acted as, seemingly paradoxically, both the forerunners of social transformations and the tide players of marketization, both self-appointed enlightenment leaders and "hooligan" antiheroes who mocked any grand narratives.[42] "Information" among this constellation of contradictions and contesting forces was a magic, chameleon-like buzzword that connoted both a liberal politics of information flows and market-oriented new economic policies and price reforms. It functioned simultaneously as the foremost medium of enlightenment and the manipulating power of marketing strategies in the burgeoning market economy of post-Mao China, and it conveyed both the remaining socialist utopian impulses and the futuristic imaginations to overcome the past. Precarious mediation in the end highlights the indispensable processes of mediation amid the information fantasies in negotiating the uncertainties on the eve of China's entry into the global capitalist system, as well as the reshuffled social relations and powers and destabilized human agency and identities. This precariousness of mediation was also manifested in the ways in which media technologies and the environment facilitated the emergence of postsocialist subjectivities in transformation. By underscoring the precariousness of mediation, I reveal how the technical was conditioned by and always imbricated within the complexity of postsocialist politics and cultural production.

One crucial aspect of this precarious mediation can be observed in the interrogations of the ontology of images by filmmakers and critics and the reflections on the ethics of mediation at a time full of contradictions and crises, as well as possibilities. The understanding of "media" became destabilized when the representational role of the media came under question in the late 1970s. During the Mao era, socialist realism was the dominant mode in literature, film, and art. Although socialist realism may be mixed with other modes, such as revolutionary romanticism, or appropriated traditional, folk, and foreign forms, the task of literary and art works was to represent the "reality" of socialism, even though this "reality" may be idealized.[43] This representation is not a mechanical, static copy of a given objective thing, but rather a creation of an artistic type or, more specifically, typical characters in typical environments (*dianxing renwu dianxing huanjing* 典型人物典型环境). According to

Peter Button, the philosophical ground of socialist realism can be traced back to the Western metaphysical tradition, especially the quest for the universal in the Hegelian tradition. The artistic type, or *dianxing*, is a dialectical unity of the individual and the universal, but, moreover, comes from the "enlargement, deepening and centralizing of the universality" of the thing in everyday life.[44] Socialist arts, including both cinema and literature, aim at the creation of types that manifest the universal and induce the emergence of the full human—the socialist new man. In sum, socialist realism is built on the belief that socialist ethics and socialist truth were shared, or should be shared, by all members of the socialist country. The role of the media was to represent the socialist types and educate people about the correct, Marxist way of perceiving reality. The representational capacity of the media was inseparable from their didactic function. Good representations of socialist life and ethical models should indoctrinate the audience with correct class-consciousness and in the end produce new socialist subjects—the socialist new men. The birth of socialist realism in China from the very beginning, as elaborated by Zhou Yang's reading of Maxim Gorky, aimed to "penetrate the surface of reality to undercover its underlying truth" and "wrest the true from the real."[45] In the realm of cinema, although early PRC films are not cut off from the tradition of the Chinese critical realism of the 1930s and 1940s and draw heavily from the conventions of fictional realism associated with classical Hollywood narration, the development of socialist realism gradually took a formalist turn, as Jason McGrath notes, to the extent that by the 1970s, with the adaption of the Cultural Revolution model operas, or *yangbanx*i 样板戏, this social realism culminated in an extreme formalism with highly stylized opera performances. This formalist turn was related to the "insistence by Communist theorists such as Zhou Yang and Mao himself that art must depart from reality in order to more clearly reflect the true, the ideal and the universal."[46] In other words, in its claim to socialist truth and its pursuit of the universal manifested in socialist types, socialist realism became a mere surface and vacant formalization that eventually jeopardized its own ideological function of serving the truth.

In the aftermath of the Cultural Revolution, this socialist realism came under suspicion and critique. In 1980, film critic Li Tuo and female director Zhang Nuanxin published "The Modernization of Film Language," a milestone essay that laid the theoretical and discursive foundation for new cinematic practices of the 1980s. In this essay Li and Zhang provocatively proposed that the dated forms in filmmaking should be "reformed" by learning from the formal and style experiments of postwar Western films, particularly from Italian Neorealism and the French New Wave, which they defined as examples of "modern films," posited against the clichéd "realism." The influential discussion on "what is cinema?" in the 1980s can be regarded as a reflection on the nature of the cinematic medium when socialist realism disintegrated.

Such a Bazinian question, instead of consolidating the purported media specificity of cinema, led to reflections on relations between the human body, the mind and the image, and the information environment. The new flexibility of cinematic images, on the one hand, indicated the pressure and impact of other electronic media and information technologies on cinema, and, on the other hand, played a crucial role in cultivating postsocialist subjectivities by building into the body of the viewer a rhythm to match the rapid changes in social arenas and the volatile shifts of the marketplace. Cinema thus became a medium of liminality, mediating the social tensions and contradictions at a liminal time, and itself a liminal body contiguous with other media and information technologies, such as television—a new medium in China at the time, and constantly reflecting on the crisis of representation.

As Chris Berry observes, post-Mao films in the late 1970s and 1980s "open up spaces of difference that include but cannot be reduced to referentiality and representation alone."[47] These spaces of difference, as Berry points out, constituted minor narratives in relation to the grand narratives and command of state socialist discourses. He thus regards the cinema bearing this feature as postsocialist cinema. Indeed, I would argue that the freeing of cinema and media from the grip of socialist "truth" and "types" engendered the multiplication of realities and induced the rewriting of history that challenged the official narrative of revolutionary history, as well as the exploration of multisensory perceptions that was built upon a renewed understanding of cinema and image, and various cinematic experiments that pushed the medium beyond the limits of representation. If the late 1970s and early 1980s films that Berry focuses on signals the beginning of such multiplication processes, by the mid- to late 1980s, with the increasing pressure of commercialization and the boom in "entertainment films," cinema was further pulled away from realism and representation and deeply imbricated in the precarious mediation of various social and technical forces.

In other words, the precarious mediation I discuss here indicates the advent of postsocialist conditions, which Arif Dirlik aptly observed in the late 1980s:

> By postsocialism I refer to the condition of socialism in a historical situation where: (a) socialism has lost its coherence as a metatheory of politics because of the attenuation of the socialist vision in its historical unfolding; partly because of a perceived need on the part of socialist states to articulate "actually existing socialism" to the demands of a capitalist world order, but also because of the vernacularization of socialism in its absorption into different national contexts; (b) the articulation of socialism to capitalism is conditioned by the structure of "actually existing socialism" in any particular context which is the historical premise of all such articulation; and (c) this premise stands guard over the process of articulation to ensure it does not result in the restoration of capitalism.[48]

The subsiding of socialism as a metatheory of politics, the collapse of the grand narrative of revolution, the interrogation of socialist ideology and the revolutionary past, and the suspicion and caution against the sweeping order of global capitalism increasingly built upon information technology and cybernetic loops of control, these fields of tension make it impossible to sustain a mode of representation predicated on a shared acknowledgment of socialist reality and a universality underlying socialist types. The murkiness of "reality" at an undecided historical moment provoked interrogations of the process of mediation and the mechanism of media production, which had brought to the foreground the threshold of (in)visibility, uncovered the transformations in labor forms and hierarchy that were concealed behind the fetish with a transparent, friction-free interface, and invoked self-reflections on the advent of the digital and the role of the human body in information processing.

Postsocialism as an Analytic

Dirlik's employment of the term "postsocialism" in describing the transformations of China in the 1980s suggests the possibility of unlocking the term from the well-worn temporal and spatial associations as defined by the fall of the Berlin Wall and the collapse of the Soviet Union after 1989. Often teleologically marked as the period "after" socialism and a transitory stage to a "free" and "democratic" modern society, "postsocialism" is equated with the end of the Cold War and the end of ideological differences. Yet Dirlik's definition presciently underscores the continuing negotiations and competitions of different forces even under the conditions when socialism lost its coherence as a metatheory of politics. Such dismantling of binary antagonism does not necessarily lead to the dominance of a singular ideology but draws attention to the pluralization of social forces as well as contradictions and contestations on all levels of social life.

To recuperate "postsocialism" as a critical analytic in the first place involves a reexamination of the effects of the Cold War, which are, instead of vanishing, still present to define the knowledge production of "postsocialism." Sharad Chari and Katherine Verdery, citing Nils Gilman's research on how the modernization theory as a device of Cold War politics shaped the imagination of the future, point out that one of the most important knowledge effects of the Cold War is the dominance of modernization theory in Western social science. Growing out of postwar US liberalism and emerging from think tanks at Harvard University, the Social Science Research Council (SSRC), and the Massachusetts Institute of Technology (MIT), modernization theory propagated the image of a liberal and prosperous capitalist West, especially as exemplified by the United States, as the goal of development for the rest of world.[49] Emphasizing the economic advantages of alliances with the West, modernization theory through its global dissemination and iterations aimed to squeeze "peripheral societies" into "stages" of development that presumably would lead them to a free, modern world. As Michael Latham shows in his extensive study on the relation of American social science to Cold War politics, the central challenge to modernization theorists was to "rejuvenate and project abroad America's liberal social values, capitalist economic organizations, and democratic political structures" and to defeat "the forces of monolithic communism by accelerating the natural process through which 'traditional' societies would move toward the enlightened 'modernity' most clearly represented by America itself."[50] This formulation was designed particularly to rule out the alternative development possibilities arising from the modernizing achievements of socialist countries, and it was further backed up by Western propaganda about socialism's "inefficiencies." Such axes of communist/free and traditional/modern continued to produce knowledge of "postsocialism," as (former) socialist countries are often relegated to the category of underdevelopment.[51] In this sense, Jason McGrath's choice of "postsocialist modernity," instead of employing the discourse of "postmodernity" in characterizing the sociocultural conditions of 1990s China, reveals this Cold War connection and the inseparability of this "postsocialist modernity" from the Cold War ideology of developmentalism.[52]

Modernization and modernity in 1980s China, more often than not, became synonymous with the Western mode of modernization and capitalist modernity. Although the dated discourse of orthodox Marxism was still deployed for clichéd criticism of "capitalist culture," the official ideology of Deng Xiaoping's China was more aligned with a futuristic discourse that had reproduced the notion of "modern" as opposed to socialist productive forces and relations, the latter considered as the remnants of feudalism blocking China's path of modernization. The "information revolution" and the "technological revolution" that had taken place in the West were seen as the driving forces and the foremost manifestation of modernization; Toffler's *The Third Wave* was designated as one of the mandatory political study materials, which further translated the enthusiastic embrace of modernization into information fantasies. Again, this association of information science and technology with an affluent society of modernization cannot be separated from the strategy of the United States in Cold War geopolitics and the continuous competition between socialism and capitalism that was often, however reductively, represented as the combat between the United States and the Soviet Union. Richard Barbrook, in an extensive examination of the intellectual spectrum in the United States during the Cold War, shows that a group of intellectuals and social scientists, whom he calls the "Cold War Left," worked closely with the US government in devising new ideologies to defend the nation's interest in its struggle against communism and the Russian enemy.[53] Recognizing that laissez-faire liberalism could no longer compete with communism and Stalinism, they strived to create a credible version of history and imaginary futures that would challenge and undermine Marxism. Their most powerful weapon was, however, precisely their intimate knowledge of Marxism, which they employed to devise a materialist conception of history only to rule out the existence of class conflicts and the necessity of revolution. Walt Rostow, for example, a prominent academic from the CIA-funded CENIS (Center for International Studies) at MIT, in his *Stages of Economic Growth*, replaced Adam Smith's and Karl Marx's schemas of social development with a movement from one economic paradigm to another. In his view, the United States served as the model of modernization and modernity, where workers would eventually become "car-owning, suburban-dwelling, TV-watching inhabitants of a democratic and pluralist welfare state."[54] Daniel Bell, another guru of the Cold War Left, who was a socialist in the 1930s and had thus acquired a good knowledge of Marxist theory, now shifted to an anticommunist celebration of consensual politics. When put in charge of *The Commission on the Year 2000* funded by the American Academy of Arts and Sciences in 1964, Bell and his group, which consisted of economists, sociologists, political scientists, geographers, and biologists recruited from elite universities, argued that technological innovation had become the impersonal force driving human society toward the future and presented a post-Fordist social utopia with all the rewards of socialism only without any danger of revolution. Drawing heavily from Marshall McLuhan's *Understanding Media*, the Bell commission singled out computing, media, and telecommunications as three key technologies that would determine the future of humanity. Combining their enthusiasm for cybernetics and information technology with a version of Marxism without Marx, the

Cold War Left eulogized the power of electronic media with the convergence of television, computing, and telecommunications, which they regarded as an indication of another step toward the information society and the remodeling of the social system in cybernetic logic.[55] Bell's *The Coming of Post-Industrial Society: A Venture in Social Forecasting*, along with Toffler's *The Third Wave*, was regarded in 1980s China as a prophecy for the coming of the information society and for the determining role of information technology in shaping the future.

In this context, the notion of "modern" became equivalent to economic development and the superiority of technologies, especially information technology. Zhang Xudong thus comments that the "capitalism" previously defined and criticized in textbooks was stripped of its political connotations associated with class analysis and the critique of the capitalist mode of production, and now became a positivistic "modern." He continues to elaborate: "With Deng's visits of Japan and the United States since 1979, the images of Japan's *Shinkansen* high-speed railway system against the background of symbolic Mount Fuji, and the scenes of Space Center Houston as well as those of everyday life in consumerist society, were disseminated nationwide through television broadcasts, which, along with the *Towards the Future* book series compiled by the young generation of intellectuals a few years later, fabricated the futuristic imaginations of 'modern.'"[56]

Two points should be highlighted in Zhang's sharp observations: First, this depoliticization of "modern" is continuous with Deng's developmentalist policies in the 1990s, and thus prepared the grounds for further reforms of marketization since 1992. In other words, to borrow Dirlik's words, "socialism" was already losing its coherence and even its legitimacy in the 1980s, when the notion of "modern" was used as a symbol of a more advanced society modeled upon developed capitalism. Second, Zhang astutely notes the key role of the new media networks, especially television broadcasts, in propagating the images and generating the imaginations of the "modern." Such techno-imaginations of high-speed transportation and communication in the space era were intertwined with the yearning for new lifestyles and the ecstasies of sensorial stimuli brought about by new information technologies and aesthetic forms.

It should be acknowledged that the futuristic imaginations in 1980s China were imbued with utopian impulses, to the extent that the era, often dubbed the "New Era," was regarded with a sort of nostalgia as an age of idealism, a time full of energy and possibilities. Indeed, the enthusiasm and efforts invested in creating a bright future were reminiscent of Mao's era and the forward imaginations about a socialist utopia.[57] Yet as the possibilities for alternative modes of modernity provided by socialist practices were evaporating and displaced by capitalist modernity, the future would lie somewhere else, to which technology would play the single most important role. If socialist production relations were once regarded as a revolution to the exploiting employment system of capitalism, Alvin Toffler proposed that information technology alone would transform the nature of work and end the alienation of manufacturing labor. The discourses of "information society," which emerged at a moment when the manufacturing industries shifted to the Global South and became invisible in the everyday life of advanced capitalism, concurred with and contributed to the subsiding of socialist movements in the late twentieth century. To put it bluntly, information discourses appropriated the socialist critique of capitalist industrialization and its labor conditions and displaced the socialist revolution with a technological revolution. This becomes even more obvious in our time, when drastic social transformations are often simplified as the "Facebook revolution" or the "Twitter revolution." As Neda Atanasoski and Kalindi Vora acutely observe, "The 21st-century association of revolutionary change with the novelty of technological objects and platforms and their social effects dislodges the term 'revolution' from its prior association with political and social transformation, altering the possible fields for political action."[58] In this way, information technologies and communication infrastructures, and their implication in the colonial and imperial order and their deep entanglement with Cold War politics rendered invisible, became fetishized as liberating technologies that alone would bring democracy and progress to humanity. In this sense, postsocialism should be regarded as a global condition that redefines the limits and possibilities of the political under the technical conditions of information and control. It therefore remains crucial to revisit this episode from 1980s China and uncover the historical and ideological intersections and intertwinements of "postsocialism" and the "information society."

Yet as Dirlik points out in his essay, "postsocialism" also forestalls any total control of capitalism. To unlock the potential beyond the hegemonic power of capitalism, the complicated forces and contradictions of postsocialism should first be acknowledged and analyzed. In the first place, in order to recuperate postsocialism from the Cold War framework of knowledge production, postsocialism has to be extricated from the telos of developmentalism and acknowledge the coexisting of multiple temporalities. The valorization of the "newness" of information and media technology, bearing the linearity of developmentalism that was deeply entrenched in both the media history narrative from analog to digital and the ideology of the "New Era" with Deng's Opening and Reforms, should thus be scrutinized through technological and discursive analysis. In this process, I shall uncover a complex mediascape in which old and new, real and imagined, media coevolved and constituted the conditions for postsocialist mediation and subjectivities. And from the fragments and cracks of ideologies, socialist sentiments and dreams, histories and experiences can always be detected and uncovered, now in an assemblage with shifting technical means and aesthetic forms pointing toward potentials for new forms of sociality.

Methodology and Chapters

This project takes an interdisciplinary approach to examine a wide range of social and cultural phenomena and their intertwinement with scientific discourses and technological imaginations. Methodologically, in order to re-embed science and technology into the sociopolitical context of 1980s China, I chart a landscape in which the high-end scientific studies in the areas of information and AI research interacted and intersected with the dissemination of scientific knowledge through popular science journals and with popular imaginations in fiction and films that reflected on the social consequences of new technologies. Science fiction stories, literary texts, and films thus are not fictive accounts to be excluded from historical examination, but a sensitive barometer that registers the social imaginations of new technologies, allowing the unveiling of more nuanced and complicated social scenarios surrounding the emergence of information technologies. This method of moving back and forth between scientific and technological studies and popular imaginations allows me to bring in issues such as the transformations in labor forms and hierarchies in post-Mao China that were concurrent with the pervasive discourse about a purported shift from manual, factory labor to information labor. Information work was believed to be liberating for human beings. As the labor issue remains central to both the reconsideration of socialist practices and the current information economy, which has generated heated debates around fan labor, crowdsourcing, and post-Fordist precariousness, my method gives me the advantage of situating my examination of information technologies and discourses at the juncture of both socialist legacy and technology-based utopian imaginations, both postsocialist transformations and the emergent order of global information capitalism.

Science fiction is an intricate part of the "information fantasies" that I chart in this book, not in the sense that the genre provides any predictions of the future, but because it sensitively registers structures of feeling that were yet to be articulated and the potential yet to be actualized. Steven Shaviro in a different context argues that science fiction "works to extrapolate elements of the present, to consider what these elements might lead to if allowed to reach their full potential."[59] It is in this sense that he claims that science fiction grasps "the futurity that haunts the present," "the virtual dimension of existence."[60] Drawing on this beautifully put statement, my reading of science fiction imaginations thus aims beyond merely to replicate the futuristic fantasies around information, but also to uncover the virtual future(s) of the past and the past(s) of the present.

The scope of my investigation thus includes not only film and visual materials but also literature and writing. Literature is often excluded from the area of media studies because of the disciplinary settings in North America. Such disciplinary barriers, however, neglect the ceaseless interactions and coevolution of different media forms, as well as the continually shifting boundaries of media in cybernetic environments.

I argue that the experiments in literary form in the mid- and late 1980s should be examined in relation to the pressure and impact of the transformed media environment on literary production. As "information" proliferated with the rise of the market economy and the emergence of advertising across different media platforms, the sense of literature also became a struggle between signals and noises, aesthetic autonomy and commodity economy.

The materialist approach of this project on the one hand emphasizes the ways in which the materiality of media and technology constitutes the aesthetics of experimental writings and filmmaking, and on the other hand insists upon art works as legible social forms integral to a new political economy of sensoria and perceptions that arose with shifting information technologies and practices. The focus on the entanglement of the technical and the aesthetic throughout the book demonstrates how creative and aesthetic practices shaped the formation of media to the extent that media should not be considered merely as given discrete objects. I explore on two levels the aesthetic innovations of the 1980s, from the stunning appearance of *Yellow Earth* (1984) and *Black Cannon Incident* (1984) by directors such as Chen Kaige, Zhang Yimou, and Huang Jianxin, who later were grouped as the "Fifth Generation," to the daring experiments in literary forms. First, the fascination with modernism and new forms has to be contextualized in relation to the ideology of the "modern" and considered as a symbolic construction complicit in a developmentalist order, which was also imposed on literature and arts as stages of advancement. The technics of modernism, which, as Zhang Xudong points out, created an appearance of autonomous forms, should be regarded as consistent with technological rationality.[61] Here modernist techniques and new technologies converged in the futuristic fantasies of a new order imprinted by capitalist modernity. Yet on the second level, the liberation of the sensoria and the redistribution of the sensible brought about by the experiments of aesthetic forms also captured fleeting moments of utopian imaginations, as well as the persistence of socialist experiences and sentiments, revealing a structuring of feeling that refused to be assimilated into the hegemonic order of global capitalism.

Intervening in the areas of new media and information studies, science and technology studies, modern and contemporary China studies, socialist/postsocialist studies, and film and media studies, this book unearths a neglected history of China's participation in the global production and circulation of information technologies and discourses—even before the general implementation of the internet and digital media in the 1990s. Central to my thesis is the political and sociocultural implications of a cybernetic body. The fantasies of and the frictions that resulted from integrating humans into environments of ceaseless information flows have to be understood in relation to the transformations of labor with the advent of the information society, as well as the rise of new forms of governmentality that rely on information tracking and biocybernetic technologies. Anticipating the discussions on information surveillance, data collection, and precarious labor conditions in the information economy today, this project thus provides an *ur*-history of the digital. Each chapter deals with one concept that is frequently discussed in current new media and information studies, although they are intertwined with one another throughout the book. The key concepts are: the digital, the interface, the system, noises, and liminality of cinema. By placing them in the context of the drastic postsocialist transformations in 1980s China, I hope to create a dialogue between new media theories and postsocialist studies so as to question the limits of current theoretical practices in new media studies that often fail to take into account socialist and postsocialist practices of information.

Chapter 1 begins with the anticipation of a coming information society in both scientific discourse and popular imaginations of magic waves. *Qigong* and extrasensory powers attracted immense scientific and social interest at the beginning of the 1980s. Believing that extrasensory powers and *qigong*—a traditionally Chinese practice that combines breathing techniques with meditation—would reveal a secrete mechanism of waveform communication of the human body, Chinese scientists, such as Qian Xuesen, the renowned author of *Engineering Cybernetics*, established a "somatic science" in order to find out the magic waveform medium for real-time information transmission between human bodies and information environments. The discourses and imaginaries of magic waves can be regarded as an envisioning of the digital, as magic waves were attributed with incredible flexibility and cross-media convertibility that are usually regarded as the properties of the digital. In other words, I argue that instead of defining the digital simply as binary coding, the new relations between bodies and environments, which have been discussed by Mark Hansen and other scholars as an outcome of digitization, should be reconsidered in this long history of media technology and cybernetic thinking.

Underlying the imaginaries of "magic waves" was the strong urge to reposition humans in the new media environment, a cybernetic fantasy of incorporating the human body into ceaseless information flows. Magic waves in this sense also featured a seamless interface between the human body and the information environment. Chapter 2 discusses the politics of the interface in the instance of an artificial intelligence system called the "expert system." Emerging among the post-Mao critique of class politics, expert systems epitomized the depoliticization of "information" and the neutralization of knowledge and technology. Hidden behind the fantasy of a seamless interface is the reorganization of labor forms and hierarchy, an issue increasingly prominent in the current economy of crowdsourcing, which conceals intensified labor exploitation behind code and spreadsheets. Situating the polemic of the interface in postsocialist politics, I hope to develop a critique of the interface to addresses the labor issue, but, more important, to read the interface as symptomatic of an increasingly compartmentalized and fragmented society that commands increasing affective and communicative labor to bridge gaps between segregated layers of society.

Chapter 3 engages with another aspect of depoliticization by focusing on how systems theory was adopted in analyzing Chinese history and society, particularly represented by Jin Guantao and Liu Qingfeng's characterization of Chinese society as an "ultrastable system." Depicted as repetitive cycles of crises and restoration, Chinese history was conceived as perpetually mired in the stagnant state of feudalism, the whole society resistant to changes and modernity. Set up as a "scientific" answer to the hypothetical question of why feudalism persisted in China, Jin and Liu's influential thesis was in fact driven by an anxiety of modernity, now equivalent to Western capitalist modernity, and inextricably tied to the modernization theory that was born from the Cold War strategy of the United States. This was precisely, I argue, the political and intellectual environment from which the stunning aesthetic of the film *Yellow Earth* emerged. As a milestone of the new-wave filmmaking in the 1980s, the film had mesmerized both critics and international audiences with its immobile shots of immutable rural landscapes and a temporality of eternal stagnancy. While former scholarship focuses on its connections to modern cinema traditions represented by Italian Neorealism and French New Wave and to visual arts such as traditional Chinese landscape painting, my discussion of new-wave cinema opens up new possibilities to rethink aesthetics and politics, information and postsocialism. The notion of the "system," while becoming prominent in managerial sciences and operational studies, also brought about new aesthetics in the cinematic reconfiguration of the relationship between the landscape, human society, and the human actor (observer).

Chapter 4 considers "information" in relation to the rise of the market economy, the return of advertising after its disappearance during the Cultural Revolution and its media strategy of "information bombing," especially with the emergent wireless radio and television broadcasts. Advertising studies, a new discipline that appeared in the curricula of Chinese universities, centralized upon the ways to maximize the impact of advertised information on humans. Reading several pieces of experimental writing by Wang Meng in the late 1980s, this chapter focuses on the tension between literature as an information medium and as art works of aesthetic autonomy in the complicated cultural environment of post-Mao China, in which the tides of commercialization coexisted with a declining yet still-functioning socialist system of cultural production. This chapter thus reveals an often-neglected aspect of "information" as commodified media flux to capture human attention and bodily affectivity in multimedia environments. The key term here is "noises," a term crucial to Claude Shannon's information theory. The term gained a particular meaning when information theory was adopted in advertising studies, with which the line between an environment of information and a cacophony of noises became precarious.

Chapter 5 continues to examine the transformations of cinema as modes of mediation that reflected on its own liminality among the twin simultaneous shifts to a new media environment and the start of commercialization. Situated within a vibrant multimedia environment and facing fierce competition from television broadcasts and videotapes, cinematic images gained a sort of flexibility to break away from the confines of both cinema theaters and rectangular screens, a palpable energy I see aligned with the eager anticipation of unlimited freedom and possibilities by the emergent postsocialist subjects at the initial moments of liberalization. However, this anticipation and excitement was also overshadowed by the precariousness brought about by the process of marketization and prevalent ethical crises at a liminal moment of disintegration and reinvention. Theoretical discourses of cinema that focused on the interactions of the human body with cinematic images while ushering in an understanding of cinema beyond the strictures of cinematic realism also echoed the role of the body in processing information and "enframing" images in the discourses of magic waves, which I discuss in chapter 1. This final chapter concludes with *Lonely Spirit in a Dark Building*, a horror film released in 1989 on the eve of the Tiananmen Square incident, which I regard as a self-conscious interrogation of the cinematic medium and the ethics of mediation. The film also spoke to a convergence of information fantasies and postsocialist precariousness in China of the late 1980s.

CHAPTER ONE

Extrasensory Powers, Magic Waves, and Information Explosion

Imagining the Digital

In 1979, the *Sichuan Daily* reported the discovery of a twelve-year-old boy named Tang Yu who could "read" words with his ears instead of his eyes. The story goes that the boy, when playing with others, accidentally touched the pocket of one of his playmates with his ears and immediately "saw" the brand of the cigarettes in his friend's pocket without actually looking into his pocket. The boy's ability to read without seeing aroused the interest of local officials, whose ensuing tests further developed the legend that the boy could detect with his ears not only words but also the colors of the ink in which the words were written. Some wrote English words for him to "read." Lacking any knowledge of English, Tang was able to reproduce the accurate images of the words without knowing their meaning. He said that he could start to feel the words reflected in his mind when his hands touched a rolled-up piece of paper with writing on it, as if electricity were passing through his hands. When he stuck the rolled-up paper inside his ears, the details of the characters appeared in his mind as clearly as on a screen. The author celebrated the new horizon of research that the Tang Yu case might open for further understanding of the human body. The story concludes by reporting that the authorities of Sichuan Province were urging scientific institutes to investigate the phenomenon of "extrasensory powers" (*teyi gongneng* 特异功能).[1]

The Tang Yu case was only a start. A few days after the *Sichuan Daily* report, a girl named Jiang Yan in Beijing was reported to have a similar power to read with her ears. Soon children with extrasensory powers were reported everywhere and captured immense media attention. One year after the *Sichuan Daily* report, the *Chinese Journal of Nature* (*Ziran zazhi* 自然杂志) held an academic conference on extrasensory powers in Shanghai, assembling scientists from universities and research institutes, as well as fourteen children and adolescents who allegedly possessed extrasensory powers. In the opening remarks, He Chongyin, the chief editor of *Ziran zazhi*, declared that the pivot of the current research into "image-recognition through nonvisual organs" (*fei shijue qiguan tuxiang shibie* 非视觉器官图像识别) was to uncover "the mechanisms in the human body for receiving, transmitting, processing and displaying information." He believed that this research promised the discovery of an unknown, alternative sensory system of the human body, or what he called "the seventh sense."[2] Furthermore, the mysterious medium for extrasensory powers was believed to be the information-carrying wave. Hovering between the real and the imagined, waves were central to the scientific discourse of extrasensory powers and were also a ubiquitous presence with the rapid expansion of wireless broadcast in 1980s China. These two strands, the extrasensory and the wireless, shared a cybernetic logic of incorporating humans into real-time information circuits. On the one hand, studies on "extrasensory powers" increasingly adopted the analogy of the human body to the television set as a receiver and displayer of information; on the other hand, the unprecedented expansion in wireless broadcasting and the growing importance of television as a new information channel in the 1980s fueled the imaginary of flexible and versatile waves: television became a "psychic" medium that enveloped humans in information environments.[3] Waves (*bo* 波)—a magic medium that enabled unobstructed information flows across the human body and its surrounding environments regardless of their material and structural differentiation—were accorded the extraordinary flexibility and easy manipulation that is usually attributed to digital media.

The strong interest and active engagement of scientists and research institutes soon led to a fad for extrasensory powers. Qian Xuesen, a prominent and politically influential scientist and the designer of China's nuclear weapons program, was a firm advocate of extrasensory powers

Figure 4. Cover of the journal *Ziran zazhi*, which features children with extrasensory powers. *Ziran zazhi* 3, no. 4 (1980).

Figure 5. Photo reports of children with extrasensory powers, *Huashi* [Fossil] no. 3 (1980).

as an object of serious scientific research. As with He Chongyin, he expected the research into extrasensory powers to reveal a more direct and accelerated mechanism of information transmission between the human body and the environment. This new direction of examining the human body as an information system was included in "somatic science," a term Qian coined in 1980. Writing with great enthusiasm, Qian claimed that the liberating power of somatic science might bring about "the second renaissance in human history": "If we apply toward future educational practice any discoveries we make about child prodigies, everyone will be able to become 'wise' in the twenty-first century; if we find out how extrasensory powers work, and use those principles to develop the latent power of the human body, everyone will be able to become 'omniscient.'"[4] Comparing the transformative power of somatic science to that of communism, Qian rewrote the first sentence of Marx and Engel's *Manifesto of the Communist Party* to read that "the specter of somatic science is haunting us."[5] In this sense, he celebrated somatic science as "not only a scientific revolution, but also a cultural revolution," which he characterized as a movement toward enlightenment and self-consciously distinguished from Mao's Cultural Revolution. Qian's locating the foundation of the communist future in the empowered human subject may seem to resonate with Mao's revolutionary ideas that weigh heavily on human initiative and consciousness. Yet if revolutionary consciousness is achieved through social and material practices, Qian substitutes a mysterious information mechanism for social practices. The human to be empowered is paradoxically subject to a bodily function that ironically cannot be controlled by human consciousness; *the human body is imagined as where the "revolution" is to take place, but at the same time a portal, a transparent medium through which information flows in and out.* What prompted Qian to put forth a human body synched with information flows? Perhaps more perplexing here is why the revolution that Qian so exalted hinges on communication and information media—in this case, magic waves.

In this chapter, I argue that magic waves in fact anticipated the understanding and the imaginations of the digital in post-Mao China at the beginning of the 1980s. My argument follows two concurrent strands of development and discourse in 1980s China: the first is the scientific discourse of extrasensory perception as the transmission of "amodal" information enabled by magic waves; the second is the development of wireless broadcast in post-Mao China, as well as the vision and practice of television as a hybrid information platform, which I argue heralded the convergence of media in the digital era. The two strands converged around the cybernetic logic of incorporating humans into the real-time information circuits. The centrality of the human body in the discourses about extrasensory powers and magic waves foregrounded the necessity of repositioning and tuning the human body into the new information environment. I analyze this anxiety of repositioning the human body as a response to the purported "information explosion" and the impetus on both the official and popular levels to synch up with "world time" in post-Mao China. The "information fantasies" epitomized in the discourses of "magic waves" signified the start of a sea change in Deng's China. Qian's apparently tension-ridden wedding of communism and extrasensory powers inadvertently suggests the deep-seated contradictions of Chinese society as it departed from Mao's revolutionary age and began to embark on a new order of global capitalism.

My strategy for carving out a critical space among the multivalent discourses and imaginations of wave-related media in early postsocialist China is to juxtapose scientific discourses on extrasensory powers and technological developments in information media through a reading of the period's science fiction stories. These stories should be regarded not merely as fictive imaginations but as practices that reembed technology into broader sociopolitical concerns. My symptomatic reading of these stories unveils a "structure of feeling" that captures the sentiments accompanying drastic social transformations and, more important, indicates a resistance to emergent information capitalism and its hegemonic temporality.[6] As the direction of these transformations was often obscured amid China's enthusiastic embrace of modernization and modernity, the discontent toward the emergent order of information capitalism was not fully articulated as a critical discourse of information capitalism but was registered in the stories as an ambiguity toward changes underway. I argue that the stories not only captured the aspirations and anxieties generated by information fantasies, but also provided a critique of the depoliticized "information" at a liminal moment in history with the advent of the postsocialist world.

Human-Machine-Environment System Engineering

Qian's investment in somatic science is partly a legacy of Cold War politics and is inseparable from his involvement in China's military defense and space technology. During his stay in the United States in the 1930s and 1940s, he worked closely with Theodore Von Kármán, a Hungarian American aerodynamic expert at Caltech. Qian became interested in rocket science soon after he arrived at Caltech and played a leading role in the Jet Propulsion Laboratory, which engaged in government-sponsored research on long-range rockets. During World War II, Qian was actively involved in many US military research projects and was recognized as the world's foremost expert on jet propulsion. Qian's *Engineering Cybernetics* was published in English in 1954 and translated into Chinese in 1958. However, the rise of McCarthyism ended his honeymoon with the US government and jeopardized his career. Accused of being a communist sympathizer, Qian was placed under house arrest before he eventually managed to return to China. Upon his return, the Party treated Qian with great respect. Lauded as the father of China's missile project, Qian was regarded as indispensable to China's development of weaponry systems during the Cold War. In 1962, Qian and several other scientists, including the mathematician Guan Zhaozhi, and Song Jian, who studied cybernetics in the Soviet Union, established a research office of cybernetics, mainly serving the national military defense. Song later applied cybernetics and systems theory to the studies of population control, which laid the foundation for the one-child policy. The arms race between the United States and the Soviet Union made the high-level Chinese officials realize that satellite and space technology should be given a priority amid the fierce military competition. During the Cultural Revolution, regular research activities in most universities and research institutes had ceased. But the groups working on missile development and other sensitive military projects were largely exempt from the political storms. If the "Mass Movement" became the major mode of knowledge production and dissemination in regular areas of scientific research, the research on top sensitive weapons was largely insulated from everyday economic life and regular political mobilization.

In 1967, the government approved a project of manned spacecraft named "*shuguang hao*" 曙光号 (Dawnlight). The Academy of Man-Made Satellite and Spacecraft was subsequently established in 1968, later renamed the Academy of Space Technology. As the head of the academy, Qian was attentive to research on the adaption of human beings in outer space. The Institute of Space Medico-Engineering, established two months after the founding of the academy, primarily focused on developing life-support systems and environmental control for human spaceflight. Its research ranged from issues on the effect of spaceflight on the human body to the collection of medical data on human physiological and metabolic processes for the design of life-support systems and space capsules.

After the successful launch of China's first man-made satellite, "East is Red," in 1970, the project of manned spacecraft coded "Dawnlight One" was next on agenda. In the early 1980s, Chen Xin, then a researcher at the Institute of Space Medico-Engineering, in his close collaboration with Qian, proposed "human-machine-environment system engineering," interdisciplinary research aimed at optimal system functioning by examining the transmission, processing, and control of information among humans, machines (and computers), and the environment. Distinguishing this research from what Western scientists called the "human–machine interface," Chen emphasized the environment as part of the ultracomplex system. "Environment" may refer to the large, dynamic environment in outer space, which usually is not habitable for humans, but more to a man-made small environment, such as a space capsule, which is manipulated to accommodate the biological and physiological conditions of humans.[7]

As Chen Xin notes, the manipulation of the environment and the coordination of humans, machines, and the environment fundamentally rely upon the possibility of information transmission across multiple subsystems made of disparate materials and diverse structures. Humans, as one subsystem in this complex system, are regarded as a black box, the material and structural complexity of which is suspended for functional consideration in terms of information input and output. Mainly concerned with spaceflight, Chen Xin nevertheless believed in the universal applicability of this cybernetic question in other fields. One example he gave was, echoing Norbert Wiener's classic example of cybernetic control, a pilot engaged in combat: while the pilot has to deal with different physical environments at high altitudes, he also has to watch all sorts of instruments and meters and finish a dozen operations in less than half a minute. Under these circumstances, it is necessary to work out "the distribution of systemic functions," considering the information-processing capability and speed of humans, and determine which tasks should be automated and which should be performed by humans.[8]

Such configurations between humans and machines, again, rest upon the presumption of the human being as an information system. One task of "human-machine-environment system engineering" is to build mathematical models that simulate the information processing and decision-making of humans. This requires quantitative analyses of human behavior as well as the physiological and biological data of the human body. Somatic science, as Qian Xuesen argues, treats the body precisely as an information system. Engaged in a constant exchange of information and material with the exterior world, this system always manages to maintain a relatively stable state, which means the physiological and biological indices of the body, such as brainwave activity, are maintained in a stable range. Qian called these states of the human body the "eigenstates," a term borrowed from quantum mechanics. He identified six eigenstates: being awake, asleep, alert, hypnotized, in crisis, and practicing *qigong*. Once these eigenstates are recognized, the characteristic parameters are determined through electroencephalogram (EEG), magnetoencephalogram, electromyogram (EMG), electrocardiogram (EKG), and the analysis of the chemical components in the human body. The next step is to ascertain the control variables that may enable the manipulation of the shift from one eigenstate to another through certain information input. Finally, somatic science should also establish records of physical and biological effects that accompany each eigenstate, such as that of *qi* 气 emitted by *qigong* 气功 masters.

Qi as Waveform Information

It was not coincidental that Qian singled out *qigong* as an eigenstate of the human body. To him and somatic scientists, *qigong* provided a shortcut to uncover the informational mechanisms of the human body. In his paper delivered at the Second Conference on Extrasensory Powers, referring to the report that some children with extrasensory powers had the same healing power as *qigong* masters, Qian celebrated *qigong* as an "advantage" possessed by Chinese researchers. This was because, as Qian explained, extrasensory powers were often unstable and thus posed great difficulties to researchers, whereas the same effects could be achieved by *qigong* practitioners so that they could provide reference cases and reliable statistics not easily accessible to foreign researchers.[9]

But "data" about *qigong* should not be taken for granted. Qian argued that unsystematic records and experiences from previous eras were "prescientific" (*qian kexue* 前科学) and should be transformed and reorganized into the framework of modern scientific systems. This was also his attitude toward traditional Chinese medicine, *qigong*, and extrasensory powers. In his opinion, their holistic view of the human body in relation to its environment might be relevant to systems theory. Yet, in essence, traditional Chinese medicine was part of "the prescience," and its language had to be modernized using the terminologies of such modern sciences as physiology, biology, and systems theory. Another way to modernize traditional knowledge was to verify and quantify traditional Chinese medicine through laboratory instruments and devices. To capture and study information sent out by the human body, instruments such as electromagnetic wave detectors were attached to the body of a test subject—now a cybernetic body amid information flows—to determine the variables and amounts of information exchange. Such quantitative studies would prepare for the seamless integration of the human body into environments and systems. These procedures gave rise to the "the science of *qigong*."

The link between traditional Chinese medicine and *qigong* was already established before this "*qigong* fever." According to David Palmer, as early as the 1950s *qigong* as the heritage of traditional medicine was already integrated into the health and medical institutions of the PRC. This was partly due to "the lack of modern medical personnel and the low cost of traditional healing," but also because in the political climate of an anti-West, anti-bourgeoisie tide, Chinese medicine was promoted as part of "popular democratic culture."[10] But since the 1960s, *qigong* had been condemned as superstition and a "rotten relic of feudalism." When Qian started advocating *qigong* research in the early 1980s, he had to distinguish the scientific research of *qigong* from "superstitious" practices.

But how to explain by way of modern science the ancient notion of *qi* and its allegedly healing effects? Qian resorted to "information" for an explanation: *qi* was released from a certain part of the body, or an acupuncture meridian point. *Qi* was the conveyer of information. This information was received by another object or the body of another person, which in turn sent back information that could be detected only by the *qigong* master, who was equipped with special sensors. Qian concluded that *qi* might in fact be another name for electromagnetic waves.[11]

It should be noted that Qian's explanation actually adopted a cybernetic mode, placing the *qigong* master and the person under *qigong* therapy in a feedback loop. If the human body was regarded as a system of information, the effects of *qigong* resulted from information flows within and among different systems. Yet the argument of *qi* as waves was merely a hypothesis that needed to be proved by empirical evidence and laboratory data. Qian thus proposed that the first step was to establish a "phenomenological study of *qigong*" (*weixiang qigongxue* 唯象气功学), starting with collecting and classifying previous records of *qigong*, the accounts of *qigong* practitioners, and ancient accounts and studies of *qigong*.[12]

Myriad experiments and laboratory tests had been carried out since the late 1970s to determine the exact nature of *qi*. Infrared detectors were used to capture *qi*, or waves sent out by *qigong* masters; electrostatic fields around *qigong* masters were measured when the masters were in a meditative state; the effects of *qi* on various bacteria were tested; the brainwave activities of *qigong* practitioners were recorded and analyzed by computers.[13] Similar tests were implemented on people with extrasensory powers: besides ears, hands, feet, and noses, even armpits were tested to determine their powers of image recognition; clairvoyance, telepathy, and psychokinesis were all tested under lab conditions.[14] There were as many as thirty-eight laboratory reports published in *Ziran zazhi* in this field from September 1979 to November 1981. Many of the researchers involved in these tests were from prestigious universities and institutes, such as Tsinghua University, the University of Science and Technology of China, and Beijing Normal University. The Scientific Study Group of *Qigong* at Tsinghua University had done a series of collaborative experiments with the legendary *qigong* master Yan Xin, after which major media in both the PRC and Hong Kong published a jubilant announcement of their successful confirmation about the medical effects of *qigong* and "extrasensory powers of the human body to remotely control and transform the physical and chemical substance of things even without the person physically touching the thing."[15]

This association between *qi* and information was soon adopted by *qigong* practitioners themselves as a powerful discourse to trumpet the magical healing effect of their *qi*. A legendary *qigong* therapist named Zhang Xiangyu was reported to be able to cure difficult diseases. It was said that a young man who suffered from chronic nephritis went to Zhang

Figure 6. Illustration from *Kexue wenyi* [Scientific literature and arts], no. 3 (1980). Echoing the fever for "extrasensory powers," *Kexue wenyi* reported that a woman in the Soviet Union demonstrated the power of "feeling" the words in books with her fingers when her eyes were covered by a piece of cloth.

for help. Having noticed his suspicion toward *qigong* therapy, Zhang required him to believe in the "science of *qigong*" before she could start healing him. By way of assurance, she sang out a "song of information." She claimed: "Usually *qigong* therapists send out *qi* to dispel diseases. If you are gifted with the power of vision (*yan'gong* 眼功), you could see white *qi* driving away black *qi*. When the black *qi* is gone, the disease is cured. But I use 'information language' instead to cure diseases. It works the same way. . . . People should not take medicine in the process, for medicine would conflict with the 'information' I send out to disperse the black *qi*."[16] Preposterous as the story sounds, nonetheless it was the discourse of information prevalent in the 1980s that transformed the word "information" into a mystical signifier.

Magic Waves in the Age of the "Information Explosion"

As "information" became a buzzword in various official and popular media, the fascination with extrasensory powers and magic waves arose to address the anxieties that accompanied the "information explosion" in post-Mao China. In 1976 there were 542 periodicals published in China. By 1979 the number had soared to 1,470, an almost threefold increase. This burgeoning of print culture, on the one hand, responded to a liberal demand for the lifting of restrictions on publication, reflected in the well-known slogan at the time that "there should be no forbidden zone in reading." But on the other hand, it also created a "hunger for information." Referring to the new pressure that individuals felt to absorb the sudden flood of new knowledge, this "hunger" was also a discursive construction, creating an image of the "opened-up" China of Deng's regime as opposed to the "sealed-up" China of Mao. People who had suffered from a "paucity of information" under Mao were now exhorted to embrace a new era of information proliferation. In other words, although this discussion of "information overload" on the surface resembles similar discussions elsewhere in the world, it had a unique political resonance in post-Mao China. Conceiving of Mao's China as a "sealed-up" communist authoritarian state meant that "information" per se became charged with liberal connotations. The talk about "information overload" thus reflected a new pressure on the previous socialist subject to transform herself in the emerging new order as China was rejoining the global capitalist system.

New journals (such as *Electronics World* 电子世界, see Figure 7), popular science pamphlets, and translations of monographs on various topics created a self-consciousness of "uninformedness" among people struggling to absorb the suddenly abundant information. By the early 1980s, there were numerous discussions of the strategies needed to deal with this "information explosion." In one 1987 article, "Sensory Deprivation and the Information Explosion," information was regarded as even more crucial to human life than food. According to the author, human beings nowadays were "surrounded by oceans of information": not only had three-quarters of the current stock of scientific knowledge been added since the 1950s, but the renewal cycle of knowledge production had dramatically shortened since the 1970s, thus creating a greater urgency for people to reeducate themselves. The author, echoing Toffler's 1970 book, *Future Shock*, went on to warn that the information explosion could generate physiological unfitness of the body in just the same way as information deprivation could.[17]

Despite this expanded print culture, there was an increasing awareness of the challenges to the very form of the book posed by screens and electronic devices. Jin Kemu, a renowned scholar and translator at Peking University, argued in a 1984 essay for the journal *Dushu* 读书 (Reading) that book culture was on the eve of a revolution now that a silicon chip the size of a fingernail could store millions of characters. An encyclopedia could be compressed into just a few disks. Under these conditions, he asserted, the ways in which books were "read" should be transformed as well.[18]

While Jin preserved a nostalgic attachment to book-reading, Qian Xuesen and his followers aimed to circumvent reading itself by shifting to a mode of information transmission beyond ordinary human perception. "Image-recognition through nonvisual organs" (*fei shijue qiguan tuxiang shibie* 非视觉器官图像识别) to them indicated an unmediated, real-time connection of the human body to waveform-based information technology that would eventually supplant the paper-based book culture. *The vehicle for extrasensory powers was believed to be an unknown type of electromagnetic wave*: "Biological electromagnetic waves are probably the

Figure 7. Cover of the inaugural issue of *Electronics World*, no. 1 (1979). Design by Tu Jiafang, photograph by Ying Jie.

reason to explain image recognition through non-visual organs. . . . Every human being is a sender of electromagnetic waves, and everyone a receiver too."[19] Proponents of extrasensory powers believed that once the mechanism of extrasensory powers could be reproduced, human beings would no longer rely solely on their eyes and ears to obtain knowledge. The human body could be directly fed effortlessly with constant informational streams through ubiquitous waves.

Thus the fascination with magic waves largely derived from the strong urge to absorb information in the shortest amount of time. A science fiction story, entitled "Dreams" and published in 1980, captured this sense of urgency by imagining a miracle-making sleep-learning machine. The protagonist is a little girl named Zhao Xiaomei, who by chance becomes involved in an ambitious project. As explained by a scientist in the story, this experiment attempts a race with time:

> Since human beings cannot avoid dreaming when sleeping, why shouldn't we make people study some basic knowledge in their dreams? To show the significance of this idea, let's do some mathematics: if a man's life expectancy is around 80 to 100 years, the time he spends on sleep is up to 27 to 33 years or so. . . . Once it is possible to make use of the sleep time, we can immediately shorten the learning process of human beings.[20]

Xiaomei mistakenly takes home another traveler's suitcase on her train trip. Inside the suitcase, she finds a square metal box. Out of curiosity, she presses one white button, but nothing happens. The next morning, however, to her surprise, she finds herself able to recite fluently an English essay she spent only a few minutes reading the night before. It turns out that the metal box is a memory machine that a group of scientists had developed to help people memorize what they had read as they slept. Xiaomei accidentally becomes the first human being to undergo testing with the machine.

In a story entitled "The Sleepless Son-in-Law," a stealthy-looking son-in-law who often shuts himself indoors and makes all kinds of noises in the middle of the night is subject to the secret investigation of his mother-in-law. She peeps into his room from the window and finds his whole body covered in a tangle of wires. A moment later, he starts his unusual midnight activities, beginning with physical exercises, then reading, then reciting newspapers. Pressed for an explanation for his bizarre behavior, the son-in-law finally reveals that he is experimenting on an electronic *qigong* device with the power of healing diseases, dissipating fatigue, and restoring physical strength. With the help of the device, people need little sleep and thus have more time for work and study.

The notion of an electronic *qigong* device is not a mere fabrication. By studying the mechanism of *qigong* and extrasensory powers, somatological scientists hoped to manufacture a device emitting the same sort of "information" with the purported healing effects of *qigong*. Through analyzing the waveforms of *qi* sent out by *qigong* practitioners, scientists reproduced the infrared rays that were believed to underlie the effects of *qi*. The device, called an "infrared ray information healing device," was reported to have been proved to have the same therapeutic effects of *qigong*.[21]

It is important to note that the late 1970s and 1980s also witnessed a sudden boom in science fiction in China, a development that can be interpreted as an immediate response to the eminence of science and technology in both official and popular discourse. From 1976 to 1981, about six hundred science fiction novels and stories appeared as books or in magazines. Founded in 1978, the journal *Kexue wenyi* 科学文艺 (Scientific literature and arts) became an important venue for Chinese science fiction. Other science fiction journals that mushroomed in this period include *Zhihui shu* 智慧树 (Wisdom tree), *Kehuan haiyang* 科幻海洋 (Seas of science fiction), *Shijie kehuan yicong* 世界科幻译丛 (Translations of world science fiction), and *Kehuan shijie* 科幻世界 (World of science fiction).

In these stories, the wish to change the temporality and physiological limits of the human body resonated with the ambitions of the Great Leap Forward, when images of sleepless "iron wo/man" were everywhere. Yet the relation between technology and humans is reversed in the science fiction stories of the Reforms Era. For instance, compare these stories of magic devices with a short story written by a mariner and published in 1959. Titled "Even Telegrams Are Not Fast Enough" (*Wuxiandian ye ganbushang* 无线电也赶不上), this brief sketch portrays dockworkers who continuously receive telegrams instructing them to enlarge their freight-loading capacity for incoming shipments and how they successfully managed these challenges with collective wisdom and a strong will. By the end of the story, workers managed to increase even more of the loading capacity, and this time *before* the next telegraphic instruction arrives—their innovations come even faster than telegrams can travel.[22] As this story exemplifies, socialist heroes rely on their revolutionary will to overcome the biological cycle of the body and push the limits imposed by the external environment.[23] To the scientific imagination of the early 1980s, the magic of the human will has been transferred to external influences and devices that can continuously feed the human body with information. The human body became a transparent medium for information waves to pass through. If Qian Xuesen's impassioned outlook of somatic science on the surface partakes of the optimistic investment of Mao's revolutionary mobilization in human subjectivity, nothing can be more ironic than this human subject empowered and entangled with information waves.

Why Waves? Versatile Television and Body–Machine Entanglement

Why did waves, which often remained ambiguous between the real and the imagined, become the most prominent, magic medium for instant, high-speed information transmission between the human body and the information environment? I argue that the unprecedented expansion in wireless broadcast and the growing importance of television as a new information channel in the 1980s fueled the imaginary of magic waves.

The number of Chinese radio stations increased from 106 in 1980 to 213 in 1985, and the rate of radio-set ownership doubled to 241 million.[24] Starting in 1983, local television stations (including municipal and county level) were approved by the central government. With this new policy, the number of stations surged to 202 by 1985, covering 68.4 percent of the whole population. A television set was one of the most popular gifts that the Chinese brought back to their families and friends from overseas. In the late 1970s, foreign brands occupied a large proportion of television sets owned by Chinese households. Because these devices were manufactured in different countries, their systems also varied. As a result, many technological discussions about television in the early 1980s focused on converting different systems in order to adapt imported sets to local broadcast codes. Domestic television production was also a primary focus among technological developments of consumer electronics: a 1980 issue of *Electronics World* featured a cover story about a flat-screen television developed by Hangzhou University (Figure 8). By 1987, China had become the world's largest producer of televisions, with an annual output of 19.34 million units.[25]

The rise of television in China was also marked by features that were historically specific to the early postsocialist context. During the Mao era, especially during the Cultural Revolution (1966–76), networks of wired loudspeakers ensured, through broadcast sound, centralized control by the Party even in the remote countryside. Auditory Maoist messages reached every corner of the socialist space.[26] The highly politicized space that wired loudspeakers covered, however, was undermined and eventually depoliticized by the late 1970s with the increase in the number of television sets and *wireless* broadcasts, which enabled the production of new sorts of private space.[27] This depoliticization of media technology also manifests in the understanding of television increasingly as an information medium. Information here is conveniently (if naively) conceived as neutral, nonpolitical, and utilitarian.

At the same time, television itself was undergoing deep transformations around the world, becoming *a versatile information platform compatible with various media forms*. Chinese media technicians and developers closely followed the recent developments and expansion of the medium. It is no exaggeration to say that television was placed at the frontier of new audiovisual technology. Thus it is often the television screen, instead of the film screen, that was evoked as the psychic media in the cases of extrasensory powers.

One author, when introducing the notion of "digital TV" to Chinese readers, traced the origins of digital technology to the invention of Morse code, and argued that the method of pulse-code modulation (PCM) invented for voice communication in 1937 by an employee of International Telephone and Telegraph in France (an engineer named Alec

Figure 8. Cover of *Electronics World*, no. 1 (1980).

Reeves) laid the foundation of binary digital coding. However, it was not until the appearance of large-scale integration (LSI) after the mass production of transistors that digital television became technologically possible.[28] This genealogy debunks the myth of the "newness" of the digital, revealing the continuity between old and new media.

More significant transformations occurred at the interface at the user's end. It was expected that microprocessors installed within television sets would enable the user to enlarge images, to pause and replay sequences, and even to watch several channels at the same time. Televisions could also be used to receive other textual and diagrammatic information, such as weather forecasts, commodity prices, and news. The Teletext service first created in the UK was one such information-retrieval system that was used to send what was called an "electronic magazine" along with TV signals. The texts might include subtitles in multiple languages, government notices, sports news, and advertisements.[29] If Teletext was a one-directional information transmission, Videotex promised a more interactive interface. Connecting their television sets with information centers through cable television lines or telephone lines, users could request information, send messages to other users, manage bank transfers, and do remote shopping.[30]

The Chinese translation of "videotex" as "visible data" (*keshi shuju* 可视数据) indicates that the television screen was becoming more and more aligned with the functions of data retrieval and display rather than with the medium of film, to which television is more commonly linked. Another example was the development of the "EIDAK" system, a machine that fetches information from somewhere else for its user.[31] In fact, the most popular home computer or personal computer in the US and Japanese markets in the mid-1980s was the Sinclair ZX81 (manufactured in Scotland by Timex Corporation), which was made of a microprocessor with a television screen. Consumers enjoyed additional functions of their televisions enabled by microprocessors and the new life of the old electronic device.[32] This was also a period that witnessed a fast increase in the importation of microcomputers in China, mostly used in the areas of financial management, accounting, and data processing in governmental units and enterprises. In 1984 alone, about twenty thousand Apple computers and sixteen thousand Apple clones—imitations of Apple or imitations assembled from imported parts—appeared in China.[33]

But the presence of personal computers did not generate a discourse of the digital as a competitor or a linear successor to the analog. Nor did it supplant the key role of television in the 1980s imaginary of information technologies. In the context of China in the 1980s, where television sets were used for purposes other than receiving broadcast television signals, all sorts of screens (except those in movie theaters) were called "television screens." For example, a popular Chinese television journal reported on an electronic device for the blind invented in the United States. With a television screen attaching to the head of the user and a pulse-sensor attached to her wrist, a connected microprocessor could guide the person around and out of the way of obstacles.[34] Exceeding the common conception of television in the broadcast era as simply a home device and a receiver of broadcast signals, such screens were conceived as a highly versatile medium that could be connected with different devices for diverse purposes.

A new medium associated with television around this time was the videodisc, or "television disk" (*dianshi changpian* 电视唱片) in Chinese. First produced as the Television Electronic Disc by a German company, and followed by other companies such as National Panasonic and Phillips, this technology was often regarded as a forerunner of the DVD. Faced with severe competition from magnetic video recorders in the home media market, videodisc was most welcomed in the realm of education. This was because videodisc was more an information system than simply an audiovisual medium. It could accommodate different forms of media so that microfilm, film strips, 35-millimeter slides, printed materials such as newspapers and journals, and computer output could all be displayed on one screen. Images on the disk could be located immediately through its search engine.[35] Such expanded functions of television made the medium a perfectly flexible passage to digital information systems.

Videodiscs were not the only locus for discussions of televisual education in China. The use of broadcast television as an information channel was also adopted for pedagogic purposes in order to meet the challenge of the "information economy"—thus connecting it in a concrete way to concurrent fantasies about instantaneous knowledge transmission through magic waves. The plan to build a nationwide broadcast network for higher education was approved by the central government in 1978.[36] A year later, China Central Radio and TV University was founded in Beijing. Soon, more than twenty-eight areas and provinces around the country had established provincial radio and TV universities and prefectural branch schools. More than one million students enrolled in the first four years. Classes were broadcast by China Central Television thirty-three hours per week, supplemented with offerings from local stations, local evening classes, and recordings of lectures distributed through the mail system and the local radio and TV universities. Enrollment was flexible, with options for full-time and part-time study. Unlike regular college admissions, students were not age-restricted and included young people awaiting employment, factory workers, and professionals who were interested in further education.[37] After the introduction of satellite television broadcasts in China in 1985, 368 transit stations were set up, many of which were scattered in remote areas (e.g., 70 in Guangxi, 27 in Qinghai), as well as 1,607 receiver stations across the country.[38] Long-distance education provided a highly effective alternative mode to regular higher education. Stories of magic information-carrying waves reflected this crucial role of wireless broadcasts in distributing information, but they also addressed anxieties about the "information explosion." Wireless broadcasts provided a new information distribution channel as an alternative to traditional publication and education and established new modes of knowledge transmission before the coming of the digital age. Information acquisition was no longer confined to the limited hours and four walls of the classroom. Instead, ubiquitous waves could wrap the human being in an information environment.

This new information channel also transformed traditional college education. In 1978, the Ministry of Education built the Institute of Research on Modern Education Technology in East China Normal University (Shanghai), with an emphasis on developing the educational application of computers and satellite television. In the same year, the institute started a graduate program, offering master's degrees in two areas: computer-aided education and the transmission and processing of images for educational purposes. A year later, East China Normal University founded the Center for Electrified Education in order to popularize such media technology as slide shows, film, radio, television, microprocessors, and computers in teaching.

Discussions of "electrified education," as in a pair of articles by Yu Wenzhao from 1983, introduced perspectives from systems theory, which regards human beings as part of human–machine closed-circuit systems.[39] Education in this environment was seen as information transmission between machines (which stored and presented information) and human beings (who gave feedback based on what they received and processed). Machines were supposed to push the limits of the human sensorium by capturing and displaying instantaneous changes that would otherwise be unnoticed by human beings. In his articles, Yu also points out that the methods for human beings to send feedback to machines were not as robust. Thus, researchers began looking for ways to transmit the bioelectric currents of the human brain and the physiological signals of the human body directly into machines.[40]

A cartoon about "electrified education" from the first issue of *Electronics World* in 1979 dramatizes this human–machine/machine–human pedagogy in which analog and digital technologies were mixed (Figure 9). On the left, beside a television monitor featuring a prominent antenna and hooked up to a reel-to-reel tape recorder, a scientist "programs" the brain of a cylindrical robot reading a printed book. A curling wire connects the robot to the television. The caption above reads, "I teach it." On the right, the robot teaches a young girl who writes in a notebook while looking at a computer. The computer, in turn, is hooked up to the brain of the robot and to a reel-to-reel tape machine, which is in turn connected to the earphones worn by the student. The caption reads, "It teaches me."[41]

It is exactly against this backdrop of massive expansion of wireless broadcasts and the recognition of television as both a new medium and an information channel that the discourses and imaginaries of magic waves emerged in 1980s China. Magic waves became the foremost medium for information transmission. The parallel between this development in media technology and the conception of extrasensory powers as waveform

Figure 9. Hu Yongguang, "Dianhua jiaoyu" [Electrified education], illustration from *Electronics World*, no. 1 (1979).

information was evidenced in the analogy between the television screen and the human body in various accounts about extrasensory powers. He Chongyin, the chief editor of the *Chinese Journal of Nature*, in a speech regarding the phenomena of "image-recognition through nonvisual organs" (*fei shijue qiguan tuxiang shibie* 非视觉器官图像识别), compiled a set of questions to consider: If television sets relied on complicated electrical circuits to process information, could the mechanism of the human body be similar to this? His hypothesis was that unknown types of waveforms were the fundamental vehicle for extrasensory information, just as electromagnetic waves were for wireless broadcasts. Furthermore, could certain parts of the human body function specifically for information display, just as a television screen does?[42] Another group of researchers based in Shanghai brought in a group of people who presumably possessed the power of parapsychological transference for laboratory tests, and discovered what they called "screen effects" in the process of transference. They characterized the "screen effects" as having several aspects: transferred information, even Chinese characters, always appeared as pictorial information. The receiver did not have to understand the transferred content, nor did it need to know the characters in order to receive the information. If there was a large amount of information, the transference might resemble the scanning process of a television screen, appearing portion by portion. The characters scrolled across their minds from one side to another just like credits crawling across a television screen.[43] It should be noted that the way they described "screen effects" was more analogous to the scanning process and information transmission of television than to the preconstituted frames of film images.

While these examples shared an emphasis on the role of the human brain in processing information, other body parts, such as ears, palms, or even armpits, were also believed to be capable of sending and receiving extrasensory information. This emphasis on the brain continues the Cartesian tradition of prioritizing the brain over other parts of the human body, but in a significantly different way: no longer a "sacred" seat of human rationality, the brain is an information processor, not so different from other parts of the body. The brain is regarded as part of the larger information system of the body, although a most active part.

Waves as the Digital

These developments of television and its applications in both China and other regions suggest that television was increasingly conceived as an information platform of great flexibility so as to accommodate different media forms. Such flexibility and convertibility between different media forms is often regarded as the outcome of the digital. Friedrich Kittler, for example, believes that "the general digitalization of channels and information erases the differences among individual media." He once predicted that "once movies and music, phone calls and texts reach households via optical fiber cables, the formerly distinct media of television, radio, telephone and mail converge, standardized by transmission frequencies and bit format."[44] This standardization and the ensuing erasure of medium specificity led Mark B. N. Hansen to claim an unprecedented flexibility for digital media and "the possibility for the universal and limitless inter-conversion of data."[45] Yet the aforementioned developments of television, although definitely empowered by the digital, indicate a flexibility of the medium and a convergence of media that did not necessarily depend on the advent of the digital. In fact, the waves, attributed with flexibility and endless convertibility, were believed to have the power of enabling obstruct-free information flows among different material entities, from the human body to various electronic devices. If the discussion about the "information explosion" and various descriptions of physiological unfitness indicated the necessary retuning of the human body, flexible waves were imagined as most effectively interfacing the body and information systems. The understanding of extrasensory powers as magic waves reflects the renewed necessity to reposition and readjust the human body in the information environment.

The interest in extrasensory powers was nothing new in human history. The question of whether one could "see" without using one's eyes, according to Mark Paterson, was part of an Enlightenment fascination with the relation between perception and knowledge. The famous "Molyneux question" raised by the French philosopher Denis Didcrot tells the story of a blind man in the town of Molyneux who asserted that he could "see" with the touch of his hands. The debates on the "Molyneux question" among philosophers divided into two sides: one side, including Berkeley and Locke, insisted upon the specificity of each sense and the incommensurability of different sensory systems; the other side conceived sensory perception as *amodal*, which denoted the existence of sensory information "prior to its processing as specifically audile, visual and tactile." As Paterson shows, the division was actually a disagreement between an empiricism that denied any "general ideas" prior to sensory experiences and those who argued for the existence of "innate concepts."[46]

This question about "visualization" in the blind had also attracted interest among neuropsychologists. Oliver Sacks, for example, has documented various cases of "visualization" experiences in the blind. Sacks draws on studies published since the 1970s on the phenomenon of various adaptations in the brain to demonstrate "a certain flexibility and plasticity in the brain." He argues that sensory modalities can never be considered in isolation. As he puts it: "The world of the blind, of the blinded, it seems, can be especially rich in such in-between states—the intersensory, the metamodal—states for which we have no common language."[47] He continues to ask whether a visual image could be built on nonvisual information, a question for which Qian and other Chinese cyberneticists also sought an answer in their "somatic science" investigation into "extrasensory powers." In other words, extrasensory powers at the beginning of the 1970s in the eyes of many scientists were serious questions worth probing into.

In this climate, the Chinese Association for Somatic Science was soon established, with He Chongyin and other researchers from different regions serving as the executive committee. The association convened frequent conferences, demonstrations, and symposia and formed an expanding network. At first, the *Chinese Journal of Nature* served as an important platform for the discussion on somatic science. With the association publication of *Correspondence on Somatic Science*, and eventually the foundation of the *Chinese Journal of Somatic Science*, somatic science quickly became institutionalized as a new interdisciplinary research area all over the country. Chinese researchers also participated in international exchanges in this area. In 1982, two Chinese representatives were sent to Cambridge University for an international conference organized by the Parapsychological Association and Society for Psychical Research. One of the representatives was Chen Xin, who also worked closely with Qian Xuesen. They gave a talk entitled "Research on Extrasensory Powers in China." Upon their return, they wrote a report introducing the history of parapsychological research in the UK and the US and provided an overview of the current state of research in other countries.

It should be noted that this revival of shared interest in "image-recognition through nonvisual organs" among both neuroscientists and cyberneticists appeared *exactly at the moment* when digital media became a more visible presence in the 1970s and 1980s. While digital media produced amorphous data that no longer pertained to media specificity, sensory perceptions were also perceived as "amodal" information not limited by an isolated sensory channel. To Qian's followers, *"extrasensory" information was "amodal" information*: that is, the differentiation between the visual, tactile, auditory, and/or any other specific sense does not apply to extrasensory information. Such "extrasensory" data was expected to surpass the specificity of each sense.[48] By freeing itself from the specific materiality of individual sensory organs, such extrasensory information obtained a plasticity, or universal convertibility, that could be directly connected to other waveform information, and therefore admitted no obstacle in the information circuits between the human body and the surrounding environment.

This prospect is also what Friedrich Kittler identifies in his essay "The History of Communication Media" as a possibility provided by the mathematical coding of waves. The electrification of sensory input data through telephone and other technical media enables the conversion of sensory data into waveforms that surpass the specificity of the senses. Digitization, according to him, further standardizes the coding of waves, facilitating waves with easier convertibility and connectibility. Kittler ends the essay by suggesting that the ongoing research on biological circuitry and the simulation of brain functions would be crucial to achieve "multidimensional signal processing in real time," which would itself eventually end the history of communication technologies since information transmission would by then no longer rely on humanity.[49] In other words, human beings are the final obstacle to the limit of communication technology, to the formation of an all-inclusive, real-time system of information circuits. Kittler's prediction of a future all-inclusive communication system should be historicized against the backdrop of digitization. If the start of massive digitization in the 1970s and 1980s means the convergence of media to Kittler, it also led him to speculate on the full incorporation of the human body into information circuits. The flexibility of the digital becomes fetishized to erase even the material and structural difference of the human body.

Qian Xuesen's interest in extrasensory powers in the 1980s in an environment of increasing media convergence was driven by a similar desire to reduce feedback time and turn human beings into highly efficient information-processing machines. Extrasensory information was imagined as no different from, and thus easily communicable with, the ubiquitous waveforms of information technology. *Extrasensory information therefore can be regarded as "digital" in its universal convertibility and connectibility with other waveforms.* This is to say, both Kittler's argument on communication media and Qian's understanding of extrasensory powers were driven by a strong urge to find an expedited communication between the human body and information environments.

But Qian still wanted to reserve a place for the uniqueness of the human body, cautioning his coworkers against any overemphasis on similarity but neglecting the differences between plants and animals, between inferior animals and more advanced ones. Asserting that humans are "the soul of the universe" in a correspondence with Chen Xin, Qian insisted on a humanistic view.[50] But it was unclear how this humanist value could be compatible with the cybernetic vision, a similar unresolved tension that Katherine Hayles detects in Norbert Wiener's thought.[51] Qian stated that the human body should be seen as an open complex giant system, for which Hermann Haken's synergetics—the study of the formation and self-organization of patterns and structures in open systems—simply falls short. This open complex giant system is constantly evolving and developing in its interactions with the universe around it, and thus the somatic science should adopt a view of the "human-heaven" relationship (tianren guan 天人观), which he believes, curiously, would be compatible with Marxism.[52] For this reason, he reiterated how his Marxist-informed system theory should be more comprehensive than the tradition of systems theory developed from Ludwig von Bertalanffy, the Austrian biologist known for his general systems theory. Yet it remains puzzling how and to what extent he could claim his somatic science to be following dialectical materialism. These contradictions and tensions reveal the uneasy efforts of Qian to navigate and negotiate between cybernetic visions, philosophical traditions, and complex social forces in Post-Mao China.

Similarly, the human body in this cybernetic view is imagined to be strangely irrelevant to human consciousness but at the same time empowering to the human mind. Because the body can absorb information without the participation of human consciousness, the human, just like a computer plugged into networks, will be continuously synched and updated. The aforementioned stories about turning "idle" sleep time into the "useful" and "productive" time of sleep-learning are representative of this pursuit for instantaneous, nonstop information transmission.

Once sleep is overcome, the human body can be turned into a ceaseless information-processing machine. Although speed and temporality were also repeatedly emphasized in Mao's China, the regulation of temporality then was driven more by central planners and Party authorities than by the market and the pursuit of profits as in capitalist society. Because of the reliance on central planners to allocate production resources to achieve centrally made production targets and due to the frequent shortages of production supplies that resulted from the centralized allocation system, socialist workers proceed with their jobs more in a rhythm of fits and starts, a temporality that is distinctive from the steady and continuous machine-rhythm of capitalist Fordist factories.[53] Therefore, the emergence of the cybernetic body for ceaseless, instantaneous information transmission signaled new rhythms of the body and labor at a time of post-Mao economic reforms and marketization and the rise of the discourse of an "information economy."

Discontent with the "Information Body"

The emergence of this "information body" was closely related not only to the "information explosion" in the 1980s but also, more important, to the anticipation of an "information society" and a "knowledge-based economy." In an interview published in *Renmin ribao* (People's daily), a major Communist Party newspaper, Alvin Toffler summarized his argument in *The Third Wave* by asserting that "a new mode of production based on 'information' and characterized by 'rapidity'" had challenged the "conventions of industrial civilization," and "knowledgeable information workers" would soon supplant "muscular laborers."[54] Alongside Toffler's book and his personal visits to China in the 1980s, Daniel Bell, a Harvard sociologist, was another voice who predicted the diminishing of physical labor with the coming of a society that would be optimized by new "intellectual technology." The central thesis of his *Coming of Post-Industrial Society* was the rise of the intelligentsia, including professionals and technicians such as scientists, engineers, and administrative managers, whose role in social planning and management was becoming increasingly prominent because of their professional knowledge and technical skills. Bell's book was translated into Chinese in the early 1980s as well, and thus converged with the technocratic, developmentalist schema of Deng's China, as well as the elevation of mental labor over physical labor.

This elevation of "information work" was also part of the politics of depoliticization in post-Mao China. "Information" here is conveniently conceived as neutral, nonpolitical, and utilitarian. Left aside are the highly politicized proletarian subjects during Mao's era that compromised workers, peasants, and soldiers. This transformation of social value was accompanied by a new hierarchy of labor division and the growth of anxieties and desire among peasants to get rid of the urban–rural division that already existed in Mao's era, but now had expanded as a marker of a new social hierarchy. In "A Lost Dream" (*Diushi de meng*), a story published in 1983, a country girl who yearns so much for a college education that she tries to commit suicide when she fails the college entrance exams. The daughter of peasants, she abhors her future as a peasant and manual worker like her parents and rests all her hopes on becoming an intellectual and engineer by getting a college education. This reverses the glorification of the muscular body of peasants and workers performing physical and factory labor in Mao's era as seen in both the visual and literary culture of that period.[55]

Fortunately, she encounters Dr. Di. A cognitive scientist, Dr. Di promises to turn her instantly into a highly knowledgeable woman by means of a certain mysterious medium, whose efficiency of information transmission surpasses "old media" such as language and writing. The girl agrees, and goes to sleep "covered under white bed sheets in the observation room.... Around her head, a dozen electronic eyes are watching her closely, collecting every single small fluctuation in her brainwaves." As information transmission begins, the effects of Dr. Di's mysterious medium are displayed as waveform graphs on a twenty-four-inch monitor: "Several waves are swirling in torrents, accompanied by flashing flames and sparkling spots, as if they were fireworks at festivals, or flying bullets in the battlefield.... Gradually, the confusing, overlapping waves are replaced by continuous, beautiful sine waves of symmetry and harmony."[56]

Thrilled with this display, Dr. Di celebrates his success in achieving immediate and massive information transmission: "I know her brain is a land in drought now, hungrily devouring torrents of information. It is absorbing, filtering, categorizing, and storing. She is undergoing the most dramatic transformation ever in her life; her millions of neurons are experiencing unprecedented stimulation. Every one of her nerve endings is trembling with bioelectric currents."[57] On awaking, the girl finds herself fluent in French, English, Russian, and German and erudite in mathematics, physics, and biology. This is just one of many science fiction stories published in late 1970s and 1980s that imagines direct information transmission to human beings, even when asleep. The acquisition of information is no longer registered by human consciousness but actually becomes a subliminal function of the body.

However, examining closely the affective description of the graphs in the passage cited at the beginning of this story, it is worth asking how an entirely different category of things, from astronomical phenomena to a land in drought, from bullets to a symphony, all are bound together through a series of metaphors. They bridge the interior of the brain and exterior phenomena, as if there are correspondent structures between the framework of human brains and other things in the world. The interior and the exterior, the abstract graphs of waves and the activities of life, are all analogous to each other so as to make their boundaries and differences irrelevant. The effect of technological sublimity in this passage comes exactly from the power of this universal analogy, which breaks the boundaries of individuals and bodies.

Katherine Hayles points out that analogy is the cornerstone of Norbert Weiner's cybernetics theory, in the sense that "analogy is not merely an ornament of language but is a powerful conceptual mode that constitutes meaning through relation." In Weiner's formula, analogy is "constituted as a universal exchange system that allows data to move across boundaries."[58] Analogy, as Hayles acutely points out, indicates an impetus toward a universality that transcends the specificity of myriad things. However, analogy in this story plays out in a way that, paradoxically, returns to the tangibility and concreteness of "ordinary" sensory perceptions. As is seen in the paragraph, similes and metaphors describe the

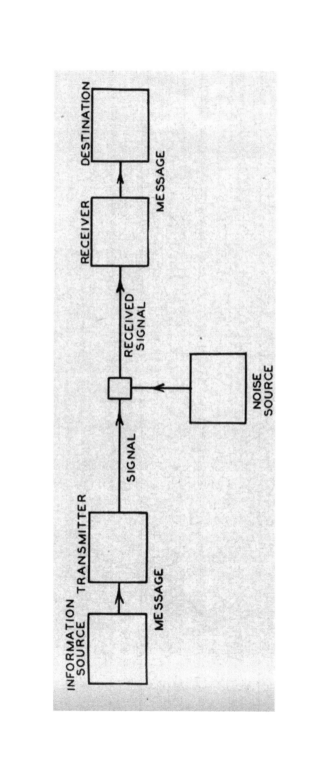

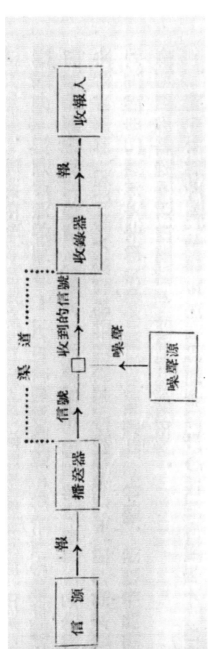

Figure 10. Top: Diagram of a general communication system. From Claude Shannon, "A Mathematical Theory of Communication." Bottom: Chinese Translation of Claude Shannon's diagram of a general communication system. From Wang Shouren, *Xinxilun yu shuxue lilun* [Mathematical theory of information theory], 1957.

abstract waveforms, but the vehicles (such as torrents and symphony) often overpower the tenor (the abstract waveform), to the extent that the passage is filled with sensory excitement. The "universal" power of the waveforms is transferred into the concrete sensations of each vehicle. If the monitor replaces the body with abstract graphs, the metaphors and similes evoke the materiality of the body by framing information as a corporeal experience.

The story does not end with the girl turning into an information worker as she desires to be. A few years later, when Di goes to Suzhou for a vacation, he is intrigued by all sorts of legendary tales about a "Tofu Sister." He goes to her tofu stand and finds a girl with "clouds of black hair covered exquisitely by a piece of white and blue homespun cloth, and a silver hairpin in her bun."[59] He is shocked when he realizes that this traditionally attired country girl is the perfect, intelligent creature he has created and whom he talked to years ago about the most complicated and abstruse scientific theories. Now she cannot recall a single English word. As if to mock the redundancy of the transmitted knowledge to her present situation, she asks him: "What's the use of theories of relativity and probability, quantum mechanics, or Riemannian geometry for a Tofu-making woman? They are no more useful to her than pickled mustard root, dried shrimps, sesame oil, or fish sauce."[60]

The girl thus renounces one type of knowledge—knowledge as information torrents that are indifferent to her individuality—for another type, namely, knowledge of concrete things as embodied in her dancelike movements in making tofu. Such an opposition between the two types of knowledge interestingly reenacts the division between the extrasensory information and sensory perceptions that Qian Xuesen and his followers demarcated. While the former is driven by a pursuit of universal exchangeability, the latter pertains to specificity. In other words, the body that tenaciously resists its dissolution into information flows is pitted against the body that is abstracted as a node for universal information exchange.

This abstract information body is implied in Claude Shannon's now well-known diagram for communication (Figure 10).[61] Conceiving communication as the transfer of information from the source to the destination, Shannon in fact presumes the coexistence of the source and the destination in an even, homogeneous space. The body as the receiver and processor of information is accordingly an exchangeable spot in such a spatial layout of communication networks. With this presumption, Shannon and other cyberneticists aim at the engineering possibilities of shortening the information transfer time between two spatial spots and reducing the response time between devices and humans. Real-time instantaneity of the cybernetic logic is built precisely upon this assumption of homogeneous space.

In this sense, the sensuous, irreducible corporality depicted in opposition to abstract information in this story should be read as a resistance to the homogeneous space in which everything becomes exchangeable. This homogenous space is further problematized at the end of the story. With her renouncing an information body, the girl also goes through dramatic recodification, now conspicuously marked by folk-style attire, as if this were the only way to refuse the reduction of her body into a blank silicon chip. The conscious invocation of the local through her attire and her intimate connections with the folks in a closely bonded community produces an imaginary of the local that is of irreducible particularity. The story ends with an idyllic country scene, in which "a skiff is drifting alongside with the silvery ripples on the river. A stout man with thick, black eyebrows and a gallant, full beard is standing at the prow of the boat. . . . The evening wind lifts up his white short gown, exposing his sturdy browned upper body."

The corporality banished by the informational mode of communication returns in this passage as an almost spectacular muscular body, a body that is imagined as an "organic" component of the country that stays out of the ineluctable network of information flows. This dualism of abstract information versus tangible corporality should be read as an effect of the story to inadvertently bring under critical attention a new round of regulation and discipline of the body under the emerging information economy. Incorporating human beings into information systems is not simply a technological question of digitizing the human body but always involves the contention of social interests and power. The hypersensualized bodies of the girl and the boatman thus become the imagined but tension-ridden site to fight against the encroaching power of information capitalism.

Figure 11. Illustrations from Wang Songyin, "Diushi de meng" [A lost dream], *Xiaoshuo Lin* [Forest of stories], no. 3 (1983).

In a similar way, the tension between the ostentatious "folk" display and high level of theory and knowledge in the story should also be read symptomatically as a constructed dualism. Around the time the story was published, "the folk" reemerged as a powerful discourse and literary imaginary. By the mid-1980s, "roots-seeking literature" had become popular, with its flag-bearer, Han Shaogong, claiming that roots-seeking writers "found in themselves a strong desire to discover the uninterrupted traditions of folk life."[62] Such an impulse toward "the folk" should be read side by side with the anxieties over the radical historical shifts China was undergoing as it was reincorporated into the global system of capitalism. In other words, the obstinate materiality of the body and the irreducible particularity of the local could be seen as a resistance to the rule of universal exchangeability of the capitalist market, the similar logic of exchangeability that is also manifested in the interconvertability of digital data.

By invoking the irreducible locality and denying the homogenous space presumed by information theory, this story also challenges the cybernetic logic of nonstop, real-time instantaneity. If such cybernetic instantaneity underlies the fascination with the unlimited flexibility and convertibility of the digital, this story, by questioning nonstop, instantaneous temporality, also invokes a critique of the digital. While the discourse of magic waves in the post-Mao 1980s encapsulated the information fantasies as China was joining a world of information capitalism, this story evokes an imagined alternative to this order. However, this imagined alternative with its recourse to *an ahistorical past* symptomatically erases the socialist past. The muscular body is no longer a body of the laboring proletariat in Mao's era.

Nonsensical Waves and the Unreadable History at the Edge of the Liminal

"Dreams" is not an isolated case about the role of science fiction in this "information fever" in post-Mao China. Besides the mushrooming science fiction journals, mainstream literary journals also showed a strong interest in science fiction. For example, "A Lost Dream" was published in a "pure literature" journal called *Xiaoshuo lin* (Forests of stories). The genre of science fiction in China since its birth in late imperial time has always foregrounded the ideological functions of modern science and technology in relation to the issues of modernity, national identity, developmental discourse, and the imaginations of utopia/dystopia.[63] The boom in science fiction in the 1980s is no exception. This wave of science fiction was spawned by the shift of the CCP's policy in the late 1970s and Deng's elevation of science and technology as the first productive force. Deng Xiaoping's speech at the National Conference of Science in 1978 was lauded as the start of the "spring of science" in China, which indicated a reversal of Mao's intellectual policy and the reestablishment of professional researchers and experts as the main force for science and technology development. Under this political climate, unsurprisingly, Qian Xuesen believed that the warfare among nations in the future would be "an intellectual war" primarily in the realm of science and technology.[64] Science fiction was thus seen as useful in disseminating scientific knowledge among the masses and educating the masses with a scientific attitude. This understanding of science fiction as a tool for "science popularization" (kepu 科普) was well accepted in the 1950s. But with the change in the political climate and the rise of a different system of knowledge production and dissemination, this genre disappeared during the Cultural Revolution. Its resurgence at the turn of the 1980s therefore evidenced a shift in official ideology from class-struggle politics to economic development and a mode of technocratic governmentality.

But science fiction is not merely a docile tool of official ideology. The crackdown of this genre during the campaign against "Spiritual-Pollution" in 1983–84 suggested the incongruence or even conflicts of science fiction writings with the political agenda of the Party, as well as contradictions and conflicts of ideology inside the Party.[65] The critical view of the story "Dreams" toward futurist information technology and a knowledge economy expresses the tension of this genre with the dominant ideology of science and technology. My reading of these stories uncovers a "structure of feeling" that captures the volatile, not fully articulated, but nonetheless significant sentiments and discontents accompanying the drastic social transformations. In this sense, these stories become a sensitive barometer of the sensibility and sentiments of a society at a liminal moment in historical change.

One story turns the imagined waves into a(n) (anti-)medium for the liminal "structure of feelings." In "Destiny Club" (*Mingyun yezonghui*), Di Dingyuan, a once sent-down party cadre, investigates a series of bizarre suicides outside the "Destiny Club" and soon finds himself lost in hypnotic confusion once he enters the club. As if under a hypnotic spell, he is almost killed by a car. All he can recall after the nightmarish experience is that he was listening to a club singer named Lin. In the lyrics he detects "exceptional clanging sounds of bronzes and stones" that burst out of the "mellifluous and sentimental melodies," which remind him of his generation's now-lost aspirations for a socialist utopia. The lyrics that capture him go like this: "Oh, the glorious dreams, the swift wind / Once I sent my dreams along to the spirits / Accompanying them to the Mt. Kunlun and the East Sea / My dream crashes into pieces under the wheel of history / Into smoke, into dust and shadows, gone with the wind." The "mellifluous and sentimental" melodies might not be far removed from the songs of the Taiwanese singer Deng Lijun (Teresa Teng), who in the late 1970s quickly conquered the audience in mainland China and transformed the soundscape dominated by the "clanging sound of bronzes and stones" of revolutionary model opera. The popularity of Deng Lijun's songs, mostly about lovesickness and pastoral nostalgia, indicates immense transformations in both political and social life. As Chinese scholar Cai Xiang points out, Deng Lijun provided "an illusion of private life," which satisfied "people's desire to escape from the control of public politics, to live a relaxing, free, wealthy and even sentimental style of private life."[66] As the myth of revolution and its grand narrative fell apart, in its place stood commoditized forms of individual desires to fill in the ideological gap. However, the mixed-coded songs in the Destiny Club, despite their mellifluous, commercial form, still preserve utopian sentiments of the sent-down generation by referring to their "glorious dreams," evoking their aspirations with the images of "Mt. Kunlun" and the "East Sea," and reflecting on the ties of individual fate to the "wheel of history."

But it seems futile to probe into the meaning of the lyrics. The secret actually lies in an ultrasonic device that is hidden inside the piano. The manager of the club, Xu, reveals the imperceptible ways in which the ultrasonic waves emitted by the device work on the human brain:

The human brain is a sensitive and fragile machine. The mechanism of brain activity relies on bioelectricity, the frequency of which varies individually. If the frequency of the ultrasonic device and that of a person's brainwaves happen to constitute a certain functional mathematic relationship, the possible resonance of the two waves may magnify the intensity of bioelectric currents in the human brain, and cause stimulations too strong for the nerve system of a man to bear.[67]

Beyond the audible range of the human ear, ultrasonic waves nonetheless act directly upon the human body.[68] The effects of ultrasonic waves on the human body are irrelevant to the meaning of the lyrics. The way the ultrasonic device works also draws attention to the contingency associated with imperceptible waves. As Xu mentions in the story, it is entirely random as to who will be the next victim of the ultrasonic waves, for the frequency of the waves emitted by the device varies all the time. The flexibility accorded to waves here becomes a play of chance. The operation of the device becomes a game of randomness, over which no one, not even Xu, has control. Ironically echoing Shannon's exclusion of semantic aspects from the technical issue of information transmission, the story works on two separate levels: Di's desperate search for meaning and the significance of the lyrics and curious suicides, and the nonsensical, random waves sent out by the device. In the end, the latter almost cancels out the former, for the suicides are just capricious effects of the device. The search for meaning becomes futile when it comes to the random waves. Waves, the magical medium for information transmission, in the end are devoid of any communicative capability.

This randomness crystallized the disorientation at a liminal moment in history when the remnants of the Mao era coexisted with the new sociopolitical order still in formation. Xu, the manager of the Destiny Club, turns out to be none other than Di's supervisor in the sent-down years, a former power-holder. He reveals that the ultrasonic device was first tested on some sent-down cadres during the Cultural Revolution before it appeared in the club. To Xu, the random waves speak precisely to the uncontrollable destiny of individuals engulfed by the unpredictable forces of history. The device that obeys no logic but randomness is fetishized as the ultimate determinant for the complexity and contingency of history. This mystery of randomness also empties out any meaningful experience of time, for the suicidal consumption of stimuli in a nightclub and the violence of the Cultural Revolution can be lumped together and attributed to a play of chance.

The imaginary of the waves thus lent form to the confused historical visions at a moment when the socialist past was abruptly denied and drained of meaning, whereas the burgeoning consumer desires stimulated by Deng's marketization were constantly called into conflicts and negotiations with the ideology and political claims of a party that still retained the name of "communism." What could be a more fitting prognostication of postsocialism than nonsensical waves working on new cybernetic bodies synched with nonstop flows of information capitalism, rendering invisible the laboring body of the socialist past?

The waves hovering between imaginary and real, as I discussed in this chapter, exemplify the imaginations and discourses about the emergent digital media, but they refuse a definite dichotomy between old and new, analogue and digital media, because "waves" are contiguous with both broadcast media, such as wireless radio and television broadcasts, and the flexible and interconvertible digital. The magic waves carry with them the aspirations of incorporating the human body into a system of instant information transmission. This dream of human–machine systems, seemingly a common cybernetic vision since the late 1940s, was of particular sociopolitical significance in the post-Mao China of the late 1970s and 1980s. The imaginaries around the waves per se invoke a critique of the fetishism of the digital and a caution against the embrace of a depoliticized "information." In this sense, the waves showcased the processes of precarious mediation, since they called attention to the unsettled social changes at a liminal moment in history when the contradictions between the socialist past and the prediction of a technologically determined future, between the rule of a communist party and its embrace of a new world order, became increasingly acute.

CHAPTER TWO

The Curious Case of a Robot Doctor

Rethinking Labor, Expert Systems, and the Interface

The strong interest in incorporating the human into ceaseless information flows, which was shown in both scientific discourse and popular imaginary in the 1980s, also brought to the fore the issue of the interface between humans and the information environment. To further propose an ideally seamless integration of humans and machines as well as information environments, Qian Xuesen proposed a few years later "a theory of metasynthetic wisdom" (*dacheng zhihuixue* 大成智慧学), which he defined as the synthesizing of knowledge and wisdom via information networks and human–machine systems to form a sort of "wisdom in cyberspace." The project, called "metasynthetic engineering" (*dacheng zhihui gongcheng* 大成智慧工程), as he elaborated, aims to build a "systematic symposium of metasynthetic engineering" (*zonghe jicheng yantaoting tixi* 综合集成研讨厅体系), an intelligent system that comprises the participatory form of an academic seminar, the C³I military system, information technology, high-speed computers, multimedia technology, virtual reality, telescience, and so forth. This intelligent system, as Qian's collaborator Dai Ruwei pointed out, signaled an important shift in the AI research from the invention of "automatic machines" to a human–machine system, the seamless integration of humans and machines into a system of unprecedented competencies and efficiency.[1] When Qian raised this notion in the early 1990s, the World Wide Web was just starting in Western countries and China to become a new information network. Excited by this potentially boundless network, Qian, when writing to his colleagues, proposed that the internet and internet users together constitute an "open complex system."[2] A study of this open complex system could facilitate the ambitious project of "metasynthetic engineering" that would eventually lead to a global human–machine intelligent system.

Dai Ruwei's acute observation on the significance of "metasynthetic engineering" to the development of AI research is no exaggeration. Qian didn't randomly choose the phrases such as "wisdom" and "Intelligence" to describe his ambitious project. His proposal actually came a long way from cybernetics and AI research, especially the observations on an AI system called the "expert system" in China since the late 1970s. A type of AI system that comprises the knowledge base of a specialized field and an inference engine, the expert system is supposed to provide professional consultation and services even in the absence of a human expert. Qian's "metasynthetic engineering" may be regarded as a response to the frustrations with expert systems, but it also anticipated the recent developments of AI based on the big data and the cloudsourcing/"crowdsourcing" of human intelligence as practiced by Google and others today.

This chapter begins with an earlier moment in AI development in China in the late 1970s and 1980s and asks how the practices of and critical reflections on expert systems may shed a new light on our current discussion on cloudsourcing/crowdsourcing intelligence. Key to my investigation is the notion of the interface, which figures prominently in the discussion of expert systems and continues to haunt cloudsourcing/crowdsourcing with its social and ethical ramifications. The interface here is understood in terms of *practices of mediation* rather than simply as media objects or substrates. Instead of understanding the interface as built-in features of machines or *a priori*, the interface invokes an ethics of relations, which, in accordance with Galloway's interpretation of Deleuze, is concerned less with devices than with the "physical systems of power they mobilize, that is, more on curves of visibility and lines of force."[3] In this chapter I will explore the politics of interface in relation to the politics of depoliticization in post-Mao China—the reorganization of labor relations and the demise of socialist ethics—with a larger goal of understanding the politics of the interface as precarious mediation under postsocialist conditions. My argument revolves around two lines: the first line follows the practices and discussions of the AI expert systems; the second line reads the imaginary of AI, especially in the science fiction of the time. I shall focus on *A Curious Case* (*Qiyi de anjian* 奇异的案件) published in 1981, a story about a robot doctor, which I argue with its complex interweaving of intertextual and contextual references ingeniously places AI at the intersection of issues such as labor and work ethics, which are crucial to postsocialist transformations.

A Robot Doctor: Inside and Outside the Text

"A Curious Case" tells of a lawsuit concerning a robot doctor accused of murder. Fangfang, a robot believed to be "the highest achievement in artificial intelligence research thus far," is an amazingly efficient doctor in diagnosing and conducting medical operations. A perfectly designed robot, she is able to "examine thoroughly the viscera of a patient, not missing even one problem in his or her nerves, blood vessels, muscles, or even a small cell." On her first day of work, she already diagnoses and solves more than twenty difficult medical cases. The plans she chooses for each surgery are the best possible and the operations she conducts are precise.

This imagination of a robot doctor who puts humans to shame was not merely a fabrication of the author Wei Yahua. Chinese information scientists were intrigued by the prospect of transferring human knowledge and experiences to computers. The idea was to collect the professional experience and knowledge of the experts in a certain field and store it into computer information systems with reasoning and inference engines, thus enabling those systems to provide professional services even in the absence of a human expert. With the development of medical expert systems in the West, such as the MYCIN system pioneered at Stanford University, Chinese scientists were eager to catch up.

The notion of expert systems was first raised and developed in the 1960s by Edward Feigenbaum, a computer scientist at Stanford. According to Feigenbaum, "The goal of an 'expert system' project is to write a program that achieves a high level of performance on problems that are difficult enough to require significant human expertise for the solution."[4]

Most postwar founders of AI research, significantly influenced by the biological models of cybernetics, approached AI through brain modeling. Their design, as Paul Edwards points out, was oriented toward a machine that would achieve complex behavior through interaction with their environments.[5] The next intellectual generation, however, represented by John McCarthy, shifted to a formal-mechanical mode, placing the emphasis on "symbolic processing" in the sense that intelligence was conceived as a symbolic manipulation process, which can be modeled through computing. As the operation of computing functions at a number of levels (hardware, machine language, compiler programs, and higher-level languages) that are conceptually independent of one another, in AI modeling the lower-level processes such as neural nets were deemed irrelevant to the symbolic system of intelligent activities. Instead of interacting with the world, symbolic AI started with formalizing knowledge of the world and injecting it into computer systems. Edwards thus incisively comments that, in its attempt to "enclose and reproduce the world within the horizon and the language of systems and information," symbolic AI thus "constructed minds as miniature closed worlds," mirroring the closed-world geopolitics and ideology of the Cold War.[6]

This formal-mechanical mode soon proved to be restricting. Feigenbaum himself was exposed to this symbolic processing approach when he was studying at the Carnegie Institute of Technology (now Carnegie Mellon University) in the 1950s. Influenced by AI experts such as Herbert Simon, Allen Newell, J. C. Shaw and others, who were fascinated with the idea of a "thinking machine," Feigenbaum collaborated with them in the development of an AI program called the General Problem Solver. His own research focuses on the modeling of information-processing activities underlying human cognition. The shift from General Problem Solver to expert systems that focus on a restricted, narrow domain, according to Hubert L. Dreyfus, reflected the unresolvable impasse that AI research encountered in programming "common sense." Knowledge engineering proposed by Feigenbaum thus retreated to microworlds of isolated domains by avoiding the daunting task of computer symbolic representation of the full range of human intelligent behavior.[7]

Feigenbaum stated repeatedly that knowledge is a scarce and valuable resource. Yet what should be counted as knowledge? The design of expert systems presumes a system of discretion that defines this project of knowledge engineering. He believed that what made a person an expert in his field was his possession of professional knowledge in his domain. Extracting knowledge from human experts and coding it into computable forms can greatly reduce the costs of knowledge reproduction and exploitation.

The earliest expert system Feigenbaum developed was called "DENDRAL," a system for identifying unknown organic molecules based on a mechanism for automating the decision-making processes and problem-solving behaviors of organic chemists. The 1970s went on to witness the birth of several pioneering expert systems of medical consultation, including MYCIN for the diagnosis of and the drug prescription for infectious diseases, CASNET for glaucoma, and INTERNIST for internal medicine, among others.

Expert systems were celebrated as a breakthrough in AI. They were further brought to the center of attention when in 1981 the Japanese government announced its investment of $450 million in developing the Fifth Generation of computers. The Fifth Generation, as Feigenbaum and his collaborator, Pamela McCorduck, explained, departed significantly from the general, fundamental design of previous generations of computers for its knowledge-information-processing systems with the ability to reason; and it was different from the data processing of conventional computers, which were limited in filing and retrieving data of numbers and characters. These fifth-generation intelligent machines would be "easy enough to use, and intelligent and fast enough in their responses, to come close to the kinds of transactions intelligent human beings are used to having with each other."[8] Japan's fifth-generation plan was perceived as a threat to the leading position of the United States in the realm of AI and information industry. Echoing arguments of a coming postindustrial society by Daniel Bell and others, Feigenbaum and McCorduck elevated the issue of expert system development to the level directly related to "the new wealth of nations"—a reference to Adam Smith's *Wealth of Nations*:

> Their Fifth Generation plans say unequivocally that the Japanese are the first nation to act consciously upon the realization of the new wealth of nations can be viewed as something besides financial capital, secured from manufactured good or land rental, as it was in Adam Smith's time. . . . The World is entering a new period. *The wealth of nations, which depended on land, labor, and capital during its agricultural and industrial phases—depended upon natural resources, the accumulation of money, and even upon weaponry—will come in the future to depend upon information, knowledge, and intelligence.*[9] (italics in original)

AI developers self-consciously related information technology and intelligent computers to a new and immanent wave of capitalist development that was believed to supersede industrial capitalism. This would result in reshuffling the power of nations in the world system.

The development of expert systems in China started in the late 1970s alongside the "information craze," epitomized by the wide circulation of American futurologist Alvin Toffler's book *The Third Wave*, as well as his visits to China in 1983 and 1988. The book, a huge success among its Chinese audience, predicted that a third wave of development based on information and new energy would soon supersede the previous wave of industrialization. In an interview published in *People's Daily*, a major Party newspaper, Toffler asserted that "a new mode of production based on 'information' and characterized by 'rapidity'" had challenged the "conventions of the industrial civilization," and "knowledgeable information workers" would soon supplant "muscular laborers."[10] Daniel Bell, a Harvard sociologist, was another prominent voice predicting the diminishing of physical labor with the coming of a new form of society in his *The Coming of Post-Industrial Society*, and the rise of a knowledge class, which would eventually invalidate Marx's formula of a polarized society made of capitalists and the proletariat. High officials of the CCP soon adopted this notion of a coming information society. In October 1983, then-premier Zhao Ziyang gave a talk entitled "A Worldwide New

Technology Revolution and Our Strategies." With a sense of urgency as to China's place in the global competition, he asked: "What should we do if the new technological revolution is coming?" He called attention to the crucial role of information and microcomputers in future developments and the recent shift from labor-intensive industries to knowledge-intensive industries.[11]

It was against this backdrop that AI research drew increasing attention. Developments included the establishment of the China Association for Artificial Intelligence in 1981, the seminars on artificial intelligence held at Ji Lin University in 1980, the large international conferences that involved both Chinese AI researchers from the China Academy of Sciences and Peking University and foreign experts, as well as the visit of Herbert Simons, the foundational person of American AI research. With all these activities, expert systems became a highly active field synonymous with the most cutting-edge research. Inspired by their achievements in medical consultation systems, Chinese information scientists became fascinated with the prospect of developing traditional Chinese-medicine-based expert systems. This was partly driven by the anxiety about a looming loss of traditional medical knowledge as the elder generations of practitioners aged and passed away. The engineering of knowledge through expert systems addressed this anxiety by promising the preservation of this knowledge and making it commercially reproducible, but also modernizing this knowledge by way of the computerized language. In the process of developing expert systems, information engineers collaborated with experienced practitioners of traditional medicine, examining the process of their decision-making and then coding their knowledge into computer programs.

Different from the types of robots that are designed to replace manual labor, expert systems rest upon the premise that knowledge is a valuable resource for exploitation. With the ascendance of the information economy, expert systems appeared particularly appealing because they promised expert support while reducing the cost and time in human expert training. By the late 1980s, Chinese information scientists and engineers had developed hundreds of expert systems for weather forecasting, transportation management, oil detection, medical consultation, and other uses. To cite just a few examples, a system for diagnosing skin diseases developed by Jilin University and a traditional medicine expert system developed by Dongnan University were quickly put into use in the mid-1980s.[12]

Expert Knowledge and Frictions at the Interface

This seemingly perfect doctor named Fangfang, however, soon exposes its/her defect and almost becomes a murderer. When Lin Caihong, a patient who also happens to be an assistant to Fangfang's designer An Xiang, consults the robot doctor over a headache, Fangfang unexpectedly decides to vivisect Lin. She wants to open up Lin's skull to solve the medical enigma of her headache! Discoursing on the backwardness of the current research on the human brain, she announces that the vivisection will significantly expand progress in neuroscience, uncovering the pathogenesis of many neural diseases. The terrified Lin is forced to jump out of a window and is badly injured. It turns out that by the end of the story the design defect of Fangfang lies in a part that Lin Caihong forgot to install in the robot doctor, a missing part that contains important legal information and moral rules to regulate Fangfang's behavior.

What the story imaginarily resolves by installing a missing part, however, is a most daunting issue in the design of expert systems. Despite the myth of its ingenuity, the expert system emerged, as Dreyfus pointed out, from the setbacks in AI research and the insurmountable impasse in coding "common sense." Even Feigenbaum, the father of expert systems, admitted that the limited success of those systems came from "a design trick": "If you want a machine that's smart, keep its area of interest narrow. If you want to pile up enough knowledge to make a difference—and knowledge is power in expert systems—then you have to pile it up in a very narrow pile, because that's all we can do today."[13] As a result, expert systems are "experts in tiny areas, little islands in the ocean, and around them is this big ocean that they can't swim around in."[14]

In accounting for the difficulty in developing expert systems, it was often bemoaned that empirical experience that experts accumulated through their practices was unsystematic, ambiguous, and highly specific to each case. It thus remained a challenge for AI developers to translate the empirical experience of experts into a computer language that is predicated on systematic categorization and logic of mathematics. In order to simplify the problem of "knowledge coding" (*zhishi biaoshi*), expert systems were often restricted to a narrow domain, for the computer representation of knowledge in a neighboring domain might require a completely different set of coding. That restriction made expert systems much less efficient and reliable when they were called on to resolve an issue bordering on several neighboring domains. Arriving at a different domain, the "expert" became "an idiot." Coding "common sense" became the bottleneck of expert systems. One article in the journal *Jisuanji kexue* 计算机科学 (Computer science) argued that the solution to this bottle-neck rested upon future software technology and "a universal method of knowledge coding and processing."[15]

Even in the domain of their expertise, "transcoding" from expert knowledge to computer codes costs immense human labor. According to Feigenbaum, two types of knowledge are key to the performance of expert systems: the first type is "the facts of the domain," the widely shared knowledge that can be easily transferred from textbooks, journals, and lectures; the second type is called "heuristic knowledge"—the "knowledge of good practice and good judgment in a field." This type is "experiential knowledge, the 'art of good guessing' that a human expert acquires over years of work."[16] It is hard to "mine" heuristic knowledge from the experts, as they themselves hardly recognize what it is. To build up the knowledge base of an expert system, a knowledge engineer, the miner of heuristic knowledge, has to work with individual experts face to face for extended periods of time. First she must familiarize herself with basic facts and background materials in the field and establish a personal connection with the expert in order to observe him working. She asks the expert to articulate the ways he solves a problem and collects initial information to give to programmers, who code the problem-solving process into computer programs. The knowledge engineer goes back and forth between expert and programmers in order to extricate and "translate" heuristic knowledge of problem-solving into expert systems. In other words, in order for an expert system to work in a narrow, highly specialized field, the knowledge engineer has to interface among different fields—in the first place, between the domain of the expert and the field of computer programming.[17]

On the surface, interfacing work appears as merely an engineering issue of translating between different languages and codes. The widely used slogan "user-friendly interface" is based on this assumption that built-in features of the machines will ensure smooth translation and interaction, even for a user who has no knowledge of computer engineering. A "user-friendly interface" was seen as key to future expert systems, as Feigenbaum and his collaborators outlined:

> Expert systems of the first era were largely "back office" assistants, in places like trading rooms and laboratories where awkward interactions are tolerated. In the second era, the systems will be moving out into front offices and into places of public exposure and use, in, for example, sales situations or in consumer-advising roles. "Naturalness" will be essential.[18]

The bottleneck for "naturalness" is the mode of human–computer interactions. Complaints have been made about the use in interface design of technological jargon specific to computing. Instead, a "general language" accessible to laypersons is preferable. However, first of all, what constitutes a "general language?" Does every user share the same general language?[19] Can an "expert" born from the design trick of an extremely limited domain speak a general language to a layperson? The second-generation expert systems that emerged in the 1970s in the West often adopted natural language in designing the access point between the user and the machine. For example, a system called YHW-CTMEST was developed for traditional Chinese medicine that combines knowledge mining with consultation services. As it provided an intelligent editing program that was based on the successful instance of a previously handcrafted expert system, the system must have sophisticated dialogue capabilities, so that the expert can interact with the program to build up the system even if the expert has only limited or no computing knowledge—in this instance the previous work of knowledge engineers becomes formalized as a program to perform knowledge mining. Such dialogue capabilities are also important in real-time consultation, as the operator has to interact with the system in order to complete the diagnosis. The developers therefore regarded the connecting points as "the windows for human operators."[20] The YHW-CTMEST provides a selection menu, dialogue boxes for hinted requests, and limited natural language input. Its developers believed that these three means of interaction had greatly improved the "naturalness" of the system.

Yet the "naturalness" is far from friction-free. Even though the use of natural language was common for the human–machine interaction of the second-generation expert systems, the limited natural language was in no way "general" enough. Figure 12, from *Building Expert Systems*, published in 1983 and immediately translated into Chinese as a foundational textbook, shows the "dialogue" record of an expert system called PUFF in diagnosing an obstructive-airway disease. The enigmatic acronyms and the technical language adopted in the interpretation indicate the obstacles that a layperson would encounter in interacting with this system.

"The Curious Case" exposes the friction at the interface precisely by playing on the gulf that exists between the "tiny islands" of specialized domain. This is not to equate Fangfang with medical expert systems, but clearly the developments and limits of expert systems defined the imagination of AI in the story. The problem of a "general language" emerges in this scene when Fangfang is summoned to court to be indicted for murder:

> Seated in a soft chair, Fangfang eyed the people around her as if in astonishment. Suddenly she addressed the judge: "What is your name?"
> Dumbfounded by her unexpected question, the judge still managed to produce an answer: "Li Yongqiang."
> "You are sick with calculus of kidney. The renal stone is about twelve millimeters in diameter, four point two grams in weight. Your case demands surgery as soon as possible. Do you approve?"
> The judge answered in embarrassment: "Dr. Fangfang, I am not here for diagnosis."
> "Please return to the lobby then. Next patient please."

The comic effects come from Fangfang's unawareness of the limits of her highly specialized language. The language for medical diagnosis creates friction when the interactions extend beyond medical settings. Furthermore, both the court and the hospital are spaces that require particular sets of professional protocols and languages. Fangfang's exertion of her expert authority in the wrong space inadvertently mocks the authority of the judge. The judge is also a patient; the doctor is simultaneously a

```
19-Nov-79 14:41:28
*PUFF*

(PUFF asks the user for pulmonary function test results and
patient data and then executes rules to reach conclusions in
interpreting the tests.)

PATIENT-7
  1) Patient's identifying number:
     ** 7446
  2) Referral diagnosis:
     ** ASTHMA

(RV, TLC, FVC, etc. are the lung test measurements.)

  3) RV/RV-predicted:
     ** 261
  4) TLC(body box)observed/predicted:
     ** 139
  5) TLC(DLCO)observed/predicted:
     ** 111
  6) FVC/FVC-predicted:
     ** 81
  7) FEV1/FVC ratio:
     ** 40
  8) The slope F5025:
     ** 9
  9) The FEV1/FVC threshold:
     ** 77
 10) MMF/MMF-predicted:
     ** 12
 11) The DLCO/DLCO-predicted:
     ** 117
 12) Change in FEV1 (after dilation):
     ** 31
 13) The change in resistance (after dilation):
     ** 2.0
 14) The severity of coughing:
     ** NONE
 15) The number of pack-years of smoking:
     ** 17
```

Figure 12. Dialogue Record of PUFF. Hayes-Roth, *Building Expert Systems*, copyright 1983. Reprinted by permission of Pearson Education, Inc., New York.

defendant. Yet each "tiny island" of their expertise assumes a pseudo-autonomy that demands extra labor to swim across the "vast ocean."

This "interface friction" should be read as the symptom of a technocratic society increasingly atomized and fragmented in all layers of social life. Anthony Giddens, writing about the consequences of modernity, uses the term "expert systems" in a broader sense to refer to "systems of technical accomplishment or professional expertise that organize large areas of the material and social environments in which we live today."[21] He regards expert systems as part of the abstract systems that are "intrinsically involved in the development of modern social institutions." Modern society is built on the trust of people in abstract systems in the form of "faceless commitments, in which faith is sustained in the workings of knowledge of which the layperson is largely ignorant."[22] Giddens calls the encounters of lay actors with the abstract systems the "access points," at which a division is made "between 'frontstage' and 'backstage' performances"—a metaphor interestingly echoing Feigenbaum's proposal of moving expert systems from "back office" to "front office." Giddens points out that the essence of professionalism lies in the control of the threshold between the front and backstage. Experts at work always keep a good deal of what they do out of sight, which functions as a means of reducing the impact of human fallibility and contingency in the workings of abstract systems so that lay individuals will feel more reassured by the systems.[23] In other words, professionalism as the work ethic of modern society ensures and reinforces the boundaries of specialized areas as well as the boundaries between experts and laypersons, which are key to the operation of social institutions and abstract systems.

The Fallible Human Doctor

Just before the publication of "The Curious Case," another story of a human doctor falling sick because of overwork had generated a nationwide discussion and garnered new attention for the status of the intelligentsia. This doctor, named Lu Wenting, is the female protagonist in Shen Rong's story "At Middle Age"(*Rendao zhongnian* 人到中年). Lu, a middle-aged ophthalmologist of great skill and professionalism, demonstrates a high regard for her patients, often working overtime at the cost of her own health. She finally faints beside the operating table after performing three consecutive operations.

This image of a doctor devoting herself wholeheartedly to her work renewed the lineage of the "new socialist men." Doctors, for their close connections with death and life, are often elevated in the public realm as models of devotion and self-sacrifice. Norman Bethune, the well-known Canadian physician who served the Eighth Route Army at Yan'an during the second Sino-Japanese war and eventually died at his post, was lauded by Chairman Mao for his "utter devotion to others without any thought of self," as "a man of moral integrity and above vulgar interests, a man who is of value to the people."[24] This image of a selfless doctor striving to save the lives of his patients was reincarnated in a 1950 play entitled "Brotherly Love amid the Same Class" (*Jieji zhi'ai* 阶级之爱) as Dr. Liang, who insists on staying at his post on New Year's Eve, even when he knows his own son is very sick.[25] To highlight the dramatic conflict between individual interests and the interest of his "class brothers," two competing voices are arranged to speak to Dr. Liang simultaneously: on the one side is the nanny of his only son, who urges him to go back to his sick son, "whose lips even have turned black because of high fever"; on the other side is his coworker in the hospital, who informs him of a patient in need of urgent medical help. With little hesitation, Liang goes to the patient, without even asking about his own son. In a contrast to the selfless Liang, his coworker Dr. Gu, an elder doctor subscribing to the ethics of "the old society"—referring to a pre-PRC "dark age"—cares more about his reunion with his family on New Year's Eve, and leaves for home even when patients are flooding in. By the end, Gu is educated by Liang's selfless contributions and determines to transform himself with a new class consciousness and to show his solidarity with and love for his patients. All the happenings in the play are concentrated in the workspace of the hospital, marginalizing the domestic space and personal life into invisibility.

"At Middle Age" interestingly follows a similar plot: Lu Wenting's daughter is sick with a high fever, but Lu, too busy with her patients, has to leave her daughter in the kindergarten and bear the blame for her failure to take care of her family. However, in contrast to Liang's strong-willed determination, Lu is tortured by her feelings of guilt—she never stops blaming herself for her failure to be a good mother and wife. Though devoted to her work, she still struggles to perform all sorts of domestic duties. The story details how she rushes home to cook lunch and dinner for the family, take care of her two kids, and do mending even after a whole day of heavy work. The story, instead of focusing solely on the hospital space as in "Brotherly Love," shifts between the hospital and Lu's home, a cramped, little room for a family of four. The domestic space and personal life invisible in "Brotherly Love" resurfaces here with a vengeance, significantly modifying the image of "new socialist men."

Critics immediately sensed how this image of Lu Wenting diverged from the previous lineage of new socialist men. The grand heroes of the Mao era were giving way to Lu, an "average-looking" woman who is not even a Party member. Instead of a grand hero who belittles any obstacles, we see a woman who is troubled by everyday menial problems, and who has to eat and drink and take care of her family just as common people do. As one critic wrote: "Lu is such a common person in real life. How familiar her appearance, her work and life sound to us! However, as an ideal of a new socialist man, this image is also unfamiliar to us."[26] The unfamiliarity detected by this critic derives in part from the hyper-visibility of her personal life in the story. The revelation of her continuous menial troubles in everyday life, the incorporation of her domestic space into the story, and the depiction of her profound love and care for her family make this hard-working woman more "human," but less an embodiment of the "spirit of revolutionary romanticism" than her predecessor, Dr. Liang. The "humanness" of Lu no longer rests upon her political devotion, but on her emotions and feelings as a "common" person.

Such modifications were not uncontroversial. With the story's adaptation into an eponymous film, a series of heated discussions began with a volley of severe criticisms that accused the story of lauding a passive and pessimistic character who "surrenders to troubles in life."[27] Lu's lack of revolutionary, romantic passions was singled out as politically suspicious. But this criticism was soon refuted. Lu's case was read as a consequence of the inhuman, bureaucratic state. As one critic asked: "Why is Lu Wenting, in the eyes of some leaders, no more than 'a good scalpel' to serve the eye operation of a minister? Why is she just a 'supporting pillar' in this famous hospital? This is not a problem simply resulting from the Cultural Revolution, but a problem within our socialist system. It touches upon the question of the role and value of human beings in our society."[28]

The discussions generated by the story cannot be separated from the contemporaneous Marxist humanist critique of the Mao era in the late 1970s and 1980s. Drawing Marxist humanist critique of state socialism and the Soviet Union from the West and Eastern Europe, such as Poland, Czechoslavakia, and Yugoslavia, Wang Ruoshui, then deputy editor of *People's Daily* and one of the most insistent voices of Marxist humanism in China, proposed that human beings should be "the starting point of Marxism." He criticized the lack of attention to human values and the problem of alienation that arose in Mao's era. Following Marx's criticism in his *Economic and Philosophic Manuscripts of 1844* of political economists who ruthlessly took "the worker as a working animal—as a beast reduced to the strictest bodily needs," Wang questioned in a similar vein: "Isn't it against the principle of socialist humanism to take the planned production targets as everything, whereas workers become negligible? Shouldn't it be noted that human beings have the need not only to work but also to improve their material and spiritual life?"[29] Along with the heated nationwide debates around the Pan Xiao case, self-sacrifice was questioned as a hollow slogan and a systematic dismissal of individual value.[30]

In this regard, the case of Lu Wenting reflected the shifting social values of Deng's China. Lu Wenting appeared with a "human" face with "human" needs. But this humanist critique failed to address the issue of invisible labor as computers and AI systems were increasingly incorporated into various aspects of social and professional life, not to mention the devaluation of other forms of labor and the drastic marginalization of workers and peasants when the voices of humanism resonated among the intelligentsia and public discourses. Yan Hairong pointed out that the discussions triggered by "At Middle Age" set the stage for a large influx of maidservants from rural areas into the city, which was accompanied by a hierarchy of labor division that reversed the value of the Mao era and a redistribution of labor that reinforced the inequality between the city and the countryside, the mental and the manual.[31] This new development is captured by a 1983 story entitled "Baomu" 保姆 (Maidservants). The story tells of a young girl named Ling who works as a maidservant in Professor Shen's household. Dissatisfied with previous maidservants from the countryside, Professor Shen is happy to find in Ling, a Beijing girl free of the "defects" of country girls, an ideal maidservant. But soon Ling faints, as Lu Wenting does, because of overwork. To his great surprise, Professor Shen finds in her bag a manuscript on Tang poetry and realizes that Ling is not a maidservant but an intellectual just like he is![32] The dissatisfaction of an intellectual with his country maidservant signals the social disparities resulting from the division of labor, which could only be appeased by an imagined intellectual maidservant who turns out not to be a maidservant.

Moreover, this human doctor is too "human" as to be susceptible to fallibility. Compared with human doctors, robot doctors are "advantageous" in that, as Fangfang attests, they have "no need to eat and drink, to rest or consume, and neither parents, siblings nor any social relations to tend to." They can work twenty-four hours a day, and they exist solely for their work. Fangfang therefore proclaims herself "a selfless nonindividualist," who "transcends any class categorization." Fangfang's remark is a retort to the accusation of her complicity in the murder case, which was seen as a political incident plotted by "a class enemy in camouflage." The person who accuses her is the father of the victim Lin Caihong, a "peasant-looking" man in a "washed-out military uniform" who represents a die-hard Maoist. Fanfang's retort, an ironic poke at socialist ethics, nonetheless reveals the fantasy behind every expert system: a machine that can replace humans but dispense with human needs. As one advocate of expert systems in the 1980s remarked, human beings could be subject to fickle emotions, irrational decisions, and unproductive conditions such as sickness, exhaustion, or other distractions that might result in errors or negligence. Robots wouldn't have such problems and thus promised a rapid improvement in productivity.[33]

Indeed, this inhuman robot doctor is more desirable than the human doctor, who falls sick after three consecutive operations and is constantly distracted by her family troubles. Even today it is still the dream of technophiles and various tech industries to produce inhuman "artificial" intelligence that is not flawed with human traits, as Kevin Kelly, a co-founder of *Wired* magazine, puts it:

> Intelligence may be a liability—especially if by "intelligence" we mean our peculiar self-awareness, all our frantic loops of introspection and messy currents of self-consciousness. We want our self-driving car to be inhumanly focused on the road, not obsessing over an argument it had with the garage. The synthetic Dr. Watson at our hospital should be maniacal in its work, never wondering whether it should have majored in English instead. As AIs develop, we might have to engineer ways to *prevent* consciousness in them—and our most premium AI services will likely be advertised as *consciousness-free*.[34]

This requirement of inhuman and "maniacal" focus on work without distraction best exemplifies the rule of rationalization driven by the pursuit of efficiency in modern society, but it also reflects the operation of abstract systems that are based on discrete areas of specialization, as discussed by Anthony Giddens. This maniacal focus is expected not only for AIs that are supposed to perform without fallibility, but also for human workers as the rule of professionalism, the essence of which, as Giddens points out, is to reduce human fallibility and ensure the smooth function of the systems. Inhuman AIs are the perfection of human workers who are immaculately professionalized as robots with no other distracting human needs.

Professional "Coolness" and Affective Labor

In "At Middle Age," we see that Lu Wenting makes a strong effort to banish her sick daughter and family from her mind once she starts working. She has to focus on the surgeries to be performed instead of obsessing over the troubles at home. The solemn atmosphere in the surgery room immediately separates this space from the rest of the world, from whatever might be taking place outside the surgery room. The setup in the hospital requires professional coolness. People working in the room are equally solemn, their other identities and social relations suspended:

> Everyone here wears a long, sterilized, white robe, their forehead tightly covered by a sterilized, light blue hat imprinted with the words "surgery room." Everyone wears a big mask, leaving bare merely their eyes. No distinction of beauty or ugliness, man or woman among these people. They are just doctors, assistant doctors, anesthesiologists, and instrument nurses.

The patient's face is covered by a white cloth pad, leaving only the eye visible for surgery. Once the ophthalmologist is positioned in front of the operating table, all she sees is the impaired eye of her patient:

> She skillfully injected some Novocain into his lower eyelid. Then with needles she fastened both the upper eyelid and lower eyelid of the impaired eye to the surgical pad. The eyeball, the vision of which had been blocked by something white and cloudy, was thus exposed in the bright light of the operating lamps. Lu had now forgotten whom the person lying there was. She saw only an impaired eye.

Anything else is irrelevant to her work, regardless of whether the patient is male or female, a peasant or a minister. The story repeatedly describes Lu Wenting's vision of eyes without faces, indicating her professional devotion and impartiality. As Lu Wenting wields shining "scissors, needles, forceps with and without teeth, fastening tweezers, porte-aiguille, mosquito forceps, retrobulbar injection needles, crystal scoops and other exquisite devices for surgery" that are neatly placed in a rectangular tray, she exudes a professional "coolness." The substantial, even ostentatious, display of medical terminology in the text may immediately strike readers with no medical training as alien, yet nonetheless it creates a halo surrounding the "cool" expert. Jean-François Lyotard notes that the pragmatics of scientific knowledge requires a denotative language, which assumes a statement's "truth-value" as the criterion for determining its acceptability. Scientific knowledge is "in this way set apart from the language games that combine to form the social bond."[35] This language distances itself from everyday language, consolidating the exclusiveness and specialization of knowledge through institutions "run by qualified partners (the professional class)." In other words, the terminology in "At Middle Age" reinforces the autonomous space of a profession, which produces a sociolect—a social dialect that is restricted to members of the profession.

A similar exactitude and "coolness" of technology can be found in "A Curious Case." The litany of diseases that Fangfang diagnoses runs as follows: "leukemia, lung cancer, cerebral vascular thrombosis, coronary heart disease, Keshan disease, later-stage hepatoma, myocardial infarction, lepriasis and etc." With her specially designed eyes, Fangfang can conduct "chest x-rays, intravenous pyelographic surveys, tomographic surveys, ultrasonic sounding, isotopic examination, liquid crystal examination" in less than one minute. The accessibility of this highly specialized terminology to common readers matters less than their effects: their distinct register mystifies the expert knowledge that Fangfang embodies and reinforces the "coolness" of professionalism to maintain the threshold between abstract systems and laypersons.

Despite Lu Wenting's professional "coolness," the story also zooms in on her "feminine touch" at work. To her little girl patient Wang Xiaoman, Lu Wenting is "not only a surgeon, but also a doting mother, a nurse in a kindergarten." She whispers gentle words into her ear while conducting the operation, calming down the restless girl. Anticipating the anxieties of her patients on the operating table, Lu always begins her operations by calming them with her lullaby-like voice: "We are starting soon. Don't be nervous. You won't feel any pain once I give you anesthetic. The operation will be done soon." This chanting has become her signature so that one patient of hers ten years ago immediately recognizes her from her tone. This "feminine touch" of Lu at work shows that her work consists not only of wielding scalpels but also "motherly" care, which infantilizes the patient and provides a cushion that softens the shining coldness of scalpels. When she orders her patient in a commanding tone to stop fidgeting once the operation starts, even the minister Qin feels like "a trouble-making little boy" in front of her. She is at the same time the expert system with professional knowledge and the attending physician who mediates between the layperson patients and the cold apparatus and systems in the hospital.

Michael Hardt and autonomist critics, in writing about the transformation of labor in the current economy of informationalization, which is "defined by a combination of cybernetics and affect," use the term "affective labor" to describe the types of labor that do not fall into the industrial mode of labor that produces tangible industrial products but instead produces "social networks, forms of community, biopower."[36] In this sense, the "facework," as described by Giddens, that mediates at the access point between laypersons and abstract systems can be regarded as a form of affective labor that binds together layers of society increasingly fragmented by and atomized with the specialization and division of labor. Affective labor is often gendered as a "feminine touch" because it overlaps with women's emotional and caring work in the sphere of reproduction, which under the conditions of industrial production is rigidly separated from "masculinized" factory wage labor. From this perspective, the doctor who dutifully plays the role of mother to her patients becomes the female Lu Wenting, conveniently replacing the male doctors in the lineage of socialist heroes from Norman Bethune.[37] But this also suggests that affective labor is not restricted within the domestic realm but is generalized across all spheres of work with the expansion of abstract systems in all realms of social life. Lu Wenting, who combines professional coolness with a "feminine touch," became a model of professionalism precisely at a time when the crisis of socialist ethics occurred, and the neutralization of knowledge and technology in the post-Mao late 1970s and 1980s began as part of postsocialist depoliticization.

Depoliticized Knowledge versus the Mass Line of Knowledge Production

If the theoretical frameworks of Lyotard and autonomist critics address the specifics of highly developed capitalist and postindustrial Western countries, the professional "coolness" and affective labor performed simultaneously by this new professional model, Lu Wenting, has to be understood in the context of postsocialist depoliticization. Lu Wenting, this average-looking, gently-speaking woman "as slight as a thin straw," once in the surgery room, displays unquestionable authority that even conquers the impertinent Red Guards who attempt to stop her from completing surgery on a persecuted Party cadre during the Cultural Revolution:

> Lu Wenting was wearing her white surgery robe, green plastic foam slippers, a blue-cloth hat, and a big mask, leaving bare only her eyes, as well as her hands, soon to be covered by rubber gloves. The insurrectionists were stunned, perhaps because of seeing the unusual outfit for the first time, or sensing for the first time the solemnity in the surgery room, or witnessing for the first time the bloody eyeball beneath the snow-white sheet on the operation table. Dr. Lu remained seated on her high stool, emitting a few words from beneath her mask:
> "Please get out!"
> The insurrectionary red guards looked at each other in consternation, as if realizing this was the wrong place for insurrection, and left.[38]

In this setting, Lu's coolness and rationality are set against in her eyes the irrational fervency of political fanatics. In fact, Lu's expertise was even more respected for not being "politically prejudiced" because of her nonparty affiliation. Members of the intelligentsia were expected to be politically "neutral," never letting their political beliefs meddle in their judgment. "Objective truth" and "universalism" became the new values embraced by the Chinese intelligentsia. One author, in reviewing Alvin W. Gouldner's *The Future of Intellectuals and the Rise of the New Class*, criticized the way intellectuals were judged for their political views in Mao's era, for political views should be regarded as irrelevant to their knowledge. Their knowledge being objective truth, intellectuals should be considered as the inheritors and discoverers of scientific truth that belongs to all human beings rather than to any specific sociopolitical groups.[39] After its publication in the Anglophone world, Gouldner's book was immediately reviewed in Chinese journals, such as *Guowai shehui kexue* 国外社会科学 (Social science abroad) and *Dushu zazhi* 读书杂志 (Reading magazine) among others. His view of the intelligentsia as a "universal class" and the "most cosmopolitan of all elites" was read by his Chinese reviewers as a confirmation of the role of the intelligentsia in "eradicating class prejudices."[40]

In line with this new view about the intelligentsia, one writer, Gu Xin, advocated "meritocracy" in a future society in which authority would be predicated on knowledge and competence. He further distinguished "authority" from "power": "Authority is built on individual gifts, learning, skills and other competence" and is recognized by "people's judgment and ethical principles," whereas "power is obtained through violence, coercion and other means." The formation of scientific elites, according to him, reasonably followed the principle of rationality and universalism, whereas its opposite, egalitarianism (*pingjun zhuyi* 平均主义), by rejecting any authorities and demanding the power to be shared by the masses, slipped into "anti-intellectualism." He denounced "the submission of the authority of professors to students and workers" during the Cultural Revolution as "a ridiculous farce." Finally, he concluded that a meritocratic society, though not necessarily one of equality, would bring justice, for the acquisition of social status through knowledge and talent would ultimately award individual efforts rather than inherited privilege.[41] Gu's advocacy of "authority" based on knowledge and professional skills carefully marked out an autonomous space divorced from socialist ideology. This authority was described as nonoppressive, representing a rationality and universalism that transcended "class prejudices" and ideological conflicts. At the same time, Deng's government started to reverse the intellectual policy during the Cultural Revolution and build an expert advisory system in order to incorporate experts into the decision-making process.[42]

This privilege of professional authority over political commitment reverses the dynamics in the 1950s play "Brotherly Love." Dr. Liang, in the eyes of his Western-trained colleague Dr. Gu, lacks interest in pursuing medical knowledge and theories from books, but wastes his time in seeking treatments for diseases that even medical books have pronounced incurable. As Chinese critic Cai Xiang points out in his discussion of the play, the conflicts between the two derive from their different understanding of "science" and the social production of knowledge: Dr. Liang's challenge to existing medical knowledge is motivated by his "love for his class brothers," which Gu presumably lacks. Cai places Dr. Gu in the lineage of "conservative, aloof and arrogant" experts in Mao-era literature, arguing that this literary image conveyed a cautionary message against the technocratic "expert despotism."[43]

Cai Xiang is right in invoking a different mode of knowledge production during Mao's era. Although there were always disagreements and conflicts inside the CCP about its science and technology strategy, a prominent feature of Mao's policy was the "mass line." This "mass line" led not only to the reorganization of or even interruptions in regular activities of universities and research institutes but also the movement of "mass technical innovations," which was built on the belief that technical innovations should come from the masses—peasants, workers, and other frontline production participants—instead of experts confined in their own labs and offices. The effects of this "mass line" were not always coherent and they received mixed evaluations. One important outcome of this "mass line" is the emergence of a rural cooperative medical system, which operated on a three-tiered system comprising medical institutions at county, commune (township), and village levels. This system included both full-time medical workers and "barefoot doctors"—referring to part-time medical workers "who served their communities after basic training in Western medical techniques and indigenous Chinese treatments."[44] Selected from workers, soldiers, and mostly peasants, barefoot doctors still performed their regular work, but they also played a key role in providing primary health care and basic treatment. Designed to address the lack of medical workers in the countryside, this medical system was also aligned with Mao's "mass line" of disseminating knowledge among the masses and encouraging knowledge production at the grassroots level. This "mass line" can be observed in other areas, such as systems of earthquake prediction and paleoanthropology, which advocated collaborations between professional workers and amateur, grassroots participants.[45]

In the realm of electronics, engineers and workers were reported working together to design machines and write computer programs in order to best address specific problems and issues in everyday production activities. Workers in oil fields, textile factories, and even in commune factories, the workers of which were mainly lowly educated women, who were reported to study electronic engineering enthusiastically and actively participate in modifying computer technology and devices in order to adjust the machines to their concrete working conditions.[46] This mass line of scientific development also attracted intense interest in radical science activities. According to Sigrid Schmalzer, one radical science organization, Science and Engineers for Social and Political Action (SESPA, better known as Science for the People, which arose from the antiwar movement in 1969), in selecting its delegates to China in the early 1970s, was especially concerned with understanding the "connections of the professionalism to class position and bourgeois society."[47] The delegation was impressed with the "barefoot doctors" who brought primary health care to even the remotest villages, and spoke positively of the mass-line scientific practice, as "sending scientists into the fields to work with peasants helped the scientists better understand the practical applications of their research," while "integrating college engineering classes and electronics production offered benefits for students and workers alike."[48] Fa-ti Fan thus proposes an evaluation of Mao's mass science that differs from the Western institutionalization of science in modern times: "Maoist Programs of mass science, such as earthquake prediction, barefoot doctors, and various attacks on 'elite science,' were based on the tenets of integrating experts and the masses and combining indigenous and Western Science. The underlying political doctrine asserted the class character of science, exalted everyday epistemology, and projected a utopian vision of scientific and political modernity."[49]

Such an approach to knowledge production and the affirmation of the class character of science are also manifested in the character of Dr. Liang in "Brotherly Love." Liang is a far cry from the professional "coolness" and expertise embodied by Lu Wenting. In fact, he constantly questions the "iron" rule of science, believing that the human will, as long as you have it, can push science beyond its limits. This strong will is driven by his deep devotion to his brothers, to whom he is bonded by class interests and feelings. The play repeatedly documents his efforts to save wounded soldiers, even when other doctors decide that they are helpless. Disregarding scientific exactitude, the play turns the blood transfusion into Liang's all-purpose remedy for his endangered patients. In one scene, the already exhausted Liang volunteers to transfuse his blood to a hero wounded in battle, but another comrade, a patient whom Liang has previously saved through a blood transfusion, volunteers to take his place. Blood circulated among these bonded brothers eschews its medical definition, inviting a metaphorical reading of the blood transfusion as a symbol of mutual "brotherly love." In this sense, although Lu Wenting's care for her patients on the surface resembles that of Dr. Liang, their political contexts and implications cannot be more different: while Dr. Liang's insistence in serving his patients meals and assisting them to the toilet is driven by his feelings of class belonging, Lu Wenting's affective labor is predicated on her nonpolitical "neutrality" and simultaneously registers her professional detachment and scientific distance.

This transformation from politicized knowledge and the class character of science to "neutral" professionalism registers the politics of depoliticization in contemporary China. The depoliticized politics in contemporary China, as Wang Hui points out, are closely related to the negation of the revolutionary history of China from 1911 to 1976. Depoliticization manifests itself as the annulling of political subjects of the peasants and the working class and the transformations in the role and function of the state, as well as the change in the party's identity, as it no longer possesses "its own distinctive evaluative standpoint or social goals" but can "only have a structural-functionalist relationship to the state apparatus." While depoliticized politics did not start with post-Mao China, the new order since the late 1970s consolidated the hypothetical separation of the economical and political realm, a separation on which the notion of the modern market economy is built. This separation also entails the neutralization of technology, as technology now is tied with efficiency and scientific rationality and is conceived as politically neutral.[50] If the depoliticized autonomy of expertise knowledge underlies Lu Wenting's "coolness," then the developments in expert systems and the imaginary of robot doctors, by allegedly separating expertise knowledge from the human subject, magnify the fantasy of this depoliticized autonomy and neutrality.

The Interface Revisited and the Politics of Life

As discussed above, the development of expert systems in the late 1970s and 1980s converged with the politics of depoliticization in post-Mao China and signaled the rise of a depoliticized professionalism. The discussions and imaginaries of the AIs, at the same time, bring to the foreground the politics of life. If the robot doctor Fangfang, who can work twenty-four hours a day with "no need to eat and drink, to rest or consume, with neither parents nor siblings nor any social relations to tend to," represents a professional ideal of human experts with no human "flaws," isn't it *life* per se, not merely knowledge, that is sucked into the machine of total efficiency?

An "intelligent" machine that replaces human beings is merely an illusion. For a medical expert system to work "automatically," it requires not only transferring expert knowledge into computer programs but also using the collective labor of knowledge engineers and computer programmers, as well as attending physicians, that "interfaces" between different media layers. In this regard, the interface means more than the built-in features of machines. The understanding of the interface as built-in features, as Johanna Drucker criticizes, presumes individuals as "autonomous agents whose behaviors can be constrained in a mechanical feedback loop," and a user who exists as an a priori entity. Drucker instead proposes a constructivist approach, positing the interface as the "very site of construction" modulating the cognition and sensorium of human agents, and thus destabilizing the boundaries of the "human."[51]

This problematization of autonomous human agency appears in "The Curious Case" as a controversy as to who should be held responsible for the medical accident, the robot doctor Fangfang or her manufacturer-designer, the latter conveniently simplified as the chief engineer. The problematic here is to locate one single autonomous agency: while some in the courtroom argue that the robot doctor is nothing more than a tool, just like a car, others contend that the robot should be considered as a human equivalent, an independent agent. This argument of tool versus independent agent rehearses a similar discussion in the 1960s. The plot of "The Curious Case" resembles a story entitled "Siema" by Anatoly Dneprov. Translated and serialized in *Kexue huabao* (Science pictorial), the story follows the process of a scientist making an intelligent robot named "Siema." With enormous information input and an advanced sensory system, Siema soon becomes an incomparable expert of neuroscience, who eventually threatens to vivisect her own inventor. A student from Peking University criticized the story for "distorting the relationship between humans and machines." Writing in 1966 on the brink of the Cultural Revolution, the author contended that robots, no different from any other types of machines, were "products of human labor," and thus merely tools. His criticism echoed the general discourse on cybernetics and robotics of that time, which criticized the promotion of robotics superiority as an ideology of capitalism that conceals the real source of value.

However, the revisiting of the agency issue in "The Curious Case" subscribes neither to the human-centered doctrine nor to the version of posthumanism that fantasizes freeing human from labor by machines or the obsolescence of the human. In the story, not only is the human-object division troubled, but the notion of culpable agency is also thrown into question, since it turns out that the making of the robot is collective labor in which even the victim-patient herself was involved. In the end, the story raises the question as to how to understand new conditions of labor as it is transforming with the networks of things and humans, as well as the transformation of the "human" per se.

Lydia Liu, in addressing the impact of cybernetics on the very notion of "human," uses the term "Freudian robot" to refer to "any networked being that embodies the feedback loop of human–machine simulacra and cannot free her/him/itself from the cybernetic unconscious." Including cyborgs, androids, and robots within "Freudian robots," she raises a provocative question: Does the "Freudian robot" also apply to human beings who usually "prefer not to associate themselves with cyborgs and machines"? She argues that the question of whether human beings become masters of, or slaves to, their machines is a wrong question, because it neglects the transformation of human beings in their interactions with intelligent machines. Yet she also warns against a celebratory notion of cyborgs, for the new human–machine entanglement entails political and psychic consequences that need to be acknowledged.[52] In other words, the redistribution of subjectivity and labor around the human–machine interface neither consolidates the human mastery of "tools" nor easily slips into a posthuman celebration of the disappearance of the physical human body. The complex involvement of physicality, affectivity as well as intellectual competences in the human–machine interface, leads to an unresolved question in "The Curious Case": Should Fangfang be regarded as an equivalent of a human agent? By raising this issue, the story in fact questions the understanding of "human" as a transhistorical and pregiven subject, an assumption implied in the Marxist humanist discussion. Between the human and the machine, Fangfang in fact symptomatically reveals the invisible labor and life subsumed into and spread around the processes of the human–machine interface. The ambiguous "hybridity" of Fangfang anticipates a politics of labor and life that is closely tied to the redefinition of the "human" in the era of digital media and networked society.

The predicaments arising from the development of expert systems and AIs challenge the conventional dichotomy of the man versus his tools. Marx refers to knowledge and "scientific power" that is objectified in the system of machinery as the "general intellect." He argues that the development of machinery as a manifestation of the "general intellect" shows the degree to which general science and knowledge has become "an immediate productive force." There are two forms of technology crucial to this "general intellect" in Marx's *Grundrisse*, as explicated by Nick Dyer-Witheford: "One is the development of production systems based on 'an automatic system of machinery . . . consisting of numerous mechanical and intellectual organs, so that the workers themselves are cast merely as its conscious linkages.' The other, to which his allusions are more scattered but equally persistent, is the network of transport and communication integrating 'the world market.'"[53] Automation, according to Marx, will eventually reduce direct labor and the individual labor time required in production. Indeed, automation at every stage is also the dream of AI developers. Bemoaning the time-consuming and painstaking process of knowledge acquisition—the process in which a knowledge engineer extracts knowledge from a human expert for the development of expert systems, Feigenbaum hoped to change the "cottage industry"-like process with automation so as to eventually dispense with the labor of the knowledge engineer.[54] To a certain degree, Feigenbaum's dream has already been realized by combining the two aspects of general intellect, making the network of communication indispensable to the automatic system. Now every click and keying on the keyboard by the user helps train the Google AI.

Kevin Kelly recently announces in an article published in *Wired* magazine that Artificial Intelligence, after the long winter of meager progress and stagnation, has finally been unleashed on the world and has a bright future in view. He forecasts that the business plans of the next ten thousand start-ups will be: "*Take X and add AI.*" But instead of expecting the HAL 9000 as in Stanley Kubrick's spectacular film *2001: A Space Odyssey*, Kelly predicts that AI in the future will look more like cheap and reliable Web Services provided by Amazon. This vision is supported by his recent visit to the IBM research labs, where a new generation of AI system named Watson, different from its predecessor, which is made of "10 upright, refrigerator-shaped machines" and is contained "within a wall of cabinets," is "spread across a cloud of open-standard servers that run several hundred 'instances' of the AI at once."[55] He is not the only one who perceives aspiring breakthroughs in AI research with the advancement of cloud computing. Baidu, the biggest Chinese-language search engine, has launched its ambitious AI project called "Baidu brain," and recruited Andrew Y. Ng, an AI and machine-learning expert at Stanford University, the founder of Google Brain, to be its Chief Scientist. Baidu's heavy investment is just one scenario in the fierce competition among the IT industry in the field of AI research. Google, Yahoo, Intel, Dropbox, and Twitter have all purchased AI companies in the past several years and have aggressively pushed research in this direction, observed Kevin Kelly.[56]

If the future AI no longer appears to be the HAL 9000 type, what can it do? A vice president of Baidu gave an example: if you see a purple flower, and want to know its name, instead of asking people around, you can just upload a picture of the flower and consult the Baidu Brain.[57] This scenario of the seeming replacement of human beings mystifies Baidu Brain as an omniscient superintelligence. But the way it works is less mysterious. For search-services providers like Google, every one of its users is contributing to the development of its AI system:

> Every time you type a query, click on a search-generated link, or create a link on the web, you are training the Google AI. When you type "Easter Bunny" into the image search bar and then click on the most Easter Bunny–looking image, you are teaching the AI what an Easter bunny looks like. Each of the 12.1 billion queries that Google's 1.2 billion searchers conduct each day tutor the deep-learning AI over and over again. With another 10 years of steady improvements to its AI algorithms, plus a thousand-fold more data and 100 times more computing resources, Google will have an unrivaled AI.[58]

In fact, Amazon has already developed this "artificial/accumulated" intelligence into a business mode with its launch of Amazon Mechanical Turk. The name refers to "The Turk," a chess-playing automaton of the eighteenth century, which later was revealed to be manipulated by a chess master hidden inside. Amazon Mechanical Turk achieves "automaticity" with precisely the same method by distributing tasks to invisible human workers hidden behind its interface. Lilly Irani thus comments that Amazon Mechanical Turk "has allowed canonical AI projects by simulating AI's promise of computational intelligence with actual people."[59]

This "automaticity" is realized through the replacement of the wage labor of individual engineers with the collective labor of anonymous mass users. Marx's prediction of the reduction in wage labor with the increasing importance of the general intellect in social production did not anticipate the unprecedented domination of information capitalism. In the view of Paolo Virno and other autonomist critics, Marx's prediction derives from his equation of the "general intellect" with fixed capital, which fails to consider living labor as an indispensable component of the "general intellect." In their interpretation of *Grundrisse*, Paolo Virno and Carlo Vercellone take up Marx's notion of the "general intellect," considering it no longer merely as part of fixed capital and external to living labor. Criticizing Marx for neglecting "the way in which the general intellect manifests itself as living labor," Virno understands living labor as "a depository of cognitive competencies that *cannot be objectified in machinery*" (my italics), which includes "the faculty of language, the disposition to learn, memory, the capacity to abstract and relate, and the inclinations towards self-reflexivity." He further argues that "thoughts and discourses function in themselves as productive 'machines' in contemporary labour and do not need to take on a mechanical body or an electronic soul."[60] These machines without "a mechanical body" indicate the continuous distribution of human labor in the human–machine interface. Virno thus sees no separation of living labor from automatic machinery in capitalism's mobilization of the general intellect.

The production of economic value is also accompanied with the production of subjectivity in the age of information capitalism. This, as Lazzarato comments, "demonstrates how capitalist production has invaded our lives and has broken down all the opposition among economy, power and knowledge."[61] The ubiquity of the human–machine interface connects various aspects of social life to the capitalist productive machine, turning the society into a factory to the degree that Hardt and Negri claim that "social life itself becomes a productive machine."[62] The network of communication integrates not only the "world market" but also human beings into ceaseless information circuits and capitalist productive machines. Work is no longer restrained to particular sites, nor can the boundary of work and life be maintained by the conventional division of the public and the domestic.

From Dreyfus to Qian Xuesen

Amazon Mechanical Turk, in the view of communication scholar Lilly Irani, is a trick to fulfill the "automaticity" dream of AI developers. But instead of seeing the involvement of actual people as a fake AI, I would argue that this inadvertently reveals the indispensable human labor in any AI project, in spite of the dream of AI developers of replacing human beings. Irani refers to traditional AI as "the field of computer science that attempts to develop algorithms that can represent, model, and demonstrate human intelligence," a long-standing dream yet to be realized.[63] It is this understanding of AI that drives both fans and critics of AI to focus on the question of whether an AI system can replicate human cognitive activities. This prompted the renowned philosopher Hubert Dreyfus, a most audacious critic of AI, to argue against any possibility of a machine as intelligent as a human being. He argues that most projects of artificial intelligence by the 1980s had shared the wrong assumption that human behavior can be formalizable in terms of a heuristic program. This assumption followed the Western philosophical tradition from Plato to Descartes, which separated human intelligence and reason from the human body. Partaking of Merleau-Ponty and phenomenology, Dreyfus emphasizes the indispensable role of the human body in pattern recognition, global anticipation, and other intelligent behaviors. Nonformalizable sensory motor skills underlie all "higher" rational functions, which were assumed by AI researchers and engineers as logical and detached forms of intelligence.[64] In the 1980s, Hubert Dreyfus cowrote with his brother Stuart Dreyfus *Mind Over Machine: The Power of Human Intuition and Expertise in the Era of the Computer*, in which they continued to criticize the assumption of disembodied reason and calculative rationality shared by AI researchers at that time who dismissed intuition and skills.

Dreyfus's insightful critique of the absence of the body in AI projects reveals the deep-rooted metaphysical tradition of Western philosophy that valorizes disembodied reason. On the other side of the Pacific, Chinese researchers and scientists, dissatisfied with the too "expert" expert systems, were also looking for ways to make machines more "intelligent." Qian Xuesen wrote in 1988 to Ma Xiwen, a professor of mathematics and artificial intelligence at Peking University, after he read Hubert and Stuart Dreyfus's book. He believed that their critique of the state of AI research in Western countries further confirmed the striking lack of a theory of intelligent machines.[65] The key here is how to define intelligence. Obviously frustrated with expert systems, Qian wrote to Ma in a different context: "The problem is that each of these existing expert systems has serious limitations. Their so-called 'intelligence' is just so-so.

The next step is to adopt the method of fuzzy mathematics and find a solution among the various expert systems and knowledge bases. In this way we may be able to remove the limitations step by step and work towards higher 'intelligence.'"[66] Sharing Dreyfus's aversion to cognitive science and its fetish of formalist reasoning, Qian since the late 1970s had been promoting "noetic science" (*siwei kexue* 思维科学), a term he coined to differentiate from the tradition of "cognitive science" in the West, which he believed had too narrowly focused on logical thinking. Qian's "noetic science" more ambitiously intended to uncover the secrets not only of logical thinking but also of image-thinking (*xingxiang siwei* 形象思维), intuition, and the source of inspiration. Noetic science, he firmly believed, would eventually lead to breakthroughs in AI.[67] In his letter to Ma, Qian turned the relationship of the two around, arguing that intelligent machines should be the entry point for noetic science since experiments on intelligent machines could facilitate forming a theory of human thoughts. This shifting around indicates the unspoken assumption about the coupling of human and machine. In fact, by the end of the letter he spoke highly of Ma's recent talk on the human–machine integration system.[68] Just a few years later, he proceeded to what he called a "metasynthetic engineering" project, aiming at a seamless human–machine interface.

By incorporating humans into the system, the human–machine intelligent system circumvents the problem of the absence of the body that resulted in the predicament in the earlier developments of AI. But the human–machine interface also renders the human body invisible, as the interface often appears as the built-in features of a system, as a technological accomplishment. In the case of Amazon Mechanical Turk, millions of workers whose labor is absorbed into the interaction points of the Turk become invisible and "bodiless." Aren't workers from the less developed countries more and more integrated into the global networks of cybernetic machines and digital media, their life and labor sucked into the capitalist machinery and rendered into virtual ghosts? Isn't it too good a dream for advanced capitalism to have all the work done by foreign laborers yet whose physical existence is completely erased and no longer a concern to the capitalist productive machine? Lilly Irani is thus right in commenting that Amazon Mechanical Turk "helps ameliorate the contradictions of intensified labor hierarchies by obscuring workers behind code and spreadsheets."[69]

The alleged replacement of human labor by machines turns out to be the restructuring of labor under varying socioeconomic conditions. The development of AI necessarily entails the new division and forms of labor, as well as the shifting line of the visibility/invisibility of different types of labor. This restructuring also generated discourses and debates on the definition of the human per se, which exposed the paucity of humanist discourse in the face of drastic changes in post-Mao China. The disappearance of the physical, laboring body from social and intellectual discourses in the late 1970s and 1980s converged with the politics of depoliticization in post-Mao China, as well as the dismissal and disintegration of the working class, not only in China but also in postindustrial capitalist countries, reflective of the global conditions of postsocialism. As ubiquitous cybernetic machines transform the conditions of life per se under information capitalism, a new politics of life emerges in the horizon. If the symbolic processing mode of the earlier AI, as Paul Edwards suggests, mirrors the "closed-world" of the Cold War, the all-inclusiveness of "metasynthetic engineering," with its ambition to cover all ranges of human knowledge from the past, all sorts of human capacities from cognition to intuition and bodily affect, and all kinds of communication and information media, indicates an ever-expanding network, and the rapacious appetite of the machine: everything is incorporated into the system and coupled with the machine, serving the irrational rationality and efficiency. In this regard, isn't the robot doctor Fangfang, who can work 24/7 and "has no need for eating and drinking, for resting and consuming, and no parents nor siblings or any social relations to tend to," and who insists upon vivisecting her patients, no longer a robot, but instead is a perfect metaphor for the productive machine that continuously sucks in life?[70]

CHAPTER THREE

The "Ultrastable System" and the New Cinema

While the prospect of a human–machine integrated information environment generated immense excitement among both scientists and the general public, Chinese filmmakers found a stunning aesthetic to reflect on the relations of human beings to their living environment. Filmed at a high point in China's economic reforms, *Yellow Earth* (*Huang tudi* 黄土地) threw its audience into a barren and bleak landscape that seemed out of synch with the ongoing, ambitious project of modernization. The immobile images of the sprawling yellow earth that engulfs any characters on that land almost became a symbol of a backward, stagnant China, which Chinese intellectuals of the 1980s returned to again and again to address their anxieties about China's modernization process (Figure 13).

Such fascination with the landscape was not unusual at the time. In *River Elegy* (*Heshang* 河殇), a controversial television miniseries first broadcast on China's Central Television in 1988, the deserted yellow earth is seen as the creation of the Yellow River, which ruthlessly swallows the female protagonist Cuiqiao in the film. The miniseries adopts the "yellowness" of the Yellow River and yellow earth as a symbol of the "yellow civilization" of China, in contrast to the "blue civilization" of the Western world, building up dichotomies of East versus West, land civilization versus ocean civilization. The landscape of the yellow earth, across which the Yellow River runs—usually regarded as the origin of

Figure 13. A still from *Yellow Earth*.

the Han civilization in textbooks—thus became an iconic image. Yet, the land evoked "revulsion rather than admiration" in the heart of Xia Jun, a young CCTV director at the time, who was the chief producer and creator of the miniseries. The first time he saw the real Yellow River, as he accounted, he was "shocked not by its idealized, eternal magnificence, but instead by its ugliness, poverty, and hidden crisis."[1] Thus, in *River Elegy*, the landscape is inextricably tied to constant crises of Chinese civilization, as the male narrator questions: "Why did our feudal system, just like the torrents of the Yellow River, never end? . . . History transpired in China just like the Yellow River dragging slowly and laboriously through its mud-filled channel."[2] The analogy between the landscape and Chinese history was further developed in the argument that the flooding of the river shared similar chronic cycles with the rise and fall of feudal dynasties. This argument was sanctioned by a scholar who appeared in front of the camera and claimed Chinese society as an "ultrastable system," a system in which chronic disruptions of history, such as peasants' rebellions, only led to an even more stable and viable feudal society.

That scholar was Jin Guantao, whose own fame was established on his theory of the "ultrastable system." Collaborating with his wife, Liu

Qingfeng, Jin generalized the thousands of years of Chinese history as following the patterns of an "ultrastable system." Starting with an article published in the *Journal of Guizhou Normal University* (*Guizhou shifan daxue xuebao* 贵州师范大学学报), the couple continued to elaborate on the idea in *Prosperity and Crisis: On the Ultrastable Structure of Feudal Society in China* (*Xingsheng yu weiji: lun zhongguoshehui de chaowending jiegou* 兴盛与危机：论中国封建社会的超稳定结构), published in 1984. Acclaimed as the first works that adopted systems theory and cybernetics to study Chinese history and society, these works proposed that a society could be studied as a complex system consisting mainly of three interacting subsystems: the economic, the political, and the cultural and ideological. The interconnections and interactions of the three subsystems, through the circulation of functional inputs and outputs, would together achieve homeostasis and result in the stability of the whole system. This system was considered the "interior environment," which in turn constitutes a larger system that encompasses both human society and the natural world. The ultimate question Jin and Liu raised in the book was: Why did feudalism persist in China? Their answer was that the "ultrastable system" barred a "stagnant" China from progressing toward modernization.

The stagnancy thesis, which can be traced back to orientalist discourses, was nothing new in itself. For example, Hegel notoriously proclaimed that China was still outside the "World's History," because, as he accounted, "as the contrast between objective existence and subjective freedom of movement in it, is still wanting, every change is excluded, and the fixedness of a character which recurs perpetually, takes the place of what we should call the truly historical."[3] Particular worth noting about the "ultrastable system" thesis is the widely disseminated understanding of human society as an intricate information system and the deep embroiling of this knowledge production in Cold War geopolitics. How did the notion of an "ultrastable system" become such an ideologically invested term that was used to characterize Chinese society but also pervade the cultural discussions of the 1980s and impact cinematic discourse and aesthetic experimentation? Despite its presentation of a seemingly insulated space, the cinematic images of *Yellow Earth* were in fact borne from a discursive network that deployed information sciences, postwar modernization theory, and the aesthetics of modernism.

In this chapter, I begin with a genealogy of system theory–based analyses of society and its entanglement with the Cold War modernization theory, which, through the mediation of Max Weber, resonated with the culturalist understanding of modernization among Chinese intellectuals in the 1980s. By placing the thesis of the "ultrastable system" in the discourse networks, I will uncover its implication in Cold War geopolitics. Then I move to explicate the postsocialist politics surrounding the new authority of scientific rationality, which undoubtedly lent the thesis of ultrastable structure new appeal despite the archaic nature of the question it addressed. This "ultrastable system" thesis also moved into cinematic theory and criticism, and converged with a vocal voice to advocate the "modernization of cinematic language," thus informing the practices of a new aesthetic emerging around iconic films such as *Yellow Earth*. The complicated relations between human agency and the environment, between the intellectual observer and the system in *Yellow Earth*, indicate the "strange loops" of geopolitics and the global networks of knowledge production in which post-Mao intellectuals were caught. Crucial here is the reevaluation of history in relation to modernization. Yet the "belated" modernist aesthetic does not necessarily follow the linear temporality of modernization discourse; instead, it suggests the overlap of multiple temporalities between a postsocialist world and an unevenly developed global capitalism. I will conclude the chapter with a reading of *Black Cannon Incident* (1985) by Huang Jianxin, which I argue, through its self-reflexive aesthetic, captures a structure of feeling that cannot be assimilated into the dominant modernization discourse.

The "Ultrastable System" and the Modernization Theory

Jin and Liu did not invent the term "ultrastable system." Their direct inspirations came from W. Ross Ashby's *Design for a Brain: The Origin of Adaptive Behavior*, a recognized classic of systems theory. Ashby used the term to describe the ability of a system—of both biological and nonbiological forms—to adjust itself in accordance to the changes in the environment so that the fluctuations of the system are restricted within certain limits in order to maintain its own stability. To Ashby, this is important for the survival of a biological entity. The interactions between the biological entity and the environment are realized through feedbacks inside the large system that comprises both the entity and environment. When Jin and Liu adopted the term to describe Chinese society, underlying their argument was the presumption that Chinese society could be viewed as a biological entity capable of adapting itself to the environment. If to Ashby the self-organized closure of the entity is crucial to maintain its identity, Jin and Liu interpreted this closure projected onto Chinese society as a negative that precludes any significant changes.

To be sure, Jin and Liu were not the only ones who tried to apply systems theory to the examination of human society. Qian Xuesen, along with his two collaborators, Xu Guozhi and Wang Shouyun, in 1978 proposed using the methods of systems engineering to organize various areas of social activities.[4] Tracing systems engineering to the organizational methods of large and complicated military projects that involve hundreds of thousand people and the coordination of different parts, such as the development of atomic bombs, Qian and his collaborators developed the method of systems engineering into a "general design" (*zongti sheji* 总体设计) in the national defense department that treats the project as a system comprised of several subsystems and aims to optimize the operations of the system. This, along with corporate "management science," usually called "Operations Research" in Western universities, applied systems theory to the management of a project, a corporation, or a department of the nation.[5] In an article published in 1979, Qian Xuesen and Wu Jiapei further argued that the operations of a project, an institute or a work unit, should be considered a small system in relation to the larger system of the nation. Based on the methods of systems engineering, this "social engineering" project involves large-scale collection of information, data analysis, computational modeling.[6] The use of cybernetics and systems theory in economic management, population control, price reforms, and other areas indicated that human society was understood as a huge, complex system.

If Qian and others explicated the war origins and military associations of "Operations Research," the adoption of systems theory in social sciences was also historically imbricated in Cold War geopolitics. American sociologist Talcott Parsons, adopting the analytics of systems theory and cybernetics, had similarly argued that the variables of the system of human society are interdependent, and that the stability of this system is maintained through the "equilibrium" reached by different forces. Parsons's theory is representative of structural-functionalism in Western academic sociology. Its emphasis on the "oneness" of society, as opposed to Marxism's emphasis on division, internal contradictions, and class conflicts, as Alvin W. Gouldner commented, addressed the anxieties of the middle class about "the emergence of Communist power in the Soviet Union," and it reflected "the common concerns of relatively advanced or 'developed' industrial societies whose elites defined their problem primarily in terms of their common need to maintain 'social order.'"[7] The Parsonianist conception of society as a self-maintaining, homeostatic system privileges the established order and the benefits of the status quo. Gouldner also pointed out that at the time of his writing in 1970 there was increasing interest in Parsons's theory inside the Soviet Union and the Socialist Bloc, mainly for two reasons: first, because of the crisis of classic Marxism in addressing the new social order in the Soviet Union and other socialist countries, Parsonianism was regarded as an administrative sociology to keep their system running within the existing framework; second, while Parsons stressed the integration of the system, he also affirms the functional autonomy of each component, which Soviet scholars read as a support for their liberalizing demands and a possibility for a more humanistic culture.[8]

As early as the 1960s, introductions and reviews of Parsons's works had already appeared in Chinese journals, such as *Guowai shehui kexue wenzhai* (Digest of foreign social sciences) and *Shijie zhexue* (World philosophy). With the revival of Western sociology in China in the early 1980s, Parsons became a high-profile Western sociologist featured in various social science journals. Jin Guantao and Liu Qingfeng in their 1986 book *Lun lishi yanjiu de zhengti fangfa* (On the wholistic method of historical study) admitted the similarity of their work to Parsons's theory of social systems. Though Jin and Liu revealed that they had not been exposed to Parsonianism when they started writing in the 1970s, there are certainly parallels in their work with Parsons's theory. For example, Parsons's notion of the interdependent system, as pointed out by Gouldner, was "a polemic against those models that stressed the importance of 'one or two inherently primary sources of impetus to change in social systems.'"[9] Obviously, one of the models Parsons wrote against was classic Marxism. Orthodox Marxism was also Jin and Liu's strawman in their book. Against the thesis about the determinant role of the economic base, they proposed instead the vision of society built upon systemic interactions among its components. Similar to Parsons's obsession with "oneness," Jin and Liu were preoccupied with "systematic totality," a mode of analysis that Wang Jing notes, "pledges alliance with a totalizing scientific rationality, a rationality that allegedly enables and liberates the mind but at the same time encloses real human beings and human history within a superstable macrostructure."[10] Although the "oneness" of the system to Parsons meant the positive stability of the social order, which on the surface differed from Jin and Liu's view, they both consciously resisted the analysis of society based on class conflicts. More important, their shared positivist view implied that science could overcome ideological and religious differences.

Writing about this "coincidental similarity" between Jin and Liu and Parsons, He Guimei points out the mediating role of Max Weber. Weber's emphasis on the role of culture in the rise of capitalism, to them, could be an effective argument against the Marxist priority in the economic base. In fact, Weber's theory on the rise of capitalism in the context of the 1980s was read as the saga revealing the secrets of Western modernization. This mediating role of Weberian theory of modernization between Parsons and his Chinese readers was evidenced in the publication of the 1980 Chinese translation of Weber's *Protestant Ethic and the Spirit of Capitalism* via Parsons's English translation by a group of graduate students at Peking University. Parsons himself was a key figure for establishing the foundation of modernization theory in postwar American social sciences, which aimed at providing a scheme of industrialization and modernization in non-Western, underdeveloped countries and regions. Scientism and developmentalism, two pillars of the modernization theory, became the ideological weapon of the United States to compete with the Soviet Union. At the turn of 1980s, with the rise of neoliberalism and transformations inside the socialist bloc, the ideology of modernization gained growing influences among former third-world countries and appeared as a universalized path globally.[11] Repacking the not-so-new imperial notion of Western superiority and teleological narrative into new languages, modernization theory played an important role in the foreign policies and strategies of the United States to contain the danger of communism in "backward" regions, and it was "resurrected in post–Cold War analyses celebrating the collapse of state socialism and the transformative power of capitalist markets."[12] By turning the Weberian thesis of culture and capitalism into a universal theory of modernization, Parsons and his colleagues successfully explained the "superiority" of the West as that of culture, concealing the history of colonial expansion accompanying the rise of capitalism. As He Guimei points out, this privileging of the culture by the modernization theory renders the issue of modernization into a result from the internal functioning of the system and the values of a society, obscuring the interrelation of different societies.[13] With Max Weber as a key figure in modernization discourse in 1980s China, this cultural thesis not only emerged as a counteraction to Marx's economy-based social analysis, but it also shaped the "cultural fever" in 1980s China. We can observe this in Jin and Liu's thesis of "ultrastable systems." Though they proposed three subsystems as an interacting system that maintains homeostasis status, in the end the persistence of Confucian culture was considered pivotal in helping restore the system each time after its disruption. In this way, an examination of the "deep cultural structure" naturally became the manner in which Chinese intellectuals explained the absence of modernization in China.

The Post-Mao Politics of Scientific Rationalism

Jin and Liu's treatise could be regarded as part of the general intellectual efforts at this time to seek "scientific solutions" to social problems, an enterprise no doubt backed up "with quiet blessing of the top leadership, which was actively searching for rational means of revitalizing the country."[14] In a manuscript Jin coauthored with Chen Fong-ching, Jin characterized this as "a movement away from orthodox Marxism-Leninism toward Scientism, that is, a worldview and social theory based directly on the principles of natural science."[15]

Indeed, this faith in scientism cannot be divorced from post-Mao politics. Jin Guantao was a student of chemistry at Peking University when the Cultural Revolution began in 1966. He developed a strong interest in philosophy through reading Marx and Hegel. When underground reading became a fashion among the intellectual youth, Jin, like his colleagues, was enthusiastic in hunting for "internally circulated" books, which were prohibited from being publicly circulated and were supposed to be restricted within limited circles of high Party cadres. Jin avidly devoured books on science, from mathematics to physics, and felt that "the challenges of the ongoing scientific revolution to our society had not been well discussed."[16] He thus abandoned Marx and Hegel, which he regarded as "dated" nineteenth-century philosophy, for scientific rationality. His reading notes were circulated among friends, a process through which he became acquainted with Liu Qingfeng, a former student of physics and Chinese literature at Peking University. The pair earned their initial publicity for a small book published in 1981, entitled *Open Love Letters*, which Liu Qingfeng composed based on their own correspondence during their sent-down years.

In this epistolary novel, the fictive female protagonist Zhenzhen is perplexed with future prospects of her own life as a college student sent down to the remote countryside. Her friend Laojiu introduces her to the new world of cybernetics and bionics, as he writes with enthusiasm: "My dear friend, you should stand up bravely from where you fell down, and march toward the road of science, which can never be wrong. It is science that always gives us the strength and power. Living in a time like ours makes us realize that the right answer to everything lies only in the most advanced scientific thoughts and achievements, the criteria against which everything at the present and in the past should be tested."[17] Laojiu recounts that amid the high tide of the Cultural Revolution, distanced from factional fights, he relied solely on reading to seek answers to his puzzles about his own time, only to find that he should abandon philosophy for science. He asserts that all previous philosophical thought should be reformed through science. Unsurprisingly, the philosophy that ought to be reformed in his opinion is above all Marxism and its related treatise on dialectics, which once Jin had been intrigued with, as he confessed in his autobiography. Laojiu also feels sorry for the "benumbing religion" of previous generations of scientists, who harbor their faith in communist ideals and ethics. He believes that only science can serve as the true faith.

This belief in science is intermingled with the affection between the lovers. Interspersed with epistolary correspondence between the lovers are their recent serendipitous encounters with books, scientific knowledge, and serious intellectual discussions. Their correspondence reflected the networks among intellectual youth even when they were sent down to the countryside. Such networks did not fall into the boundaries of academic disciplines but instead constituted a common intellectual ferment in the years following the end of the Cultural Revolution.

The argument of prioritizing science over political faith was typical in the post-Mao political environment and amid the widespread disillusion with socialist ideals. If the Cultural Revolution was regarded as irrational and inhumane, science was invested with the power to transcend ideological conflicts. This belief in science and rationality lies at the core of Jin and Liu's theory, and their application of systems theory and cybernetics to examine the not-so-new question: Why did feudalism in China persist? To be sure, their use of "feudalism" was not unquestioned. Jin Guantao summarized in 1988 the critical voices toward his book as such:

> On the surface, the question we raised about why feudalism persisted in China is ungrounded. First of all, it is quite controversial that we named as "feudalism" the long period from the Qin Dynasty (from 221 BCE) all the way to the Qing Dynasty (which ended 1912), because "feudalism" is too generalized a term that often refers to the Middle Ages in Western Europe. Moreover, how do we determine whether the endurance of feudalism in China was long or not? According to what criteria? The implicit idea is to take the history of Western Europe as the standard model of historical development. Why don't we ask why the feudal society in Western Europe was short-lived? In fact, this

question is still Europe-centered. It sounds like a biologist asking why the head of a deer is not on the shoulders of a horse.[18]

As a delayed response to these sharp but fundamental questions, Jin contended: "The real significance of this inaccurate question lies in its refreshing understanding of Chinese history. Implicit in this question is a comparison of the *deep cultural and social structures* between the West and China.... What led to their disparate roads of development?"[19] In other words, the real question for them was: What was missing in Chinese culture and society that prevented China from traveling on the road of modernization modeled by Western Europe? In an interview, Jin made the political urgency of his inquiry even more explicit:

> The disaster of feudalism during the Cultural Revolution prompted historians to inquire again into the reasons for feudalism's long endurance in China.... If feudalism had been abolished (as some scholars argued), why did it hit back during the Cultural Revolution? We believe that it is the ultrastable system that produced alternate patterns of peace and chaos that kept traditional Chinese society from advancing into a modern one, despite its once-prosperous commercial economy.[20]

Apparently, "feudalism" in Jin's linear view of history is a signifier for backwardness and irrationality, which also was the fundamental cause of the Cultural Revolution. Such chaos could only be eradicated through the pure reason of science. Undoubtedly, it was the purported scientific theory of cybernetics that gave Jin and Liu their confidence in the validity of their own argument. Though the same question has been discussed before, they refuted all previous studies as unsatisfactory. With the aid of systems theory, they believed that they had provided a comprehensive answer to the question.

Such passions with scientism were supported by state institutions and the Party-run publication system. After joining the editorial board of the *Journal of Dialectics of Nature* in 1978, Jin and Liu developed the journal as an important site for disseminating modern cybernetics and information and systems theory. The *Journal of Dialectics of Nature*, originally the

Newsletter of Research in the Dialectics of Nature, was overseen by Yu Guangyuan, who headed the science section of the Propburo and was known for his translation of Engel's *Dialectics of Nature*. In the late 1970s, he revived the *Newsletter* under the name of *Journal of Dialectics of Nature* after it fell into dysfunction during the Cultural Revolution. He entrusted Cha Ruiqiang and Li Baoheng as the managing editors of the journal. Li, who personally received Alvin Toffler during his visit to Shanghai, in turn recruited Jin Guantao. Around 1984–85, Jin became a key figure in organizing the publication of a book series called *"Zouxiang weilai"* 走向未来 (Toward the future). Dedicated to introducing Western thought and promoting science as the remedy for China's impeded modernization, the series was one of the most influential in the 1980s, along with the *"Wenhua: Zhongguo yu shijie"* 文化：中国与世界 (Culture: China and the world) book series edited by Gan Yang, and the *"Zhongguo wenhua shuyuan"* 中国文化书院 (Chinese Culture Academy) series by Tang Yijie and Li Zehou. Jin and Liu's *Prosperity and Crisis* was abridged as *Zai lishi de biaoxiang beihou: Dui zhongguo fengjian shehui chaowending jiegou de tansuo* 在历史的表象背后：对中国封建社会超稳定结构的探索 (Beneath the surface of history: A thesis on the ultrastable structure of Chinese feudal society) and republished in the "Toward the Future" series.

The "Toward the Future" series covered a wide range of disciplines, from modern physics and mathematics to linguistics, art theory, and economics. For example, *The Limits to Growth* by the Club of Rome was a pessimistic prediction of the human future resulting from limited resources, which later generated the discourse of information as an inexhaustible resource for future society, as exemplified in Alvin Toffler's books. Julian Simon's *The Ultimate Resource*, a counterargument to *The Limits to Growth*, was also translated and published in an abridged form. Besides translation, there were also monographs by Chinese scholars, such as *Xinxi geming de jishu yuanliu* 信息革命的技术源流 (The technological origins of information revolution) by Song Desheng, *Jingji kongzhi lun* 经济控制论 (Economic cybernetics) by He Weiling and Deng Yingtao, and *Furao de pingkun* 富饶的贫困 (Rich poverty) by Wang Xiaoqiang and Bai Nanfeng, an investigation into the "backward" countryside of the northwestern regions. Most of these people belonged to the same intellectual circle around the "Rural Development Group" (*Zhongguo nongcun fazhan wenti yanjiuzu* 中国农村发展问题研究组) under the Chinese Academy of Social Sciences.[21] While the rural area was considered the location of "authentic" cultural roots, it was also a symbol of intractable traditions in urgent need of modernization.[22] This interest in rural areas was shared by Chen Kaige and other once-sent-down youth who were active in film and literature in the 1980s. He Weiling, active in a group composed mainly of economists and sociologists, was also acquainted with the Baiyangdian intellectual youths, the most representative of whom included the well-known poet Mang Ke. [23] Some of them served as a think tank to the government. One of the editors of the "Toward the Future" series, Chen Yizi, who initiated the Rural Development Group, was a key figure in drafting suggestions to the central government on the reform plans in the countryside.[24] Gan Yang, the editor of the "Culture: China and the World" series, recalled that Jin Guantao and his group, seeking to play a role in the policymaking of the Party, had close connections with the reformists in the CCP.[25] The popularity of Jin and Liu's work among Chinese intellectuals thus reflected common intellectual concerns and their shared discourse of modernization with the state. Given that Jin Guantao was one of the main consultants of *River Elegy*, it is unsurprising that the miniseries presented a view of Chinese history quite similar to Jin and Liu's theory of "ultrastable systems."

This understanding of Chinese history among Chinese intellectuals was also the outcome of the cultural fever of the moment. It is not to say that all these intellectual groups shared exactly the same views about Chinese traditions and paths of modernization. As mentioned above, there were mainly three active intellectual groups surrounding the three most influential book series, including "Toward the Future" group led by Jin Guantao, "Culture: China and the World" group headed by Gan Yang, and the "Chinese Culture Academy" group represented by Tang Yijie and Li Zehou. Chen Lai later accounted that the Jin group aimed at the "scientization" of humanities through quantitative analysis, mathematical models, and other methods of natural sciences, whereas the Gan group, especially Gan, inspired by modern hermeneutics, was concerned more

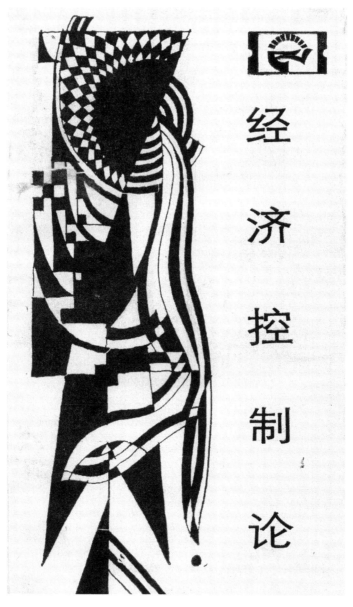

Figure 14. Book cover of *Jingji kongzhilun* [Economic cybernetics], He weiling and Deng Yingtao (Chengdu: Sichuan renmin chubanshe, 1984).

with reforming Chinese culture through Western modern culture.[26] The last group, closely associated with overseas Neo-Confucianists and fascinated with Max Weber's *Protestant Ethic and the Spirit of Capitalism*, enthusiastically pursued the question: Can Confucianism be transformed to serve the ideological foundation for China's modernization? This revival of Confucianism found official endorsement and cooperation from the late 1980s.[27] Their opinions about Chinese culture might vary, but they all shared the same concern: the relationship between Chinese culture and China's modernization project. The mutual influences and crisscrossing among the groups, according to Chen Lai, spoke to "the contradiction between cultural nationalist recognition of the tradition and anti-traditional tendency that placed urgency in modernization."[28] It was this contradiction that made the relation between modernization and the "deep structure of Chinese culture" the common concern of Chinese intellectuals in the 1980s.

The "Ultrastable System" of Film Theory and the Aesthetic of the New Cinema

Born from such general intellectual ferment, Chen Kaige and his crew developed a new cinematic language to examine the deep cultural structure of the ancient land. The most stunning feature of *Yellow Earth* for Chinese audiences in the 1980s was its immobile images. The cinematographer Zhang Yimou explained why he decided to reduce to a minimum the movement of the camera in this film:

> As film is an art of moving images, naturally, it is the strength of film to capture the movement of things. But a cinematographer doesn't have to feel obligated to move the camera all the time, as a moving camera isn't necessarily the best technique. Whether the camera should be mobile or immobile depends on the content and the theme of the film. The immobile cinematography of *Yellow Earth* is decided upon two considerations, specifically:
>
> First, we hope to convey a sense of historical feelings through the immobile camera.... *Yellow Earth* is set in the Sino-Japanese War period, so there should be a sense of historicity, and a feeling of the ambiance of

that time. The immobile camera is the most faithful and powerful way to present that ambience. . . .

Secondly, the immobile camera is also in accordance with the topography of the land. Because of the soil erosion by water, the land of the Northern Shaanxi . . . became a patch of bare earth, as if it were something serene and of incredible weight that had landed on this planet. The vegetationless land is insulated from the noises and agitation of cities, nor could any sound of the insects or wildlife be heard. We hope to capture the serenity of the land with the immobile camera.[29]

It may seem unclear what sort of historical feelings might be captured by the immobile camera. However, it was never a problem for Zhang's contemporaries to identify these "historical feelings." Film critic Zheng Dongtian had no difficulty in detecting in *Yellow Earth* a presentation of traditional culture as accumulated in the long history of "backwardness and uncivilizedness" just like the sedimentation of the Yellow River, and a critique of the "ultrastable familial structure" that sacrifices young lives like Cuiqiao.[30] Ni Zhen commented that the film "used symbolic language to present the stagnant history of the nation." He applauded the use of immobile shots to capture the rhythm of slowness and repetition in the everyday life of an agricultural society, which he saw also as a psychological rhythm passed down generation by generation.[31]

It is worth noting that in Zhang Yimou's statement, the "sense of historicity" and the unique topography of the yellow earth converge in the immobile shots. The "sense of historicity" cannot be mistaken as a realistic or faithful representation of a specific historical incident, or of the Sino-Japanese War period. In fact, some critics pointed out the incongruity between the historical setting and the costumes and props, which exposes no interest of the film in realistic representation.[32] The "sense of historicity" was conveyed more on a symbolic level. In other words, the images of the yellow earth are not a naturalist's representations of a real, concrete place, but a symbol of the old civilization. The alluvial sedimentation of the plateau in the eyes of the Chinese intellectual is also the sedimentation of China's long history. The yellow earth refers to the natural environment that interacts with human society on this land, but it also refers to the man-made environment, which is shaped by the natural landscape but altogether comes to define the workings of a human society. History in this sense was no longer regarded as a series of unfolding temporalities; rather, it was condensed in the immobile shots of the symbolic landscape. The *substitution of spatiality for temporality* resembles Jin Guantao and Liu Qingfeng's approach of replacing temporality with a timeless, ultrastable system, any changes in which could be spatialized only as insignificant modifications to its subsystems. While each of the subsystems was never entirely static, in Jin and Liu's assessment, the adjustments among the various subsystems kept society from breaking through into a new system. Although Jin and Liu claimed to examine history, their thesis, by claiming that Chinese history throughout the two thousand years had remained stagnant, in fact *ruled out temporality* from their model. In a similar way, when the camera contemplates the yellow earth, the immobile framing locks the characters and their world in a frozen temporality.

The long shots of immobile images resonate with the slow rhythm of the film. Critics of the 1980s quickly sensed its diluted, "nondramatic" narrative as a break with socialist realism. Since the late 1970s, discussions about the divorce of film from drama had been central to the aesthetic explorations of the new Chinese cinema. Film scholar Chen Xihe in his essay "Rethinking the Film Aesthetics of China" determined that the "root" of the Chinese film tradition lies in a drama-centered aesthetic. Based on "a comparison between Chinese and Western film theories in their disparate cultural and philosophical traditions," he undertook "an archeological research on the origin of the Chinese tradition of film theory." He traced this Chinese tradition to *On Shadow Play Writing (Yingxi juben zuofa* 影戏剧本作法), the earliest text of Chinese film theory by Hou Yao, a pioneer filmmaker whose screen adaption of the Yuan dynasty drama *The Story of the West Wing* remains the earliest extant silent film. Chen argued that Hou's contemporaneous film theorists in the West, such as Louis Delluc, Sergei Eisenstein, and Béla Balázs, all had focused exclusively on the design of mise-en-scène and techniques of camera work, which laid down the very fundamentals of filmmaking. Hou instead took cinema basically as a type of drama, and he overemphasized the social functions of cinema, which resulted in what he called a "shadow-play aesthetic," which was still dominant in Chinese films to date. Partaking philosopher Li Zehou's argument that this utilitarian attitude was rooted in the practical reason of the Chinese cultural tradition, Chen called this shadow-play aesthetic the "ultrastable system of Chinese film theory," which persisted in Chinese film practices regardless of any input of foreign films and theories. From this perspective, the incomplete storytelling, the reduced dramatic elements of *Yellow Earth*, Chen finally concluded, should be deemed a challenge to this "ultrastable system."[33]

Chen Xihe's essay was applauded by other like-minded film critics. It was no coincidence that Chen adopted the term "ultrastable system" from Jin Guantao and Liu Qingfeng. Critic Li Tuo, referring to Chen's essay, considered the shadow-play tradition a central ethical doctrine that prevented Chinese film from developing into a modern art. According to him, antithetical to this "didactic rule" of cinema is a "scientific" understanding of film that focuses on the technology and techniques of filmmaking such as camerawork, lighting, film editing, and the design of the mise-en-scène. For Li, the debates on film aesthetics since the late 1970s could be summarized in one question: What is cinema? This Bazinian question was, as Li understood it, a choice between a utilitarian and a scientific approach to cinema: Is it a tool for ideological doctrine, or is it a subject of scientific study? He asserted that the real significance of Bazin to Chinese film theorists was not so much about the argument of realism or documentary, but about bringing film theory to the level of scientific study.[34]

It should be noted that Jin Guantao and Liu Qingfeng in their pursuit of the question "Why did China fail to give rise to modern science?" similarly identified "ethics centeredness" (*lunli zhongxin* 伦理中心) as the attribute of Confucianism, which "always ascribed ethical judgments to the explanation of natural phenomena" and eventually led to superstition and mysticism.[35] The parallel construction by Li Tuo of the opposition between scientific values that represent the modern and ethics-centered judgments that belong to the traditional on the surface advocated for the "purposeless purpose" of science, but in fact aimed to free cinema from political interventions. Li distinguished the new Chinese cinema of the

1980s from the earlier PRC films, dismissing the latter as distorted products of power. "Science" in this context became the signifier of a new authority that contested against the political and ideological domination in filmmaking, however loosely Bazin's theory might be defined as a "science." The technical level of filmmaking, such as camerawork and editing, was no longer derogated as "formalism," but gained autonomy for its association with "the modern."

Indeed, the post-Mao new wave of aesthetic experimentation in cinema can be said to date from Zhang Nuanxin and Li Tuo's call for the "modernization of cinematic language," the title of an essay published in 1979. As Zhang Xudong points out, this pursuit of the "modern" is above all a challenge to the official mode of representation—socialist realism. Bazin was embraced as a "theory of cinematic ontology," or the "long-take" theory. For Chinese film critics, Bazin's recognition of the automatic mechanism of the cinematic apparatus rules out human intervention, which, in the context of the early 1980s could only represent political manipulation. Zhang Xudong thus summarizes this politics of cinematic language as such:

> By being transparent to the reality, that is, by letting the photographic, cinematic dimensions take over, the person behind the camera successfully maintains the political ambivalence and semantic multiplicity of his or her visual world: hence the discussion of "opacity" of the new wave films. In contrast, socialist realism is seen as privileging a monolithic, transparent political meaning by imposing the opaqueness of the medium as a visual cliché.[36]

This "being transparent to the reality" in fact posits a competing notion of "reality" over and against socialist realism. The short circuit between the clichéd language of socialist realism and its meaning is regarded as political manipulation and a distortion of reality, whereas the ambiguity or "opacity" of the "modern" cinema leaves its audience space for reflection. Central to this version of "modern" cinema and a reflective audience is a humanistic notion of subjectivity aligned with the enlightenment ideals of Chinese intellectuals, here embodied as a film audience not manipulated by propaganda but capable of rational observation. Sharing similar concerns about the agency of the audience, Chen Xihe read the scene of Cuiqiao's marriage in parallel to a similar marriage scene in *Life* (*Rensheng*, 1984) directed by Wu Tianming. He commented that while Wu used a close-up on the tears of the reluctant bride to induce the audience's identification with and pity for the bride, *Yellow Earth* employed an extreme long shot, itself a deliberate repetition of the marriage scene that Cuiqiao witnesses at the beginning of the film. Chen continued:

> This is unlike some cheap, melodramatic gimmicks to bully the audience emotionally. Rather, it achieves an effect of defamiliarization, which keeps the audience at a certain distance to see and think about the fate of Cuiqiao against the broad background of Chinese history.... The use of long shots leads not to a utilitarian interpretation of politics or ethics, but rather to modern reflections on the cultural heritage of our nation.... Class analysis can no longer reveal the richness and profoundness of our life today ... [but] cultural analysis can touch upon the more eternal and essential elements of our life.[37]

It is not hard to see that "culture" replaced "politics" and "ideology" as the pivot in critical writings of the 1980s. The defamiliarizing effect Chen associated with the long shot, according to him, prevents the audience from "losing" themselves in the scene, providing them a detached distance to "observe" the culture. This detached mode is different from that of dramatic conflicts to manipulate the reactions of the audience, which, as we can see, is inseparable from what Chen criticized as the ultrastable system of Chinese cinema that centers around ethical indoctrination. Furthermore, cinema is attributed the role of anthropological observation and cultural analysis, supplanting its role during the Mao era of inducing class identification. It is precisely with this shifting role of cinema that Chen came to privilege the long shot over the close-up, because the long shot allegedly has more capacity to capture the modes of human life in their social and natural environments. This privilege of long shot over close-up and long take over montage among both filmmakers and critics was intended to register a temporality of repetitive and long duration in Chinese society, which was posited in striking contrast to the eruptive, eventful temporality of the revolutionary narratives of socialist realism.

The plot of *Yellow Earth*, which is set in the 1930s and centers around the interactions of a Party representative named Gu Qing with local peasants in Shaanxi, where he goes to collect folk songs, evokes the narrative of revolutionary history films such as *The Red Detachment of Women* (1961): the Party influences peasant girls to rebel against feudalist oppression and arranged marriage. Yet in *Yellow Earth*, the narrative of saviorship breaks down as the peasant girl Cuiqiao fails to escape from her fate and is eventually drowned in the torrents of the Yellow River. In contrast to the low-angle close-ups and medium shots that glorify revolutionary heroes, the agent of the Party Gu is often framed in long shots against an endlessly unfolding yellow earth, which almost engulfs the characters on this land. To a certain degree, the vast landscape of yellow earth resistant to revolutionary transformation becomes the real protagonist of the film, which disintegrates the revolutionary narrative. This politics of landscape in the new Chinese cinema is sharply observed by Zhang Xudong: "What is smashed by the presentation of this landscape, though, is not temporality per se, but rather the narrative of time inscribed to a particular mode of representation, the official, bureaucratized discourse of socialist realism."[38]

The significance of the landscape in relation to human agency is explored by Stephanie Donald, who traces the landscape of *Yellow Earth* back to the landscape paintings of the Chang'an school in Mao's era, specifically, Shi Lu's *Fighting in Northern Shaanxi* (1959), a painting commissioned by the Museum of Revolutionary History.[39] The painting depicts the similar mountainous region in Shaanxi, yet the landscape is commanded by the gaze of the heroic figure in the painting, as Donald describes:

> On the mountain's top Mao Zedong stands in profile, looking out of frame right. The red massif to his left thrusts up as a satellite in comradely alignment with the Leader. . . . The background is crammed with distant ranges which snake and weave towards the foreground bloc.

This bloc is in turn defined by the standing figure whose gaze steadies the mountain in the frame, pins it down to a specific historical and political meaning, owns it.[40]

This legitimacy of the Party affirmed through the commanding gaze disappears in the long shots of *Yellow Earth*. In the final scene, when Gu reappears on the landscape, Donald comments: "He has himself become part of the horizon. His agency, which has been ironized throughout the film, is finally removed and handed to the audience on a visual plate. In this moment the Party disappears from the text and the landscape."[41] Gu Qing, portrayed at the beginning of the film as an observer of the "backward" society, is an outsider of a privileged perspective. The moment he disappears into the landscape, the observer no longer occupies a view of command, but becomes indistinguishable from the system he observes.

The Polemic of the Observer/System Dichotomy

The dichotomy of the observer/system was a crucial but daunting issue to the first generation of American cyberneticists. According to N. Katherine Hayles, Claude Shannon found that humans and machines in the cybernetic system would often be caught in a reflexive loop. For example, in W. Ross Ashby's theory of homeostasis, a human being is treated as a machine or an entity that responds to its environments in order to maintain homeostasis. The question arises: Is this man involved in the circuit an operator/observer of the system, or is he himself a black box functioning no differently from an input/output device? Cyberneticists such as Heinz von Foerster and Gregory Bateson, in attempting to grapple with the issue, realized that the problem of reflexivity posed a serious challenge to epistemology. Humberto R. Matunara and Francisco J. Varela's *Autopoiesis and Cognition: The Realization of the Living* is a classical work that addresses this epistemological challenge. "Autopoiesis" means self-making, a word Matunara coined to describe the self-reflexive circularity of a living system. Hayles summarizes Matunara and Varela's argument: reality comes into existence for humans "only through interactive processes determined solely by the organism's own organization," and such interactions "would be necessarily determined by the autopoietic organization of the observer."[42] Therefore, "a living system's organization causes certain products to be produced," and "these products in turn produce the organization characteristic of that living system," the result of which is "a circular, self-reflexive dynamic."[43]

Before taking this discussion into complicated territory, I would emphasize the blurred boundary between the observer and the system in Matunara and Varela's argument, for the observer knows the world precisely through the self-making reflexivity of her own organization. The world as seen by a frog comes out from its own construction, which in turn defines the frog's way of interactions with its living environment that makes it a frog. To put it in Hayles's words, we construct our environment through the "domain of interactions" made possible by our own autopoietic organization. Following this logic, referring back to *Yellow Earth*, if Chinese society is an ultrastable system, from whose perspective is it seen as such? Is the system the product of the observer's self-making world, or is the observer himself defined by the system's autopoietic organization? Could the observer maintain an objective distance despite his own being implicated in the feedback loops with the system he observes?

Borrowing such cybernetic terms as "homeostasis" and "ultrastable system" from W. Ross Ashby, Jin Guantao and Liu Qingfeng initially claimed that their analysis of Chinese society was more "scientific" and "objective." Jin later realized that "objectivity" was problematic for cybernetics and systems theory. In *The Philosophy of the Human: The Foundation of "Science and Rationality"* (*Ren de zhexue: Lun kexue yu lixing de jichu* 人的哲学：论科学与理性的基础), published in 1988, the central issue he explored was the subjectivity of the observer/researcher. Referring to the works of von Foerster and Muturana, he echoed their arguments about the impossibility of an "absolute reality."[44] To a certain extent, the book constitutes Jin's reflections on the relation between an observer and his constructs of the environment.

Another important book that drew the attention of Chinese intellectuals to the self-reflexive characteristic of systems was *Gödel, Escher, Bach: An Eternal Golden Braid* by Douglas R. Hofstadter, which was translated into Chinese in 1983 and included in the book series "Toward the Future" compiled by Jin Guantao. The book offers a wide range of examples of self-references and recursive structures, including mathematician Gödel's Theorem, Bach's *Musical Offering*, and Dutch graphic artist M. C. Escher's drawings. Hofstadter reads these phenomena as analogous to the modularization of computer programming, which involves a loop that "tells the computer to perform a fixed set of operations and then loop back and perform them again, over and over."[45] To Hofstadter, the ubiquity of such "strange loops" reveals the underlying hidden neurological mechanism of cognition and thinking. He regards Escher's drawings as the "most beautiful and powerful visual realization of this notion of Strange Loops." For example, in *Ascending and Descending*, the monks trudge up and down the steps, but they always find themselves ending up in loops—the repetition of the same. Another example is the bizarre and bewildering form of *Print Gallery*, which compels the question: Is it "a picture of a picture which contains itself"? "Or is it a picture of a gallery which contains itself? Or of a town which contains itself? Or a young man who contains himself?"[46] However, no matter which question you start with, you will find yourself thrust back to the beginning: "What we see is a picture gallery where a young man is standing, looking at a picture of a ship in the harbor of a small town, perhaps a Maltese town, to guess from the architecture, with its little turrets, occasional cupolas, and flat stone roofs, upon one of which sits a boy, relaxing in the heat, while two floors below him a woman—perhaps his mother—gazes out of the window from her apartment which sits directly above a picture gallery where a young man is standing, looking at a picture of a ship in the harbor of a small town, perhaps a Maltese town."[47] Such self-references across different levels bring out Hofstadter's notion of "recursion," which "is based on the 'same' thing happening on several different levels at once," and make it almost impossible to "distinguish working *within* the system from making statements or observations *about* the system."[48]

To Jin Guantao, Hofstadter's strange loops are precisely the feature of a self-organizing system, in which circular cause-and-effect relationships happen across different levels. This cause-and-effect circularity functions as the corrective feedback mechanism of a living system in order for it to adapt to the environment. The living system and the production of the

Figure 15. M. C. Escher, *Print Gallery* (lithograph, 1956). M. C. Escher's "Print Gallery," copyright 2018. The M. C. Escher Company, The Netherlands. All rights reserved. www.mcescher.com.

system also form cause-and-effect circularity, resulting in the constant expansion of a self-producing system.[49] Such an egg-and-chicken question, in the context of the 1980s, was taken seriously as invoking the problematic relationship between the human agent and his environment. If we think about how the images of the yellow earth become the environment that frames the characters within the frame, and how the silent characters in turn define the seemingly transhistorical image of the yellow earth itself, the question of circularity could hardly be evinced.

Li Tuo, for example, observed that the film "makes human beings, the yellow earth and its culture an indivisible unity, the interlocked relationship of which allows us to rethink the culture of our nation."[50] The landscape is neither external to the imagined national cultural tradition nor simply in a one-directional cause-and-effect relation to "traditional culture." Instead, the land and the people become a self-producing system as a whole that cannot break out of their strange loops.

If to Hofstadter the recursions are hard-wired in the neurological system of the human brain, Jin Guantao considered repetitive cycles that locked the society in a ultrastatble system to be the essential characteristic of Chinese culture that keeps reproducing itself. Yet as Paolo Totaro and Domenico Ninno recently argued, the recursive structure, hardly a hard-wired feature of the human brain or any culture, originates from a culture of mechanization and the wide dissemination of bureaucratic organizational models in modern times.[51] Inextricably tied to modernization and the increasing bureaucratization of social organization, recursions suggest the growing "process formalization that facilitated the designing of the mechanical equipment and their speed."[52] This formalization becomes more ubiquitous with the wide application of algorithmic computation. The modularization of computer programming that Hofstadter sees as typical strange loops in fact exemplifies this process formalization in modern times. If so, could Chinese intellectuals' adoption of systems theory in diagnosing China's lagging behind modernization in fact reflect a displaced anxiety about modernization and modernity?

Black Cannon Incident and Displaced Strange Loops

Although Hofstader uses the term differently, the notion of "strange loops" best captured the ways in which Chinese intellectuals of the 1980s perceived their relationship to the system and the culture around them. The director Huang Jianxin was open about his inspiration from Hofstader's book when making *Black Cannon Incident*, a black-humor parody of the counterespionage genre. Set in an industrialized mining site instead of the remote, backward countryside as in *Yellow Earth*, the film tells an absurd story of an engineer called Zhao Shuxin, who is suspected of being a spy because of a mysterious telegraph he sends that reads: "Black Cannon Missing/ Room 301/ Zhao." Because of this suspicious act in the eyes of Party bureaucracy, he is kept away from the German expert Hanks, with whom he is supposed to collaborate in installing a set of newly imported equipment for the company. His job as an interpeter is transferred to a colleague who has no engineering background. Eventually, an error in translation by this person causes the company an immense loss, while the mysterious "black cannon" turns out to be a minor chess piece that Zhao lost on his business trip. The plot is a strange loop, which starts with the mysterious "black cannon," and circles, through a series of random cause-and-effect links across different levels of semiotic fields, back to the minor chess piece. Yet the strange loops that intrigued Huang Jianxin more were the loops in the stiff bureaucratic system and the mindset of people.

Huang, in his "Director's Notes," explained the significance of the location of its setting: "Our decision to set the film in a developed industrial urban area was made after considerable deliberation: first, the setting is more characteristic of our time; secondly, it reinforces the theme of the script, for nothing works better than the contrast between the modern, urban environment and the theme of the script. If we chose a backward place instead, we could only repeat a natural analogy between the things we try to criticize and an environment of backwardness. Obviously, the critique would not be as profound as this one."[53] Apparently, Huang had *Yellow Earth* and other similar films in mind when he deliberately challenged the routine setting in rural areas, which he considered not reflective of the ongoing industrial modernization and urbanization in China. Here he also suggested that *Black Cannon* shares a similar sense of critique with *Yellow Earth*—"the deep structure of Chinese culture" as an obstacle to the ongoing project of modernization. Yet the film intends to reveal the very presence of this structure even in an area of urban civilization, in the very heart of an apparently modern setting. This "deep structure" is externalized in the film in the first place as a linguistic structure that leads signifiers such as the "black cannon" to mutate from an actual chess piece to a secret code word, resulting in random but disastrous consequences. The intransigent bureaucracy creates a recursive structure of code deciphering, restricting the interpretation of codes to the self-producing system of the Mao discourse. In fact, this dramatic incident is presented as a competition between different languages and codes, from the mistranslation between German and Chinese, to the highly specialized technical terminology alien to people without training, as well as the political language passed down from Mao's era. In this case, the stiff political language prevents the communication and smooth functioning of technical language, obstructing the progress of modernization.

The docile character of Zhao was seen as a typical Chinese intellectual burdened with the "inherited Confucian consciousness" of the culture. Critics of this time could hardly miss this point: "The representation of the intellectuals in *Black Cannon* continued the tradition in post-Cultural Revolution films to expose the injustice leveraged against the intellectuals.... However, when tracing down the roots of this injustice, it outsteps the limited perspective (of previous films) and goes forward to examine the mentality of Chinese intellectuals.... As we go deep into a critique of feudalism, a reexamination of the traditional consciousness inherited by the intellectuals—who are supposed to be the forerunners of the modern civilization—should be on our agenda. To perform the reforms of modernization in a country as ancient as China, the inert forces of tradition were not only presented in political and economic life, but also in people's minds and psychology."[54] Here the strange loops come back to haunt the discourse again: the system victimizes intellectuals, who inherit the residue of "feudalist consciousness" that is produced by the system, which helps the system perpetuate itself, which in turn victimizes intellectuals.... This "strange loop" invokes once again the question of within and without, human agency and the system. Can Chinese intellectuals extricate themselves from the strange loops to become "the forerunners of modernization"?

With the barren, rural setting replaced by a "modern," urban milieu, the question of how environment relates to the recursive system that allegedly blocks China's modernization comes to the foreground. Graphically, the mise-en-scène of *Black Cannon Incident* is repeatedly divided, cut across, and framed by the hard outlines of the machines in the mining quarry, accompanied by sounds of droning and hammering, honing and pounding. In a long take in the film, a gigantic machine at the distant end of the installation is seen driving directly toward the camera. We see two characters framed in the dark shadow of the machine. Against the low-frequency droning noises we hear Party Secretary Wu discussing with her colleague about not entrusting Zhao with the interpretation job. As the shadowy "mouth" of the approaching machine almost engulfs the sky and all other elements in the mise-en-scène, it stops and moves horizontally instead, cutting across and flattening the mise-en-scène between its two parallel spades (Figure 16). This scene is immediately followed by a close-up on a square-shaped black object that looks like a two-dimensional graphic. As the camera tracks out, a set of similar loops is revealed as layers of circle-in-circle graphics. Designed as 3-D op-art graphics, the loops almost appear to pop out of the screen, but in the next minute they seem about to draw the viewer into their vortex. After a moment's disorientation, the audience is thrown into a scene of a noisy rock 'n' roll performance in a nightclub. The loops turn out to be the club's stage decorations (Figure 17). The abrupt insertion of the graphics and the moment of their detachment from the cinematic settings uncannily reveals the shared abstract form of both scenes: the way in which the skeletons of the machine frame the screen space and almost devour the characters is presented as analogous to the looped squares that almost extend beyond the framing and draw the dancing figures into the loops. Later, we see similar loops in a factory scene. The rectangular outlines of a gigantic machine form a flattened loop-in-loop graphic, filling up the screen space, and inside the loops crouches Zhao, who is performing maintenance on the machine. Curiously, here the strange loops are closely associated with the machines, the very symbol of the "modern." Throughout the film the characters are always confined within a closed space framed by the skeletons of gigantic machines, as if being held prisoners in the strange loops. In the end, the question arises: Do the machines and industrial setting themselves constitute strange loops?

If Chinese intellectuals used the term "strange loops" to describe what they perceived as the obstructed modernization of China, the modernist

Figure 16. The "mouth" of a gigantic machine as a "strange loop." A still from *Black Cannon Incident*.

Figure 17. Staging "strange loops." A still from *Black Cannon Incident*.

aesthetic of abstract streamlined sets and geometric graphics of *Black Cannon Incident* inadvertently reveals another kind of loops that short-circuited between the aspirations of modernization and the increasing anxiety of being engulfed by a new environment fast transformed by marketization and the Open-up. In the cacophonous soundtrack filled with noises of machines, trains, automobiles, and electronic devices, dialogue is often overwhelmed by the humming sound of machines or the earsplitting noises of landing airplanes. Even the rock 'n' roll performance ultimately becomes an unbearable noise made up of repetitious chanting. Intended as a critique of the "ultrastable system" of Chinese society, the film inadvertently captures the ambiguous feelings in a restless world increasingly absorbed into the repetitive and programmable logic of technological rationality.

Modernization, Modernism, and the Temporalities of the "Modern"

The ambiguity of *Black Cannon Incident* brings up the question of the tension between modernization and modernism, a recurring issue in the discussion of modernism since the early 1980s. In 1982, writer and critic Xu Chi wrote an essay in response to the concurrent discussion on Western modernist literature as it resurfaced in post-Mao publications. Entitled "Modernization and Modernism" (*Xiandai hua yu xiandai pai* 现代化与现代派), the essay understands Western modernism as a reflection of the highly developed economy and material conditions of the Western world. Building direct connections between technological and artistic innovations, between modern facilities such as skyscrapers and artistic modernism, Xu observed: "Since the 1960s, the productive forces of the Western world have improved immensely along with rapid developments in science and technology to a level that indeed amazes people. No wonder that their literature and art are also full of dazzling innovations."[55] Xu's allocation of modernism to the superstructure as determined by the economic base was in line with the official discourse of modernization, and it "rectified" the name of modernism from its negative associations as a capitalist art form. Asserting modernism as a necessary product of economic developments, Xu placed modernism in a linearity of arts, which accordingly corresponded to stages of economic development.[56]

Xu's essay triggered heated debates and, more important, confirmed the significance of formal innovations of modernism. Following the publication of Gao Xingjian's controversial little pamphlet *Elementary Explorations on the Techniques of Modern Fiction* (*Xiandai xiaoshuo jiqiao chutan* 现代小说技巧初探) in 1981, critics and writers were drawn to the technical aspects of modernism. Li Tuo argued that the techniques of Western modernism could be separated from its content and absorbed into and reinvented as part of Chinese literature and art forms.[57] However, with the appearance of various experimentations in literature and art, some critics lambasted these works as "pseudomodernism," as meaningless imitations of Western modernism, for the sensibilities they conveyed, such as unsettling feelings of anxieties and alienation, were believed to "lack correspondences in real life" in China because these sensibilities belonged to the advanced level of Western modernization.[58] Therefore, the pivotal issue here was how to understand the sensibilities of these works in relation to a dominant discourse of modernization and linear progress.

Apparently the argument of "pseudomodernism" assumed a linear temporality of modernization. But few voices from the other side of the debate challenged this linear temporality. Amid the debate, Li Tuo pointed out that the sheer variety of Western modernism would not allow for its characterization as a coherent group with a stable set of techniques. If there was anything shared by the variegated, often self-contradictory modernist works, it was their rebellion against traditional Western values. Though it remained unclear what he referred to by "traditional Western values," he defined Chinese modernism in a similar way as against the "tradition," in this context, nothing other than realism. Realism thus was the shadow against which Chinese modernism had to define itself.[59] It is not hard to see that his understanding of modernism still revolved around the antinomies of the tradition versus the modern, which reduced Chinese modernism to a singular temporality characterized by a progressive teleology.

Unsatisfied with the overemphasis on the autonomy of the form that left unresolved its relation to the "modern," critic Huang Ziping proposed the term "consciousness-and-techniques" as the criteria to approach Chinese modernism. Refuting the argument that modern consciousness exists only in developed countries, he firmly defended the existence of modern sensibilities in the unevenly developed regions. Huang argued that modernism should not be understood merely as techniques but instead as *"new ways of knowing/experiencing the world."*[60] In this sense, while the techniques/forms of modernism can be circulated globally, they always become transformed and recontextualized in ways that address locally differentiated modern experiences and sensibilities. Huang's approach echoes Miriam Hansen's notion of "vernacular modernism," which she defines as a set of shared and globally disseminated idioms of cinematic language that gave form to a new economy of sensory perception.[61] The key here on the one hand is to place Chinese modernism, just as other "belated modernisms" in the Global South, in a global context of material and symbolic circulation, and on the other hand to uncover highly sociohistorically specific sensibilities not necessarily assimilable into a hegemony of global capitalism and its symbolic field. On this note, Zhang Xudong comments that the Chinese modernism of the 1980s engages in a material, symbolic infrastructure that functions as "a facilitator of transition that seems to lead nowhere but to global capitalism and its symbolic, ideological world order."[62] But he also notes, although the modernism of the underdevelopment is often built upon "fantasies and dreams of modernity,"

> modernism as an international language (or a global institution) is no longer "modern" as we understand the term historically; rather, it marks the historical crisis of modernity, namely, its "completion" in the "post-modern" space that is no longer tied to the temporal, teleological "progress" of modernity or gets distributed according to the historical hierarchy of economic development.[63]

His comment in a way echoes Huang Ziping, affirming the asynchronicity between modernism and modernization, which provides space for a critique of the linear temporality of modernization discourse. By acknowledging modernism's role in registering the "restless and perplex" sensibilities, Huang Ziping in fact indicated the deep-seated tension of Chinese modernism with the dominant modernization discourse. At the historical conjuncture of a lingering socialist cultural production supervised by the state and a fast commodification of social life moving toward the global market, Chinese modernism, as part of material and symbolic production, gives form to a structure of feeling as China was incorporating into the order of global capitalism, as evidenced by *Black Cannon Incident*'s modernist images of urban modernity.

Reflexive Self-References

One inspiration that Huang Jianxin had for his imagery of urban modernity was the paintings of the New York–based Taiwanese artist C. J. Yao (Yao Qingzhang 姚庆章). Yao was invited in 1983 to the mainland to lecture about Western art history. The exhibitions of his works, mostly photorealist paintings of street scenes in New York City, were warmly received by his Chinese audience. A recurring theme in his paintings is shop windows and glass facades of high rises in urban centers in the United States. Skyscrapers, huge advertising billboards, street lamps, neon lights, and passing pedestrians all become reflected on the surface of the windows and facades. Because of the transparency of the glass, these reflections intermingle with the interior decorations and displays, forming a plaque of kaleidoscopic images complexly interwoven to the point that one can no longer distinguish the exterior from the interior. All is flattened to the surface of the glass, vacillating between real and unreal, and becoming a bewildering mix of horizontal, vertical, oblique, and circular lines.

It is in this sense that Yao was lauded by his Chinese audience as "a lyric poet of the second-nature," for skyscrapers, neon lights, and glass facades all become the new "natural environment" in which human beings reside. In an art journal, Yao's depiction of kaleidoscopic, urban scenes was juxtaposed with rural landscapes of the yellow earth by Chinese artists.[64] Underlying such a constructed contrast of different types of human–environment relations was a linear temporality of development and industrialization. Another reviewer compared Yao's painting with European realist painting of the eighteenth and nineteenth centuries, contending that the latter was not "true realism," for these paintings nostalgically turn away from industrial scenarios. This reviewer celebrated Yao's works as "a eulogy for the material culture of high modernity."[65] The images of "wide shop windows, colossal glass walls, stainless-steel skeletons, clean and clear plastic floors, shop counters and furniture, regulated lighting and temperature, as well as effulgent neon lights, and shuttling cars and pedestrians," fueled the imagination and fantasy of "a high modern life built on highly developed science and technology."[66] This reviewer continued to comment on the dynamic feeling created by Yao's constructivist method, the effects of which often threw the audience into a drastic instability, "compelling them to find a point for support" to dispel the feeling of dizziness.[67] This feeling of disorientation suggests a complicated experience of the urban space conveyed in Yao's works beyond a simplistic eulogy of urban life, which the reviewer failed to acknowledge.

Yao's particular style of depicting urban scenarios struck the director Huang Jianxin as refreshing. Huang believed that to match the overall style of *Black Cannon Incident*, unusual camera positions and perspectives should be adopted, as he recounted:

> We decided that the camera should be placed slightly below eye level, about the height of the chest, because we believe that people often feel themselves dwindling in a city under high-speed developments.... We believe that our camera should create the same feeling.... Our cinematographer got the inspiration from C. J. Yao, and suggested adopting a downward-pointing triangular structure in the design of the mise-en-scène, for this unusual perspective allows for the coverage of a broader backdrop in each frame.[68]

In the film, the bustling urban space provides the excitement of modern flair (such as the nightclub and the Western-style restaurant where Zhao and his German friend hang out), but it is also a suffocating space that diminishes human beings into the shadows of clear-cut, streamlined architecture and colossal machines. As one critic pointed out, "The toy block-like buildings, the geometrically-shaped industrial equipment, and the modern look of colossal containers" created by the director and the cinematographer "in effect create a feeling of stuffiness."[69] The urban, industrial milieu becomes a strange loop that locks the protagonist in, as one critic astutely noted: "By placing the suffering protagonist in front of the mountains of debris, confining him in the narrow space overshadowed by gigantic machines, the film creates a distorted and closed space through low-angle shooting, conveying the deep agony of the protagonist."[70]

In Yao's paintings, human beings are sometimes shown imprisoned in cagelike scaffoldings of high rises, as in Yao's color pencil work titled *Working Man II*, which probably gave Huang Jianxin the inspiration to frame his characters among the skeletons of machines (Figure 18). In some other works, human figures often become phantasmagoric images indistinguishable from the jumbled lines and colors surrounding them. In his watercolor painting *Galleries* (Figure 19), among the overlapping chunks of colors and bewildering light and reflections of light, we see several haunting human figures. Are they customers inside the gallery, or passersby in the streets, or even models in the display window? The kaleidoscopic view of the urban space feeds fantasies and daydreams, yet remains illusory and rootless, so that in the end even the human subject is dispersed and seemingly spectral. Yao sometimes plays a joke on his viewers by depicting the multiple reflections of himself in his painting, as if the hand that makes the pictures is no more than one of the phantasmagoric images in the painting. In fact, glass and reflections are also one of Escher's favorite themes. In his *Three Spheres II*, the artist beside his writing table portrays himself as a reflection in one of the glass balls, which in turn becomes reflections in the other two balls on the writing table. Thus, as Hofstadter puts it, "Each part of the world seems to contain, and be contained in, every other part."[71] The play of self-references and the multilayered display in both Yao's and Escher's works point to the question of representation with which Huang Jianxin and other Chinese intellectuals in the 1980s were concerned: Can the observer/author legitimately claim the authenticity of his observations without projecting his own reflections? Is the observer part of the world he claims to criticize?

Figure 18. C. J. Yao, *Working Man II* (color pencil, 1981). Courtesy of C. J. Yao Art Gallery, New York.

Figure 19. C. J. Yao, *Galleries* (watercolor, 1981). Courtesy of C. J. Yao Art Gallery, New York.

As if to echo Yao's and Escher's self-referential play, Huang carefully constructs a multilayered cinematic world, in which different signifiers become cross-references to each other. For example, in the middle of the film, Zhao is seen in his room, eyes fixed on the chessboard in front of him, so engrossed in his little game that he is not even aware of the arrival of his guest, Schmidt. A similar scene appears at the end of the film: two kids are seen playing with a domino-like chain of play blocks. The kids are absorbed in their little world of the game of assembling the chain, setting the chain reaction into motion, and then reassembling it again. This time it is Zhao who becomes the intrusive observer. The naive yet serious game-players immediately strike a resemblance to the engrossed chess-player Zhao in the previous scene, who was observed by his sympathetic friend and is now observing the two little kids absorbed in their own game. This ending therefore refers back to the other scene, revealing Zhao's childlike unaffectedness. His shift of position from the observed to the observer also indicates his final realization of his role in the absurd "black cannon incident."

On another level, the domino game may refer to the happenings around the mysterious "black cannon": following Zhao's telegram, everything falls apart, as if the "real world" ruled by the Party secretary's "discretion" has become a fragile chain of dominoes, just like the little kids' game. In the end, the "real world" and the "game" are not mutually distinct but instead reflect and contain each other. On the blurred boundary between the real and the fictive, between the macroscopic and the microscopic, stands Huang Jianxin's multifaceted world, one that refuses any autonomous representation.

There is another level of reference toward which the domino game gestures: a self-referential parody of a counterespionage movie. The film follows the generic conventions: beginning with fragments of high-pitched electronic tones that often appear in this genre, it shows the fidgety Zhao sending out a coded telegram on a rainy night, which induces suspicion from a post office clerk. The close-up on the alert eyes of the clerk is an immediate citation of previous counterespionage films, in which the watching eyes of the highly class-conscious masses always keep the enemy under a seamless web of surveillance. Yet when the whole incident finally turns out to be a farce, this citation in turn disrupts the code of the genre. The outlandish but innocent intellectual character played by Zhao is also a rehearsal of the generic images such as in *Spies in the East Harbor* (*Donggang dieying*, 1978) and *Traces of a Bear* (*Xiongji*, 1977), in which the quirky intellectual character always becomes suspicious.

Yet even with these generic elements, *Black Cannon Incident* least resembles the genre. Every citation works as a parody not to reinforce the generic conventions but to reveal their disintegration, as they turn out to be at odds with the scenes of an emergent consumer society along with its agitating noises.[72] Moreover, the long takes in this film replace the often fast-paced editing and suspenseful rhythm in counterespionage films, which transform completely the syntax of this genre. In this sense, the domino game becomes a self-referential game about film per se: by playing with the semantic elements of the counterespionage genre, it takes the genre apart syntactically. The ideological function of the counterespionage genre falls apart when Huang's playful parody knocks the dominoes down one by one in a chain reaction.

With the long takes and the slow temporality, *Black Cannon Incident*, as the director explicates, relinquishes the representation of dramatic conflicts but instead focuses on "the revelation of the deep structure."[73] This aesthetic is closely tied to the enlightenment idea and the self-appointed mission of Chinese intellectuals to objectively observe Chinese society and diagnose its "arrested development" of modernization. Yet as the system theory–based social analysis and the modernization theory are deeply implicated in Cold War geopolitics, the thesis of Chinese society as an "ultrastable system" has also to be understood in the postsocialist context, in which Chinese intellectuals were placed in strange loops of knowledge production. The modernist aesthetic of the new Chinese cinema, while it enabled them to enter the symbolic realm of global capitalism, also inadvertently captured the structure of feeling at a moment of unsettling changes as this socialist country entered the global market.

CHAPTER FOUR

Affective Form

Advertising, Information Aesthetics, and Experimental Writing in the Market Economy

Ineluctable Connectivity

If the immobile shots of the landscapes in *Yellow Earth* resonated with the vision of Chinese society as an ultrastable system in intellectual discourses, the view of a society as a system of multiple subsystems responding to each other in fact could not be separated from a highly developed communication system that increasingly enveloped all aspects of social life into endless information circuits. An aspiring prospect of a closely tied world, filled with the euphoria of connections, nonetheless is also a confusing, distracting, and demanding one. In "The Blinking of the Bell," a piece written in 1986 by the veteran writer Wang Meng, the poet narrator begins by complaining that his writing is constantly interrupted by the ringing telephone. The narrator, sitting alone in his study, finds himself incessantly thrown into unexpected connections with all sorts of strangers on the other end of the phone line:

> Hello, hello, hello, who's this? Aren't you the spun-wire factory? No. *You're* the spun-sugar yam store! Are you the Tian Yuan soy-sauce brewery? Is this the Donglai Shun Restaurant? Is this the west zone 4 Matchmaking Agency? Great Wall Hotel? The air-conditioning company? Cultural artifacts store?[1]

The presence of the invisible others as disembodied voices blows out the interiority of his study, filling the mind of the poet with this or that trifle that would "squeeze dry the last drop" of his poetic inspiration. In order to defend "the chrysanthemum-like purity" of his poetry, he tries to smother the phone with a cotton quilt, only to find himself constantly tempted by "some unfathomable bit of news" that the ringing telephone might bring, as well as the desire of the invisible others on the other end of the line to communicate with him. Even when turned silent, the telephone gazes at the narrator with its green light at the signal bulb: "It winks. How painfully it waits.... I clearly see the green signal light insistently twinkling." The telephone, no longer a lifeless tool or a cold instrument, is animated with its own desire of communication, its fibers stretching out, its intense "green-eyed" gaze beckoning immediate responses. It wants to be connected.

"When does the telephone become what it is?" asks cultural critic Avital Ronell. The insistent demand to be connected, to Ronell, speaks about the "atotality" of telephone as apparatus, because "it has to be pluralized, multiplied, engaged by another line."[2] Telephonic communication is beyond one-to-one mode, but presupposes a network, of which edges can develop between any two nodes. Even when the phone is hung up, the network does not disappear. It creeps up on you, and now becomes an indivisible part of you, intimating random but almost "destinal" connectivity that defies any linear cause-and-effect rationale:

> I have heard sounds from the blinking light of the signal Bulb. I'm only afraid that after I pick up the telephone I won't understand what it's saying. But it's already too late, there's already no remedy....
> I know if I answer this call my apartment will just collapse, the gas stove will leak smoke and the nanny will quit and all my poems will be consigned to flames.[3]

The last sentence frames the unpredictable effects of the irresistible call within the knowledge of the narrator. What does it mean to know the arbitrary but inevitable consequences of a call? Is this knowledge not acquired through logical deduction? But the consequences of the call seem unrelated to what is transmitted through the line. The ring devoid of any intrinsic meaning now becomes an affective medium, a medium that in this case is the message. The connection precedes any signification. This arbitrary but inescapable connectivity also leaves its imprint on language:

> Three days ago, *that is,* five days ago a year ago two months later, he *I mean* she and it is afflicted with a cervical vertebra problem *which means* spine problem dental carries dysentery vitiligo breast cancer *as well as* a clean bill of health and assurance of longevity. Struck suddenly by a reeling dizziness on the forty-first of November, *i.e.,* the eleventh and twelfth of the fourteenth month, hence takes X-ray B ultrasound electro-encephalogram cerebral angiography for final diagnosis. Couldn't get registration at hospital couldn't find personal connections *therefore* does not see doctor *therefore* forgets dizziness plays ball swims drinks gives speeches watches TV series *in a word* nothing wrong at all with cervical vertebra *or in other words* never had cervical vertebra in the first place. Relatives friends adversaries all rushed to assure him no one said a word you are so young you are so old you are hale and hearty you are on your last legs how can you be ill how come you are still alive and kicking![4]

> 三天以前，也就是五天以前一年以前兩個月以后，他也就是她它得了劲椎病也就是脊椎病、龋齿病、拉痢疾、白癜风、乳腺癌也就是身体健康益寿延年什么病也没有。十一月四十二号也就是十四月十一、十二号突发旋转性晕眩，然后挂不上号找不著熟人也就沒看病也就不晕了也就打球了游泳了喝酒了做报告了看电视连续剧了也就沒有什麼劲椎病干脆说就是没有颈椎了。亲友们同事们对立面们都说都什么也沒说你这么年轻你这么大岁数你这么结实你这么衰弱哪能会有哪能没有病呢！

The first sentence seems to play with the linguistic rules of combination and selection that Roman Jakobson proposed in his analysis of the poetic function of language. Jakobson described the selection of signals in terms of probability: "There are features that show a high probability of occurrence without being constantly present. Besides signals certain to occur ('probability one'), signals likely to occur ('probability less than one') enter into the notion of meter."[5] As Lydia Liu points out, this discussion of probability was an influence of information theory and the development of printed English.[6] In this sentence, the list of possible subjects ("he"/"she"/ "it") and the litany of diseases are all oddly present, leveled to the same plane to the extent that there are no differences in the signification of the individual words, as if the sentence intentionally turns "signal likely to occur" into "signals certain to occur" by listing all possibilities. Does this linguistic play showcase Wang Meng's familiarity with Russian formalism and structuralism, which had just been introduced into China and became a new fashion among critics and scholars of humanities? Is this deliberate defamiliarization an experiment in the literary form? How does this play relate to the unpredictable predictability of the telephone ringing?

Interestingly, these unpredictable sentences are stretched to unusual length mainly with the help of two conjunctions: "也就是" (that is/means) and "也就" (therefore). The structure "A, that is, B" usually builds an identical relationship between A and B. Yet, in this passage this formal identification is problematic and arbitrary, to the extent that the regular signification of the conjunction is disrupted. The now meaningless pattern of "A means B, C, D" becomes an aggregation of signifiers not necessarily related to each other, or sometimes even in contradiction with one another (e.g., the list of diseases and "a clean bill of health and assurance of longevity"). While the phrase "也就是" connects nouns and noun phrases, the other phrase "也就" presumably builds causal relations between verbs and actions. Again, in this passage such a function becomes problematic. The verbs arranged in the form of a linear order are in fact arbitrary in relation to one another, so that the phrase "也就" connects but without determining the relation between actions. The words and signifiers are strung together regardless of their denotation and signification and thus become homogeneous and exchangeable. The sentences also become potentially endless, for the listing of nouns and verbs can go on with repeated uses of the conjunctions. The conjunctions become the multiplied and multiplying lines, stretching in all directions, generating contingent connections.

Such contingent connectivity is exactly the logic of telephone networks. In the piece there is arguably an analogy between the telephone line and the aggregating sentences. The strings of signifiers, detached from the signifieds, call attention to their own materiality. No longer a neutral instrument to convey messages, the flows of signifiers are the media of affectivity, the contagion of effects, reaching toward the readers, beckoning their responses.

This mode of communication follows a cybernetic logic, for every human being hooked to the telephone line is synched into ceaseless flows of information and turned into an automatic answering machine. There is no switch-off mode. He is continually kept in apprehension by the ringing bell: "Maybe it's very important? Very urgent? Very unusual? Very interesting? Very useful?"[7] Communication presupposes responses, responses that are not even subject to conscious control.

However, it would be mistaken to assume such ineluctable connectivity as indicating merely the power of the telephone. In fact, Wang Meng's writing around this period is permeated with the presence of myriad media, from radio and television broadcasts to popular journals, from electronic doorbells to home audio systems, from medical radial scanners to the then newly visible microprocessors. The years following the end of the Cultural Revolution witnessed the expansion of wireless radio broadcasts as well as a rapid growth in the coverage of television broadcasts. The number of television stations surged to 202 by 1985, covering 68.4 percent of the whole population.[8] Immersed in this new media environment, one felt not only compulsory connections to invisible others but also compelled to process incessant information input.

One media phenomenon new to post-Mao China particularly demanded responses from its audience—the phenomenon of advertising. After the establishment of the PRC, advertising had shrunk in scope when it was transformed into "socialist advertising," until its disappearance in the 1960s. The turning point came in the late 1970s, when major newspapers such as *Tianjin Daily*, *Jiefang Daily*, and even *People's Daily* started their advertising business in 1979. Consumer products, from toothpaste to Coca-Cola, from watches, cassette players to television sets and other electronic devices, increasingly became spectacles of attraction on various media.[9] In fact, as early as 1978, when China Central Television introduced the Japanese anime series *Tetsuwan Atomu*, built-in commercials of Casio products were broadcast alongside the series. Foreign corporations, followed by domestic entrepreneurs, were quick to seize the opportunity provided by the new mass medium in China—television.

This chapter examines several works of Wang Meng published in the mid- and late 1980s in relation to this new media environment permeated by advertising. Positioned as an information mechanism indispensable to the market economy, advertising studies arose in 1980s China as a study of information management and a strategy of affective persuasion, aiming exclusively at optimizing communicative effects of advertising. Information aesthetics, an aesthetic study reflective of postwar information theory, addressed this goal of communication studies, but, more important, it indicated crucial rethinking of the scope and approaches of "aesthetics" responding to an emergent information environment. In this sense, any consideration of the aesthetic discourse and literary experiments has to address this new media environment. In this chapter, I will bring to the forefront an important aspect of "information"—information as an affective medium for the marketization of commodities. Focusing on the blurry line between information and noises, as well as the viral contagion of advertising, I hope to underline the deep tension between intellectual politics and marketization, between the remaining socialist system and the commercialization of cultural production that surrounded the literary experiments of the 1980s. While the question of the (literary) form had been the center of the literary production and critical discourse in the 1980s, its deep ambivalence in an increasingly commercialized society has been neglected in existing scholarship. In a larger scope, this chapter is also an attempt to rethink the materiality of literary works in relation to media flows as a way to break down the barriers between media studies and literary studies. Katherine Hayles in her illuminating call to attention of the materiality of literature uses the term "technotexts" to refer to "literary works that strengthen, foreground, and thematize the connections between themselves as material artifacts and the imaginative realm of verbal/semiotic signifiers."[10]

Affective Form

Her notion highlights not only the technologies that produce literary texts, but also the physicality of literary works. My approach in this chapter, on the one hand, outlines the media ecosystem from which literary works emerge, and on the other hand emphasizes the material, mediating effects of literature amid the maelstrom of technical and social transformations. This in turn will provoke further reflections on mediation as a precarious process for different social forces to negotiate with and confront one another.

Advertising and Market Information

Advertising was usually conceived as incompatible with socialism. In the orthodox Marxist view that China adopted from the Soviet Union, advertising was associated with capitalist production relations, a waste of resources on creating false needs in order to superficially tackle the deep contradictions of capitalism between the irrational expansion of production and the limited buying power of workers and masses. Such a systemic problem of capitalism assumedly should be resolved with a planned economy adopted by most socialist states. Ideologically, advertising encouraged consumerism and a bourgeois lifestyle, running counter to the egalitarian claims of socialism, and heavy industry-prioritized productionist goals of most socialist states. In the early years of the PRC, advertising and its company consumerism were considered the stigma of urban corruption and relics of colonial influences. Yet in reality, advertising did not disappear altogether with the establishment of socialist states. Certain forms of advertising continued to persist in the PRC until the 1960s due to economic reality and the negotiations between difference economic sectors and the state power.[11]

"Socialist advertising," however, in China as in other socialist countries, was painstakingly distinguished from "capitalist advertising." Such a distinction was made not only in terms of the general visibility of advertising, with only a small volume in newspapers and limited blocks of time on the radio, but most important in the mode and goal of advertising. While capitalist advertisements were disparaged as full of deceitful claims that stimulated desires for unnecessary goods, socialist advertising would serve to increase people's understanding of a product, shape their consumption behavior, and advocate socialist and national accomplishments. Thus, advertisements in the PRC in the 1950s, according to Karl Gerth's study, mainly focused on instructions of how to use, maintain, and thus extend the lifespan of a product, as well as introductions to the special qualities of new products.[12] Because socialist advertising valued truthfulness, the tone of advertisements was often much more subdued than the enticing effects of capitalist advertising, and the use of advertising clichés was strictly regulated to avoid any exaggerated or unverifiable claims. The format, as a result, could be minimalist, mostly including only a product brand, a basic illustration, and a list of sales locations.[13]

Despite such cautious practices of "socialist advertising," advertising was still regarded with suspicion until the Cultural Revolution, when advertisements for products disappeared. The return of advertising to post-Mao China followed Deng Xioping's new economic and reform policies. Initially, the rhetoric of "socialist advertising" was revived to ensure a proper place of advertising in a sociopolitical system that still claimed its socialist nature. For example, a high Party official in a talk emphasized the role of advertising in "serving socialist ethics," which first required the "truthfulness" of advertisements.[14] This was because, unlike the flowery and often exaggerated language used in capitalist ads, socialist advertising should "maintain a high responsibility to the people."[15] But truthfulness per se became inadequate, as this official asserted, for the effectiveness of advertising should be prioritized, a target to achieve by carefully studying market information.[16]

Apparently the new keyword here was "market information," which lent advertising its relevance to an emerging market economy and the information society. The justification for advertising was built exactly on the two interconnected cornerstones.

An essay entitled "Several Theoretical Issues on the Function of Information Management through Socialist Advertising" started with the Marxist theory of commodity circulation, arguing that in a highly developed global market, information flows should be regarded as an arena of the same importance as the circulation of material products. If commodity exchange was crucial to Marxist theorization on value, the information of commodities, as the author asserted, played a crucial role in forming feedback loops between producers and consumers and facilitating obstruct-free circulation. Therefore, an effective advertisement should be based on a "scientific" investigation into the demands of the market, which in turn would serve as a market forecast for producers. In this sense, advertising was regarded as part of information management, which was indispensable to the market economy. Finally, the author decided that whether a piece of advertising work was successful should be determined by its power of persuasion, its effects on the audience, rather than its "artistic" accomplishment.[17]

This practical tone permeated the discourse of advertising. An essay published in Shanghai's *Wenhui Bao*, entitled "'Rectifying the Name' of Advertising," expressed concerns over "wasted time" during the intermissions of television broadcasts of sports events and stage performances. The author's solution was to add advertising: "In other countries, the slot between 7pm and 9pm is seen as the 'golden time' for advertising, the fees for which could be as expensive as 100,000 dollars per minute."[18] The author continued to rectify the name of advertising from the "stigma" of capitalism, affirming the active role of advertising in "directing the circulation of commodities and boosting sales."[19] Oddly, with all these arguments on economic efficiency, the author finally concluded that advertisements should be regarded as a form of art, which targeted the broadest range of audiences. Though seemingly contradicting the conclusion of the essay "Several Theoretical Issues," which prioritized advertising's power of persuasion over "artistic accomplishments," this association between advertising and art provoked the question of a shifting understanding of art and its relation to the new information environment and the market economy.

With these justifications, advertising soon grew into a prosperous enterprise. In 1979, the Beijing Advertising Agency (北京广告公司) was established. In the same year, the Central Propaganda Department issued a document endorsing at the policy level the advertising of domestic products on various media. *Zhongguo Guanggao* 中国广告 (China advertising), the first professional journal solely devoted to advertising studies, started its first issue in 1981. In the following year, the Society for China

Advertising Studies was founded. This society frequently organized exhibitions and symposia on the topic of advertising works and studies. By the mid-1980s, advertising had become an intimate part of everyday life. In 1981, there were 2,100 advertising agencies with 16,000 employers; by 1987, the number had increased to 8,200 with 92,000 employers. The expenses of advertising increased from 15 million yuan in 1981 to 1.1 billion yuan in 1987. Some industries, cosmetics especially, spent 5 percent of their annual income on advertising. It was constantly reported that advertising saved a certain factory from the brink of bankruptcy and turned their previously obscure products into a popular brand.[20] Advertising was thus fetishized as possessing the magical power of turning stone into gold.

Sticky Fractions

Because effectiveness was considered the primary goal of advertising, methods of "scientifically" foreseeing and measuring the effects of an advertisement became central to advertising studies. It would be too late for producers to wait until their advertisements were actually launched to see the effects through their sales record, one essay in *China Advertising* warned. Quoting recent research in Western countries, the author suggested three types of electronic equipment to determine the effects immediately: a brainwave detector to collect and analyze the data of stimuli in a consumer; a digital device to record the pupil dilation of the eyes, which was believed to be an honest indicator of interest and attraction; and a lie detector to tell the truth from the voice, rather than from the words, of a consumer being tested. These devices, as the author asserted, could provide real-time feedback to both designer and producer and help maximize the effects of advertising.[21] These tests suggested that "true effects" of an ad were indicated by physiological reactions of the body, responses beneath the threshold of human consciousness, not "feigned" responses conveyed by the words of a consumer.[22] Any literal reading of the words in their testimonies was deemed unnecessary.

If words were not to be read for meaning, it was their "stickiness" that would indicate the effect of an advertisement. How can the information of an advertisement be sticky to their potential consumers, given the fact that people are being drowned in a sea of information every day? Some laboratory tests showed that an average person could process information at the speed of only 25 bit/sec. In response to this challenge, advertising studies employed psychological and modern communication studies to find out how to manufacture sticky messages. Wang Shouzhi, a foundational person in the study of modern design in China, then a researcher at Guangzhou Academy of Fine Arts, acknowledging the fact that an audience could only remember a small portion of an ad, proposed the term "fraction" (canxiang 残象) to describe the fragments that were able to capture the attention and enter the memory of a potential consumer. Different people might get different pieces of fractions of the same ad. But the retained fraction might be ineffective, in the way that it was not exactly the piece of information that advertisers wanted their audience to remember. Therefore, as he advanced,

> It is the mission and strategy of advertising studies to locate fractions of relatively common significance to consumers, to enlarge the scope and reach of their effects, and avoid ineffective fractions at best. Psychologically, only a very limited portion of advertised information can impress the sensorium of a consumer and remain in her memory.... Once this is managed, the next task is to elicit positive reactions from the consumer that will eventually lead her to purchase the product.[23]

Wang continued that the most effective communication first of all had to avoid injecting too much information into one advertisement. It was also necessary to prioritize major messages over less important ones.

In 1983, Xiamen University formally set up a major in advertising in its Communication Studies Department, the first of its kind in Chinese universities. At the same time, discussions in *China Advertising* relied heavily on theories and methods of psychology and communication studies. Psychological studies and statistics on memory work provided the foundation for discussions on the choice of medium, form, and frequency of advertising. One article, entitled "How to Enhance the Memorability of an Advertisement," proposed that besides the strategy of regular repetition, an ad should associate itself with one word or phrase familiar to its audience, for memory images were often associated with catchy words or phrases.²⁴ Both repetition and catchy phrases would help brand the products in the minds of the audience. One example is an ad for a television set, which plays with the phonetic similarity of its brand *"jinxing"* 金星 (gold star) with the phrase *"jingxin"* 精心 (with care) like this: "Gold Star TV, designed with care, produced with care, selected with care, tested with care—Gold Star with Care (*jinxing jingxin* 金星精心)."²⁵ The repetition of the homophones was expected to impress the audience with its brand by connecting it with the catchy phrase.²⁶ In one word, advertising was regarded as the efficient transmission of information from the source to the targeted audience.

Information and Noises

Once advertising had been established as a necessity in the operations of the market economy, it was also regarded as quintessential to an information society. Two researchers of advertising studies at Xiamen University, in the beginning piece of a series of essays written for *China Advertising*, raised the rhetorical question: "What would society be like without advertising?" They continued to answer their own question: "It is acknowledged that without transportation vehicles, society would be paralyzed; similarly, without advertising, which serves as the transportation vehicle of information, any social activities and communication would be obstructed."²⁷ Here advertising is not limited to the information or the contents conveyed but is itself a mode of communication, a medium, and a channel for information transmission. Therefore, the writers argued, information conveyed through advertising would cover areas as broad as industry and commerce, science and technology, culture and the arts, political propaganda, and general publicity.²⁸ This almost all-inclusive list far exceeded the usual understanding of ads as the promotion of commodities and services. Yet the question is: If knowledge transmission, or even political propagation and general publicity, fell into the realm of advertising, would there be anything left beyond advertising?

This was not merely a game of definition and categorization, but in part concerned transformations in the roles of the still state-owned and state-operated media systems. Besides serving as the mouthpiece of the Party, newspapers and radio and television broadcasts also became the channel for information dissemination. China Central Television, for example, started a daily program called *Market Information* (*Shichang xinxi* 市场信息). Its format resembled that of a conventional news broadcast, with a host/hostess sitting facing the camera/audience, reporting updated merchandise prices, new product introduction, and offering analyses of market supplies and demands, as well as market predictions for certain products.

This shift of roles was not always smooth, though, as media became an increasingly heated battlefield in the competition of similar products. Media involved in the wars among manufacturers often failed to draw a line between their functions and obligations. For example, two hair-dye product manufacturers in Suzhou were engaged in a fierce media war against each other in newspapers and television broadcasts. One manufacturer secretly sent the product of the other to a university lab and produced a distorted report about its rival. The report was published in a local newspaper, followed by nationwide media coverage involving more than fifty newspapers and radio and television stations.[29] The distorted report, which went viral among the media networks, indicated a shaky line between the role as a news agency of the Party and the new role of serving the market economy. Obviously, this blurred line became increasingly disconcerting, as one concerned author commented:

> While media always charge for advertising on their platforms, news dissemination shouldn't involve fees—the regular practices of news agencies even pay numerations to authors who submitted their articles to newspapers. It is common belief that advertising is the self-promotion of a business-owner, whereas a news report should be an objective report of the interviewee (although the content may involve a business-owner and his product). This is the essential distinction between advertising and news reports. But nowadays some newspapers or television broadcasts send out so-called "advertised news" (*guanggao xinwen* 广告新闻), to the extent of confusing their audiences. . . . Audiences have long grown to trust what is printed in papers—this testifies to the historically accumulated prestige of the Party media among

the masses, which is the most treasured thing for the Party media networks.... If the confusion goes on, it would undoubtedly damage the prestige of the Party newspapers.[30]

This insistence on the distinction of the two in fact refuses an encompassing notion of "advertising," but qualifies it as a special mechanism of producing and circulating information. Crossing this line, the advertised information may lose its communicative efficacy. Yet the notion of "information" became blurry, as the information operations of political and public interests were becoming difficult to separate from those of commercial interests.

Another author tried to distinguish the two on a formal level: while news reports always begin with expressions such as "Benbao xun" (本报讯, literally "news of this paper"), which identify the sources of information, ads do not include such markers. In addition, news reports are always time-sensitive, whereas ads are not.[31] These efforts to draw a line between the two reflected deep-seated contradictions when introducing advertising to Party media systems and the tension between political claims and market operations. Despite the painstaking distinction, advertising spreads like a virus, transforming in every way the cultural and literary production mechanism passed down from the socialist era.

As all forms of ads and "covert" ads started to flood media channels, suddenly the life of the common people was filled with ceaseless solicitations. "An omnipresent new god with neither Sabbath nor feast day has built its temples at every corner of the city," wrote cultural critic Wu Liang in 1988. "This new god sends us his oracles every day, his preaching filling our ears, the shrine of this god now even sitting right in our bedrooms. Every second it addresses us with its doctrines in different voices and expressions."[32]

The power of this new god was so palpably felt that even Wang Meng turned his own writing into a hymn to its powers, or a parody of a hymn. He titled, not without cunning, a short piece written in 1987 "a story for the purpose of advertising BNW Hair Growth Conditioner." The middle-aged male narrator is haunted by a brownish shadow that appears on his hair. Immaterial and faceless, the shadow nonetheless asserts its own presence by following the narrator, and even speaking into his ear more intimately than any human being could do. Coming from nowhere, it fills space everywhere. Sometimes it mingles with the voices on radio or television, as if it arrives through the airwaves, but sometimes it seems to originate from the narrator's own body. The story keeps the shadow ambiguously positioned between the real and the hallucinatory as something exterior and alien but also eerily intimate to the narrator. There is some sort of ruthless "stickiness" about the shadow, adhering to the narrator's mind, seeping into the unconscious, even to the extent that its incessant, long-winded discourses wrap him inside, as if it were the air that he breathes in and out.

Obviously, this omnipresent power of advertising relied on ubiquitous airwaves that acquired almost magic powers in both scientific and popular imaginations with the rapid development of wireless broadcasts in the post-Mao late 1970s and 1980s. As television broadcasts emerged as a powerful and popular information platform, it was also considered the best venue for advertising investments. China Central Television charged fees of 2,000 to 5,000 yuan per minute, but that didn't stop corporations from throwing money at advertising on television.[33]

Yet such heavy investments would not guarantee smooth and "safe" relays of information. In one of Wang Meng's stories, entitled "Fine Tuning," a couple's excitement at acquiring a brand-new color television is soon replaced by anxieties about securing sharp signals from the airwaves, as television sets common in China at that time required manual tuning, which could be laborious:

> The wife began her adjusting. First she tried the four antennas one by one. The trouble was, none of them was better than the others. The ring antenna didn't work as well as the rabbit ears, the easy-to-pull can was not as good as the ring type, and the fishbone was less satisfactory than the easy-to-pull can. Might as well go back to the rabbit ears. But by then the rabbit ears didn't perform as well as the fishbone! Even so, she stuck to it. Extending it and shortening it, turning it first to the right and then to the left. . . . After quite a while, she was grateful that the original image was restored.[34]

The television set, rather than an automatic signal pickup and display machine, is connected to and consists of different sets and types of antennas, placed both indoors and outdoors (usually on the rooftop). The complex system requires constant manual adjustments so that the human body is actively involved in a cybernetic loop in order for information to be relayed. Thus television-watching, instead of the audience being passive spectators, is a constant adjustment between information and noises mediated through the cybernetic involvement of the human body:

> One touch and the picture went bad, even the color disappeared, leaving the screen all black or all white. All kinds of strange dots and lines showed up on screen. Voices became hoarse, eventually fading away. . . . The worst was after exhausting yourself turning fifteen degrees to the left and eight degrees to the right, then ten degrees to the left and eight degrees to the right, then pulling out the antenna three millimeters and then pushing it back two millimeters. . . . Just when you thought you'd fixed it, you are left completely at a loss. You can't even tell whether it's better or worse.[35]

When the signals are finally attuned, the husband is forlorn to find out that the live broadcast of the football game he wanted to see has been replaced by ads for cosmetics. Although the images of these ads are as sharp as "the ones from a fool's touch-on camera," they are just noises to which he becomes oblivious.

Indeed, some audiences considered advertisements boring, nonsensical, and even annoying noises. It was reported that a person who became impatient with the Citizen Watch commercial broadcast daily by CCTV even wrote to the television station to complain about the tedious, stiff format. Another survey conducted by the Beijing Broadcasting Institute showed that less than one percent of audiences were willing to watch commercials, while the majority expressed aversion to ads.[36] Coarse production, clichéd language, repetitive form—all these commercials became nothing more than unbearable noises. Far from effective communication, some ads, in order to "maximize" the expensive ad time, compacted all information from product descriptions, manufacturer information, address, and telephone numbers into "a 30-second tongue twister-like high-speed preach," which was nerve-wracking to audiences.[37] Never a perfect information transmission as it was idealized, advertising always mixed intended information with a cacophony of nonsensical noises.

Subliminal Advertising and Affective Association

If advertising easily becomes noises, can it still exert influences on audiences? How should an ad leave effective fractions of information even when the targeted audiences ignore, distrust, or even become averse to the message? A journal introduced the notion of "subliminal advertising" (*yuxia guanggao* 阈下广告), which aims to capture audiences in oblivion.[38] A term derived from psychological studies around the turn of the twentieth century, especially tied to hypnotism and psychoanalysis, the subliminal suggests that some sensations may not be perceived but still are absorbed into peoples' minds. Since the late 1950s and particularly in the mid-1960s, this term became increasingly bound to advertising and moved quickly from a highly technical, psychological purview to realms of popular culture.[39] According to the report in a Chinese journal, a movie theater in New Jersey flashed commercials of popcorn and Coca-Cola every five seconds during movie screenings. But audiences didn't become upset with the commercials. Instead, the sale of popcorn and Coca-Cola increased to 57.7 percent and 18.1 percent separately during the six-week test. The secret lies in the high-speed flashing: each commercial stayed on screen for less than a quarter of a second, too brief even for the audiences to notice. Though the stimuli of the commercials remained below the conscious level, the human body nonetheless registered them and in turn impacted human choice and behavior. "Subliminal advertising" is built exactly on this mechanism of solicitation and manipulation without being noticed.[40] Therefore, behind the term is a "history of technological apparatuses designed to verify, measure, and ultimately manipulate that zone between sensation and perception, in particular the apparatus known as the tachistoscope, which flashes images and text at extremely high and variable speeds."[41]

Though it cannot be verified whether subliminal advertising was directly adopted by the advertising business in China, the idea behind it was apparently appealing: it aimed to include audiences in cybernetic loops of stimuli and responses even without the conscious participation of the person being tested. The response could be regarded as almost spontaneous, as if it were just the natural needs of the person being tested. To elicit "spontaneous" responses, an ad should provide signs and images, with which audiences can automatically associate with their own disparate experiences and propensities, and thus transform the advertised images into their objects of desire. "The God of advertising differs from other gods precisely in that," wrote Wu Liang. "He stirs up myriad unknown desires dormant in the bodies of his followers, instills in them superfluous desires through repetitive preaching, and works them up into an irreversible state of frenetic yearning."[42] Wu thus commented in an ironic tone that what was advertised was no longer the commodity per se, but the presentation of the commodity, through the lens of which even a most banal item for everyday use would shine with beauty.[43] This was precisely what advertisers wanted to achieve, despite the repugnance that advertising had incurred. In order for the advertised product to shine with irresistible lure, designers of ads, according to an essay in *China Advertising*, had to create images that would guide the audience away from clichéd associations with the object and generate a metonymic association that seems to be remotely related. But the metonymic association at the same time had to be generative and general enough so that it could resonate in one way or another with the disparate life experiences of the audiences. Only in this way could an advertisement elicit affective resonance and active associations from the audience.[44]

Skills in creating affective associations were extensively discussed in *China Advertising* and other advertising and marketing-related publications. A taxonomy of associations was even provided: association based on time and space proximity, association of resemblance, association of contrastive comparison.[45] Some believed that such associations would awaken a dormant "collective unconscious," which, once tied to the advertised product, would prove a successful advertisement, for advertising was built exactly on the physiological and psychological mechanism that human beings had developed over thousands of years. Such strategies of advertising aimed to generate resonances from the audience, inviting them to infuse the received information with their own information, emotions, and imagination in order to complete the Gestalt psychological structure of their own.[46] This meant more than dry, "objective" descriptions of the product; instead, the idea was to provoke potential consumers to transform the advertised image into an actualized image in their own life.[47] This is not a process of rational reasoning; it is the evocation and mobilization of affectivity. At the same time, the process of eliciting affectivity by advertising was believed to be a "rational management," a controlled channeling of affect and emotions to serve its purpose, which in the end was to persuade potential consumers. If an ad worked to evoke affective responses in an audience of diverse experiences and background, their diverse affective paths eventually converged toward one single destination: the commodity. "Advertising thus comes to carry increasingly refined spiritual pursuits, emotional inclinations, artistic forms, and psychological subtleties, all of which," commented Wu Liang piercingly, "fundamentally serve the presentation of the commodity."[48] Wu also acknowledged advertising as a form of art, an art conscious of its own form, though not without reservations: "Undoubtedly, advertising unites artistic forms with everyday life in an utmost way, a unity of art and life that no other times can achieve. Yet, should it also be noted that while advertising has painstakingly advanced an aesthetic of life, has it also inadvertently lowered the standard of art?"[49] The key here is to understand the ambiguities and weight of artistic forms in the discourses and practices of the 1980s, as well as the tension inside the notion of "aesthetics" as it was torn between the avant-garde impulses of artists and intellectuals and the pragmatics of the market economy.

Viral Affectivity and Defamiliarized Form

As advertising infiltrated both public and private spaces, wrapped its audiences within millions of sticky fractions of enticing images, words, and sounds, it also posed itself more and more like an art, which constantly extended affective associations that demanded compulsive responses and prompted everyone to become a sensitive reader, a poet who infused the fractions with their own affect, memories, and desires. Thus, Wang Meng's poet narrator in "The Blinking of the Bell," bathed in the sound, light, and heat of dazzling images and words, soon finds himself writing in a style that is "brimful and overflowing":

> I write about Peking ducks soloing in a hanging oven, dreaming of romance (1); Da San Yuan's roast piglets singing, "my ice-cold little hands" in Helsinki (2); the hopeless first love between socialist realism and stream of consciousness, having failed to get a housing permit, sadly parting (3). Dr. Omnipotent, expounding on the thesis that man must drink water, sweeping away all obstacles, defeating his debating opponents, then serving consecutively as the Olympic and National Championship referee (4); a quick-turnaround reselling nylon pantyhose a free enterpriser getting to drink Yao Wenyuan's dumpling soup (5); . . . I beckon life![50]
>
> 我写北京鸭在吊炉里solo梦幻罗曼斯 (1)。大三元的烤仔猪在赫尔辛基咏叹《我冰凉的小手》(2)。社会主义现实主义与意识流无望的初恋沒有领到房证悲伤地分手　(3)。万能博士论述人必须喝水所向披靡战胜论敌连任历届奥运会全运会裁判冠军　(4)。一个短途倒卖连脚尼龙丝裤的個体戶喝到姚文元的饺子汤 (5)。 我号召生活！

Readers may be perplexed with the mixed vocabulary in this passage: brand names ("Da San Yuan") juxtaposed with transliterated loan words ("Helsinki"), literary terms ("socialist realism" and "stream of consciousness") with local gourmet food ("Peking ducks," "roast piglets" and "dumpling soup"), neologisms particular to 1980s China ("free enterpriser" 个体户 *getihu*) in the same passage with English words ("solo"), names of historical characters ("Yao Wenyuan" 姚文元) almost buried under a list of commodities of new fashions ("nylon pantyhose"). These are a tangle of fractions, which by no means follow any logic. This English translation is already an interpretation of the strings of signifiers loosely put together. For example, in sentence (3), the connection between "socialist realism and stream of consciousness" and "hopeless first love" is unclear in Chinese, and the logical connection between "failing to get a housing permit" and "sadly parting" remains undefined, although the English translation ambiguously uses prepositions and syntactic structures to define their relations. Other sentences, such as (2), may look syntactically flawless but semantically absurd. Sentence (4) more radically breaks away with semantic signification, but instead is driven by a momentum of movement between chunks of phrases. The four-character idioms "sweeping away all obstacles" 所向披靡 and "defeating his debating opponents" 战胜论敌 are strung together to impose on the word "论述" (expound) a dimension of "combat" that is originally absent in the word. Then the induced meaning of "combat" leads to an unexpected direction in relation to sports competition ("Olympics"). In extending these contingent connections, each phrase is opened up and enmeshed in a network of effects. Language, in this passage, as if having gained its own momentum, aggregates and grows by itself.

The cacophony of words and phrases of different registers, the mix of political and commercial vocabularies, trendy literary fashion and new consumerist fads, at first sight resembles the "stream of consciousness," with which Wang Meng's own name had been associated since the early 1980s. Lauded for its explorations of human psychology, this modernist skill was considered a departure from the ossified forms of socialist realism. Wang Meng was considered responsible for its revival after the end of the Cultural Revolution, and he was commended for his depiction of the psychological interior of human beings, which was seen as a lack of socialist realism. Although Wang later confessed that he had not had much exposure to James Joyce, Virginia Woolf, or other representative Western writers who worked with "stream of consciousness," he found strong resonance in emphasizing the interior world.[51] In writing about his understanding of "stream of consciousness" in an essay published in 1979, Wang commented:

> "Stream of consciousness" emphasizes associative thinking.... Associative thinking doesn't reflect the logical reasoning, synthesization and judgment processes of thinking, nor the real or fictive movement in continuous time and space that exists in real life or in memories, narratives or imagination. It is about the unbounded freedom of the mind, the unrestrained roaming of the imagination. All materials from life, once rearranged through associative thinking, will be renewed in

a new light, as if kaleidoscopic scenes are always governed by an internal logic despite their dazzling appearance.[52]

What Wang Meng highlighted here is the ultimate freedom of the human mind and the interiority, which, though not necessarily borne from rational reasoning, affirms human agency. Associative thinking in this context testifies to the creativity of the author. Yet six or seven years later, the bewildering string of words in this passage from "The Blinking of the Bell" indicates less about the interior life of the poet than a swarm of information that almost overwhelms the nerves of the poet, to the extent that his "stream of consciousness" becomes a string of random fractions of words and phrases forced upon him by an enveloping information environment. It is almost like viral contagion that blurs the boundary of human interior and environmental exterior.

"The word is now a virus," so claimed William S. Burroughs. A virus, according to him, was a very small unit of sound and image. In reference to the manipulation of sound and image by politicians and popular media in the Watergate scandal, he advanced that "scrambled" tapes and words would act like viruses upon the subject against his will. Like a body reacting to the invasion of viruses, the subject being acted upon would unscramble the scrambled words and image compulsively. The responses of the physiological mechanism and neural system to manipulated units of sound and image were not necessarily registered by the consciousness of the subject—he could not help himself. To enhance the viral effects, Burroughs proposed, the brainwave feedback and visceral response when a person was watching the tape should be recorded, cut in, and played back to the tested person himself. What Burroughs proposed, ironically similar to the tests that recorded physiological reactions in order to gauge advertising effects, are infinite cybernetic loops of stimuli and responses, in which responses become stimuli that generate more responses, and in turn are taped to affect other hosts, or "go viral." The virus-words to which Burroughs referred are conditioned by reproductive, particularly electronic technology. They are audiovisual units susceptible to playback, slicing, and other maneuvers. The eerie intimacy of virus-words with their human host is tied with a media

Affective Form

environment that constantly assaults and irritates the subject, demanding compulsive responses from the subject. In a similar way, if Wang Meng's piece can be regarded as a record of reactions to the swarm of sounds and words that cajole, entice, and assault, the writing is imbued with a viral power that captures its audience in a whirlpool of affectivities.

This cacophony of noises and information creates an aesthetic that is built paradoxically upon jargon and defamiliarization, relaying an ecstasy and agitation of being engulfed by dazzling words and sounds that dash toward you too fast to make any sense. Wang Meng obviously felt the compelling force of this new aesthetic, for at the same time as he was writing "The Blinking of the Bell," he composed another piece entitled "To Alice," which again displays such a viral effect:

> I wake up all my family at midnight, saying look isn't there a green sun in the sky because our quartz wall clock has won a Nobel Prize. Wife says I am making trouble there is no sun says fry two balloons for me to eat to stop the diarrhea increase potency.
>
> 半夜里我叫醒了全家，我说你们看天上出的绿色的太阳是不是我们家的电子石英挂钟得了诺贝尔奖。妻子说我捣乱说没有太阳说让我煎两个气球吃了止泻补气。[53]

The removal of quotation marks suggests the indistinguishable line between individual remarks and general discourses. The three verbs "say" consecutively used in one sentence without a comma or any logical connection simply dash out in an unstoppable momentum. At first glance, every sentence is syntactically immaculate, but upon further examination it makes no sense: a "green sun" at midnight is already bizarre enough, not to say frying two balloons to eat. Yet soon it can be surmised that "balloons" substitute for "eggs" in this sentence. The sun, balloons, and eggs are analogous to one another just because they are all round-shaped. This analogy becomes even clearer later in the piece:

> Bus comes but with no wheels, passengers all dig into their bags to give it some Ping-Pong balls mothballs black dates small bells huge

baked cakes as wheels. Driver refuses to drive conductor refuses to sell tickets so everyone elects me in a democratic process to push it. I push it so fast that National Athletics Commission selects me as coach of long medium shot distance runners. I resign one month later to write stories and attend writers meetings in hell and stay in hotels because leadership doesn't give me free Western suit desk lamp sofa electric mosquito repellant art diary sheepskin jacket.

汽车来了却没有轮子，乘客们纷纷掏兜给它一些乒乓球卫生球黑枣小铃铛大烧饼当车轮。司机不开车售票员不售票大家便民主推选我去推车。我推车推得太快被国家体委选去做长中短跑教练。我干了一个月嫌领导不给我发西服台灯沙发灭蚊器美术日记羊皮夹克便退职写小说并到火坑参加笔会住宾馆。[54]

Ping-pong balls, mothballs, black dates, small bells, huge baked cakes, these myriad things, despite their disparate materiality and uses, are grouped together simply because of their round shapes. This first sentence functions almost like database collecting, building up catalogue connections but at the same time smashing any established categories. The unconventional associations in this passage renew the perceptions of banal items such as mothballs in an unexpected light. A similarly endless list appears at the end of the passage, indicating the extent to which these commodities in vogue infuse a writer's life, and become floating signifiers that saturate writing.

Such a self-reference to writing is already adumbrated in the prologue, which frames the small piece as part of the "experimental writing" in vogue. The prologue tells us that the narrator, an established writer, one day is called upon by an unexpected guest who angrily condemns old men like him who "seemingly having created something new" are doing nothing but blocking the way of young writers. After his indignant delivery of invective, the young man takes off, leaving the dazed old man this "novice piece" entitled "Green Sun." The prologue thus presents the emergence of "experimental writing" as the challenge of a young generation of writers directed toward their elders. Is it a coincidence that when Wang Meng composed this piece, younger writers such as Ma

Yuan, Ge Fei, Sun Ganlu, and others started emerging into the horizon as avant-garde writers, and eventually created a fad, however brief, for experimental writings? Did a veteran writer like Wang Meng, who started writing in the 1950s, and reappeared in the early 1980s as a forerunner of modernism for his "stream of consciousness" writings, now feel pressed and dazed by the younger generation just as his narrator does? Was he, under the pressure to create a "novice piece," kept awake at midnight, staring at his quartz wall clock, watching time slipping by, thinking about the Nobel Prize? The appearance of the "Nobel Prize" here also indicates the entrance of a contemporary Chinese writer into a world market of literature ruled by Western literary conventions and standards.

Interestingly, "To Alice" also provides a parodic evaluation of the new aesthetic represented by "Green Sun." The older-generation writer-narrator, after reading the piece, announces that it is "full of crappy nonsense." "Nonsense" had been used repeatedly as a condemnation of new styles of writing since the late 1970s, from "misty poetry" to "stream of consciousness." "Nonsense" in this sense ironically captures the stereotypical stiffness of old-fashioned critics in the eyes of fashionable younger writers, mirroring the reflections of contempt toward one another on both sides. But the stern-faced critic also concedes: "There is at least something in his ability to make associations" (联想的能力尚有可取). Is he endorsing the defamiliarizing effect of substituting balloons for eggs? However, why does this old-fashioned commentator merit the "ability to make associations"?

Information Aesthetics

Indeed, metonymy, unconventional association, and defamiliarization were valued skills in literary discourse and advertising. "The consistency of advertising results in routinized effects that compel the audience to obey," observed Wu Liang perceptively, "but meantime, advertising always breaks existing consistency with its own novelty, denying certain rules and superstitions that have already been accepted by people, indoctrinating people in an extreme but also in an appealing way with the belief that: your old stuff should be replaced by the new."[55] Advertising was always the battle and negotiation between consistency and novelty, Wu acknowledged. Defamiliarization through innovative associations, and memorability through repetition, advertising has to balance between the known and the unknown, between comprehensibility and eye-catching gimmicks.

This meticulous attention to the proportion of the known versus the unknown was also a central concern to information aesthetics, an aesthetic theory based on information theory developed by Claude Shannon and his followers. The emergence of "information aesthetics" in China was related to the surge of both popular and academic interest in information theory, systems theory, and cybernetics, which showcased the efforts of humanities scholars to "scientize" aesthetic studies. This fad reached its peak in 1985, so the year was named "the year of methodology fever" (方法论热年), which witnessed myriad conferences and symposia devoted to this topic, leading to all sorts of journals and anthologies that claimed to have "applied" information theory, systems theory, and cybernetics into aesthetic and literary studies.[56] Scholars were enthusiastic in "reforming" an "impressionist" literary studies with what they believed to be more precise and objective methods. Information aesthetics, thus defined, was concerned less with the metaphysical question as to the nature of "beauty" than to the methods of measuring beauty. Relating itself to Gestalt and cognitive psychology, information aesthetics claimed "scientific approaches to literary studies."[57] In this regard, Russian formalism, the Prague linguistic circle, and analytic philosophy were considered forerunners of this scientific approach, having contributed technical methods for analyzing texts. Sharing their common interest in literary form, structure, and signs, information aesthetics also distinguished itself from orthodox Marxism, which was believed to have wrongly subordinated the form to the content. If traditional aesthetic studies were conducted in libraries and study rooms of scholars, information aesthetics would unfold in laboratories and computer centers. The latter would involve decomposing art works into signs that could be processed by computers for mathematic model building, and the like.[58]

Information aesthetics was thus in close affinity with machine translation, artificial intelligence, advertising, and communication studies. Jin

Kemu, the renowned essayist and scholar at Beijing University, in one of the most articulate pieces on that topic, pointed out that information aesthetics should be regarded as an "applied aesthetics," with the aim of communicating with optimized effects to reach the largest population. Advertising, modern design, architecture, and broadcasting, as well as television services, would benefit most from this research on information aesthetics. The key issue here remained how to measure the effects of communication. Shannon's theory provided a mathematical method to measure the quantity of information conveyed by a work of art. The definition of information, in accordance with Shannon, is inseparable from the quantitative measure of "originality," or "unforeseeability." But different from Shannon's economic principle of capitalizing the maximum rate at which information can be transmitted through a communication channel, a human receptor of aesthetic communication, as Jin reminded us, could only process a limited amount of "original" information. A certain amount of redundancy, serving as a priori structure for the receptor to receive new information, would be required for artistic communication. The goal of information aesthetics, Jin believed, would be to find out the proportion between the original and the redundancy in order to optimize the effects of aesthetic communication.[59] Such calculated measures would address the concern of both ambitious literary composers and advertising designers in their play between the original and the conventional in order to achieve the best effects of defamiliarization but without alienating their audiences.

Near the end of his essay, Jin mentioned the name of Abraham Moles, a French electrical engineer, sociologist, and philosopher who was considered a pioneer of information aesthetics. Moles's monograph, *Information Theory and Esthetic Perception*, written in French and translated into English in 1966, was the foundational work in this field. In fact, most ideas in Jin's introductory essay derived from his work. In the introduction, Moles explained the significance of developing an information aesthetics by outlining two aspects of the world that had been examined in science: one aspect concerning energy that "gave rise to the sciences of mechanics, strength of materials, thermodynamics, etc., in which man as an individual supposedly plays no role at all"; the other aspect is communicational, which "returns man to the material world," and studies "the *interaction between the individual and the rest of the world*."[60] The second aspect for a long time was subordinated to the first aspect and, as part of the second aspect, arts were believed to function "without a purpose." It was not until well into the twentieth century, especially with the development of technical media such as radio, film, and musical recordings, that a work of art was valued as "a creator of sensations, hence as a motivating force in society and not as a social epiphenomenon."[61]

Moles's notion of art thus is a far cry from the notion of "pure art," which presumes purposelessness. Rather, his definition of art in relation to stimuli and sensations is closely bonded with recent developments in media and communication technology. Obviously bearing the imprint of cybernetics, it concerns in a broader sense the interactions between human beings and environments, be it the natural or a mediated environment. Aesthetics, in accordance with this notion, shifted to focus on the transmission and process of information. No longer restricted within the presumably purposeless high art, "aesthetics" was thus open to the examination of a broader range of cultural phenomenon, including advertising. Aesthetics in this sense, as Jin Kemu pointed out, thus became an applied science, which could also serve market predication, investigation, and propagation.

If "originality" was valorized as an aesthetic feature of modernism, information theory as developed by Claude Shannon and others provided a method to quantify "originality." In this first place, Moles distinguished the "originality" of an information sequence from its length. The example he gave was that a page of orders in case of fire would give less information to a person who had known the text by heart than the simple word "fire" would in the case of an emergency. He defined originality as "a function of the improbability of the received message": the more unexpected a message is, the more likely that it will *modify the behavior* of the receptor, and thus provide more information than what appears to be contained in the length of the message.[62]

Information aesthetics thus emphasizes affective power—if an ad manages to modify the behavior of its audience, it is considered successful.

The associative affectivity valued in advertising theory and practices at this time reflected precisely this new criterion: an ad should make the advertised product associable to individual consumers, opening up affective potentialities for them to relate the product to their disparate experiences and interior life. Information aesthetics provides a framework to evaluate the "aesthetic" value of a work, be it an advertisement, an experimental piece of writing, or a classic masterpiece. An excellent television commercial should be treated with the same respect as a work by Da Vinci or Michelangelo, claimed Li Yanzu, a scholar who campaigned for the recognition of applied and industrial arts.[63] The notion of "aesthetics," as observed here, had been extended beyond classic categories of the fine arts.

If aesthetic appreciation works fundamentally in line with the originality of the information of an art work to affect people, why can a person still enjoy a symphony even though he has already known its themes by heart? To solve this question, Moles proposed a distinction between two types of information: semantic and aesthetic. The former refers to the type of information "having a universal logic, structured, articulable, translatable," while the latter refers to what is untranslatable, and the knowledge that is "common to the particular transmitter and particular receptor."[64] Moles emphasized the corporeal aspect of aesthetic information, but he also pointed out that semantic information was transmitted along with aesthetic information "by the same elements in different groupings on different levels of perception."[65] Some perceptions of certain levels may be more alert to semantic information, while others may be more alert to the aesthetic. Information sent out by art works is therefore a combination of both aspects of different proportions on different levels. His reviewer Rudolf Arnheim summarized the two aspects as "a distinction between the What and the How, between the story of a play and the manner in which it is performed."[66] This is to affirm the autonomy of the artistic form from the content per se. The aesthetic value of a work lies not so much in its content alone but more in the untranslatable aesthetic information, an aspect that cannot be judged merely by semantic clarity.

The Politics of the Form and the Market of Affect

The emphasis on the form by information aesthetics can be historically traced to the close ties between information theory, literary modernism, and postwar literary theory. Shannon's development of stochastic analysis of English writing, for example, as Lydia Liu informs us, was framed by modernist experiments pioneered by James Joyce. She comments that game theory and information theory have appropriated literature "as a shared resource of symbolic exercise through which the theorists have made their intellectual leap toward formalization."[67] This formalization of literary works by information theory in turn introduced a formalist approach to literary studies. One representative figure of this formalist approach is Roman Jakobson, the Russian American linguist and literary critic whose development of structuralist critique and literary theory was informed by postwar information theory.[68]

The form carried particular political weight in the late postsocialist culture of the 1980s. This is because an "obsession" with literary form was generally believed to be a feature of depraved bourgeois modernist literature, according to the orthodox Marxist view. Against this view, critic Li Jie argued for the autonomy of literary form, asserting that the form was not subordinated to the content or merely a vehicle of the latter.[69] A fascination with formalist experiments in the 1980s in both literary composition and critique should be regarded as an effort to break away from the straitjacket of orthodox Marxism and the dominant "Mao-style writing" (*Mao wenti* 毛文体), which with its particular set of vocabulary and syntax had transformed contemporary vernacular Chinese. To critics, "Mao-style writing" became a "preexisting structure" (先结构) that delimited epistemological horizons and ways of thinking. Thus an invention of new forms was "a rebellion in the realm of language," a fundamental step to break down the "preexisting structure" that was passed down from the Mao era.[70] Russian formalism, new criticism, and structuralism were introduced to provide techniques for a "scientific" analysis of literary forms, whereas the previous focus on the "externalities" of literature, such as sociological and biological approaches, was criticized as a symptom of the ethical obsessions in Chinese culture.[71] Such cultural critique via formalism and structuralism was adopted among "new-wave critics" (新潮批评), especially toward the new forms of writing, such as the Misty Poems, Roots-seeking Literature, and other experimental writings that emerged after the end of the Cultural Revolution. With this investment in literary form, critics enthusiastically embraced new experiments, even if some did not necessarily make sense to critics and readers: "We like those nonsensical, obscure pieces as well. Their value lies in themselves (as literary works), not in what they say. Their existence affirms that stories can be written in such an unconventional way.... The medium is more important than the meaning it conveys."[72] The nonsense of formal experiments was justified by the notion of "estrangement" from Russian formalism. Literary composition was naturally regarded as a deviation from everyday language, "a continual process alternating between destabilizing the certainty of language and establishing a new form of certainty and conventionality."[73] In other words, literature always slides between the comprehensible and the nonsensical. Resonating with Moles's definition of aesthetic information as the untranslatable, Chinese critics emphasized the peculiar and well-deliberated ways in which the stories by new-wave writers are told, to the extent that it is almost impossible to retell the stories in other ways. The plot matters less than the innovative way of storytelling. Some critics even characterized these "new stories" as a sort of "immaterial but perceptible information."[74]

A conscious formalist approach to literature thus not only acknowledged the significance of literary form but also introduced new perspectives and critical vocabulary. For example, Meng Yue, in her reading of Wang Meng's "To Alice" and "Thrilling," decomposed the sentence structures of the two pieces into three parts: the subject, the verb, and the object. For each part, she developed a meticulous analysis of the interexchangeable pronouns, the empty signifiers without references, the verbs that fail to function as a narrative or to fabricate a plausible plot, and objectified subjects that merely occupy a syntactically subject position, all of which aimed to address "the basic question of their unprecedented mode of narration."[75] After this demonstration of excellent formalist critique, Meng concluded that the two pieces "subverted symbolically a metaphysical system that defined the subject in relation to the object, to each other, as well as to the culture, and smashed up the conventional mode of fiction writing, artistic creation, and aesthetic perceptions, and in the end undermined the deep-rooted cultural and psychological structure."[76]

This move from the form to the "deep-rooted" cultural structure on the surface didn't go beyond the ambit of cultural anthropology–informed structuralism. In reality, by focusing on the literary form in relation to the deep cultural structure, she in fact invested particular political significance in literary form. The concern with the deep cultural structure resonated with the discourse of the "ultrastable system" as discussed in chapter 3. Meng diagnosed this deep structure from the perspective of language:

> The discourse of the almost demented narrator consists of three parts, or three forces to be more accurate: the first is the commonly recognized set of rules of the national culture; the second is all sorts of cultural symbols; the third is the choice the narrator makes when speaking—he fails to express himself with chosen words but instead leashed out all words without control. . . . The narrator says nothing and cannot say anything. Rather he becomes an instrument of saying, an increasingly unstable valve that controls the vast chaos of cultural unconscious under the stern rules of cultural rationality. This discursive world is not controlled by the narrator, but by the cultural unconscious and the rules of cultural rationality, the real authority of our civilization.[77]

Meng thus reveals a crisis of the subject that was deluged by discourses and had no power of speaking. Curiously, an experiment in literary form that was supposed to free the subject from the straightjacket of Maoist style and ideology in the end finds a feeble subject who stumbled in the cracks of language. To generalize this as a symptom of modern civilization as structuralists do would be misleading and ahistorical. Meng herself in fact provided a best footnote for this crisis:

> The bizarre flows of discourse in "The Green Sun" and "Thrilling" are overflowing with buzzwords from the exterior layer of our culture,

and random words and phrases from commercials and advertisements, journals and newspapers, street talks, idle talks in offices and meeting rooms.... They are a highly condensed collection of myriad absurd everyday phenomenon, modes of behavior, ideas and judgments, all of which are displayed as distorted and even messy cultural symbols.... These words are not connected in a continuous way that follows the rules of syntactic structures, but are combined in an associative, metaphoric way.[78]

Implicit in this picture is a media environment that enveloped individuals within all sorts of sounds and words that mixed information with noises and seeped into the unconscious even when audiences paid little attention. This media environment on the one hand was predicated upon the developments of media technologies, especially wireless (television) broadcasts and emergent electronic media, and on the other hand was closely tied to a market economy that not only repositioned media systems in relation to audiences, but was also drastically changing the cultural system passed down from the socialist era.

While the fascination with the form has been generally acknowledged as a highly political gesture of revolting against socialist realism and "Maoist style," the relation of the market economy to new literary forms by experimented by writers active in the 1980s is often neglected. In his reading of Ge Fei's stories of the late 1980s, Zhang Xudong sharply detected the forces of an emergent market economy and the unleashed desires and erotic fantasies that drive the narrative of the stories but also work as a symbolic registration of "the disintegration of a socioempirical totality and the coming into being of a new reality."[79] If such forces and desires are subtly transformed into a maze of narratives in the avant-garde writings, they burst forth in Wang Meng's pieces as a cacophony of fractions of information and noises, resonating with the media environment increasingly saturated with advertisements and affective solicitation.

Indeed, advertising "invaded" literature in a more direct way, as many writers by the late 1980s were involved in a new type of composition called "advertising literature." Hired by entrepreneurs, writers penned essays in the form of reportage literature, with payments of 300 to 500 yuan for two thousand to three thousand words. These essays, often published in major newspapers and literary journals, were intended to put their entrepreneur sponsors and relative products in the limelight.[80] It also turned out to be lucrative for newspapers and journals, which had suffered from financial problems in the competitive publication realm as government subsidies were gradually being withdrawn.[81] Chen Cun, one of the experimental writers active in the late 1980s, confessed that in 1988 he had composed only six thousand words of "serious" writing, whereas the advertising literature he produced amounted to thirty thousand words.[82]

It was precisely against this background that the notion of "pure literature" was raised and extensively discussed in the mid-1980s, when "serious" literary journals were faced with a severe shrinkage in readership. The rise of multimedia entertainment such as television and dance clubs in urban areas and the proliferation of "popular literature" (*tongsu wenxue* 通俗文学) were believed to have stolen readers from "pure literature."[83] Some scholars, sensing the pressure of the media environment on literature, attributed the failure of "pure literature" to its "refusal to enter the arena of mass communication."[84] "Pure literature," rather than a category that policed the boundary between "serious literature" and "popular literature," should be considered a discursive invention that addresses the deep contradictions in the late socialist cultural production: literary experiments in the 1980s indicated the strong desire and efforts to break away from socialist realism and "Maoist style." But ironically, such experiments were made possible precisely by the remnants of a socialist culture system, with space secured by state subsidies and a publication system that was not yet completely commercialized.[85] As Shao Yanjun succinctly summarizes, while the social organization was going through drastic marketization, "serious" literary journals to a certain degree still preserved the mode of socialist central planning.[86] In this scenario, readers of "serious literature" were neither customers in commercial society nor the people under the guidance of the socialist system. Experimental literature in this sense was unfolding in these contradictory forces: on the one hand, the experimental writings in the 1980s relied on a socialist cultural system that shielded them from complete commercialization and, on the other hand, these writings sensitively registered the pressure of marketization and the looming postsocialist crisis.

In this sense, Wang Meng's parodic pieces of advertising literature, with their appearance of a "nonsensical" avant-garde form and their sensitivity to the noises and information of the late socialist cultural system, reflected these contradictions and tensions in 1980s China. Immersed in a rapidly transforming media environment, his writing now looks not that different from a clichéd but also sticky advertisement:

> Hotel manager woos me in private, offers me sips of canned liquid gas, asks if I'm willing to be honorary chair of board of directors of Beauty Gruel, Inc., saying Beauty Gruel has already obtained a patent from Atlantic Trans-International Corp. and enjoys a special income tax waiver for fifteen days (a), emphasizing Beauty Gruel has Vitamin U, V, W, XYZ as well as 2,437 kinds of organic compounds and inorganic salts (b). It has won Beauty Quality Cup after government tests and after taking it single-fold eyelids become twofold and twofold become fourfold plus legs grow forty centimeters longer (c).
>
> 宾馆经理悄悄与我谈情。请我吸罐装液化石油气。问我愿不愿意担任美容粥公司的名誉董事长。说是美容粥已经在大西洋跨国公司登记了专利权并受到免征所得税十五天的特殊照顾(a)。说是美容粥内含维他命UVWXYZ和有机物无机盐两千四百七十种 (b)。经过国家检验颁发了优质奖杯服用后单眼皮变成双眼皮双眼皮变成四层眼皮而且大腿延长四十公分 (c)。[87]

At first sight, this passage is filled with numerical facts and special terminologies, high in semantic information. But the reader may soon find that they are just clichés of advertising, full of formulaic idioms and syntaxes immediately perceptible as from ads: sentence (a) lists the approvals of the product by various authorities, (b) its nutrition components, and (c) its magical effects. To an audience bombarded with similar ads every day, these formulaic sentences offer nothing new. Yet this passage also takes the formulae as an object of parody and ridicule. If "Vitamin U, V, W, XYZ" are signifiers without referents, the sentence that "single-fold eyelids become twofold and twofold become fourfold" is a tongue-in-cheek mimicry to the extent of absurdity of exaggerations commonly seen in ads. Is this an exposition of the mechanism of advertising, in which its affective persuasion overpowers its semantic signification? Is this piece of writing also a meta-advertisement?

Meshed with the discourse of advertising, this piece strives to maintain a distance through ironic mimicry; yet the subtle distance is often devoured by the incessant flows of information and noises, to the extent that this piece also becomes nonsensical wooing. Wavering between experimental literature and advertising, this passage becomes a best instance showcasing the constellation of contradictory forces of a postsocialist cultural politics that are torn between aesthetical aspirations of literary experiments and economic pragmatics of commercialization, between communicative/scientific rationality of an emergent information economy and an affective contagion of viral media.

CHAPTER FIVE

Liminal Mediation and the Cinema Redefined

> Audiences approach films as reality, and even identify them as a "higher reality." That is what Baudrillard calls "hyperreality." Hyperreality is the reflection of the audiences' self-consciousness, and audiences thus become the observers of themselves. This is because all the signs and images that constitute cinema can be regarded as a revelation of the subconscious and myths, with the pre-structure of which the audience themselves complete the interpretation of the images on the screen.
>
> —Yao Xiaomeng, *"Dui yizhong xinde dianying xingtai de sikao, shilun dianying yixiang meixue"* [Some thoughts on a new cinematic aesthetics: A tentative discussion on the cinematic aesthetics of "thought-image"], *Dangdai dianying* 6 (1986)

Written in 1986, the epigraph to this chapter might sound like a mere psychoanalytical cliché to film scholars today. Yet critic Yao Xiaomeng's work was not so much meant to affirm the authority of "Western theories," but to propose a new understanding of cinema concomitant with the appearance of a new cinematic aesthetic represented by Chen Kaige, Zhang Yimou, and other directors who had enjoyed national and international attention since the mid-1980s. Curiously here, Yao juxtaposed psychoanalysis and structuralism with Baudrillard's notion of "hyperreality." His "misuse," or appropriation, of the term should be understood in relation to the efforts of Chinese filmmakers and film critics to reexamine the question "what is cinema?" amid drastic changes. On the one hand, cultural production was quickly shifting from a socialist state subsidy system toward marketization, which directly impacted filmmakers' relation to the audience; on the other hand, with the emergence of new electronic media and information technologies, and especially the ascending status of television in 1980s China, cinema was both in crisis and reinvented in this transformed media environment. Yao's argument can be explicated and contextualized in three aspects.

First, Yao distinguished the reality effects of cinema from film's relationship to profilmic objects by redefining the "real" from the perspective of the audience. Following the severe critique of socialist realism and its didacticism after the end of the Cultural Revolution, Chinese film critics championed the so-called Bazinian realism as a manipulation-free version of realism. Yet Yao's thesis above indicated a move away from the correspondence between the film and the external world. More important, this pull away from the conventional understanding of realism arose from the repositioning of humans in a new information environment that was purchased upon media's role in reshaping the living environment, and it put in crisis the representational mode and its metaphysics. Magic waves that immediately integrate humans into information circuits, holography that was seen as a radical break from photographic images, and cinematic images that moved beyond the constraints of the screen and movie theaters, all of these led to the blurring of boundaries between representational space and living space, transforming the spaces saturated with information into a magic field of metamorphosis. In this sense, Yao's invocation of "hyperreality" incidentally indicates this shifted media condition from representation to simulacra. But without entirely relinquishing the notion of the "real," Yao curiously reasserted the agency of human beings in maneuvering the technical conditions of simulacra toward a "higher reality," though this "higher reality" remains open and contingent upon the audience's interpretative acts.

Second, implied in this new condition of simulacra was a reorientation toward the audience. This was partly a response to the pressure and crisis of the domestic film industry, which was suffering a sharp drop in theater attendance. The newly expanded television broadcasts and the availability of videocassettes contributed to the decline. But the increasing push of socialist studio systems toward marketed-oriented entertainment business introduced a new relation of filmmakers to the audience. "Entertainment films" (*yule pian* 娱乐片) that aimed at sensorial pleasure was born in this context as a way to win audiences back into theaters. Film critics adopted humanist discourse to justify the birth of entertainment films, but the tension between humanist intellectual pursuits and a commercial culture became increasingly acute and often erupted in both "entertainment films" and more experimental films. This reorientation toward the audience also suggested the role of the cinematic medium in producing postsocialist subjectivities capable of constant improvisation and quick adaption to fast-changing market information, and thus augured an economy of information that extracts value from bodily affect. In other words, this turn toward the audience ambivalently evoked a liberal, humanist discourse and responded to the marketization of cultural production.

Finally, in the latter part of his essay, Yao's invocation of psychoanalytic terms did not lead to a simplistic notion of cinema as the expression of the interior. Instead, he proposed more complicated entanglements of cinematic images with emotions, thoughts, and bodily affect via a term from classical Chinese poetics—*yixiang* (idea-image 意象). Regarded as a distinctive mode of cinematic aesthetic by Yao, *yixiang*, echoing the reorientation toward the audience, suggested that the affective power of cinema rested upon the actualization of virtual images by the film audience. Yet differing from the concept of affect in recent film scholarship as a radical alterity resistant to discourses and ideological powers, Yao's theorization of *yixiang* acknowledged that this actualization of cinematic images could not do away with cultural memories and social conventions. His articulation of *yixiang* thus demonstrated a sharp political sensitivity to the affective power of cinema in the rapidly changing media and political environment of the late 1980s.

In this chapter, I trace the reinvention of cinema as modes of mediation of liminality amid the technological, social transformations and the ethical crises in the mid- and late 1980s. "Liminality" here is multifold: first, it refers to the contradictive, overlapping, and contending forces that define the production and functions of cinema. Between state regulation and market orientation, between humanist, intellectual pursuits and new consumerist desires, cinema was deeply imbricated in the maelstroms of uncertainties and contradictions. Second, it refers to the liminal "body" of cinema contiguous with television, holography, and other information technologies, which drastically redefined the relation of the human body to images and information environments in general. Whether conceived as simulacra or *yixiang*, cinematic images were understood as incomplete without the filtering and actualization performed by the human body. It is my argument that this new relationship of body and image suggests the liminality of cinema in its anticipation of an information economy that has flourished in our digital era today. Finally, the "liminality" also points toward the limits and crisis of representation, with which images and sounds fall at the edge of nonsensical noises. Here the crisis of representation led to reflections on the ethics of mediation. The precariousness of mediation therefore resulted from not only the failure of technology, but more important, the crises of a postsocialist society in which historical memories and social values were fragmented, effaced, and reshuffled.

I will start with the critique of both socialist realism and the so-called "Bazinian realism" by filmmakers and critics around the late 1970s and 1980s, which necessarily entailed rethinking the relationship between images and thoughts. This occurred along with the technical imaginations of magic waves and holography, which evoked new coordinates of thought and image, body and information, as well as space and time, which were free from the rules of realistic representation. This in turn generated new cinematic aesthetics responsive to the transformations of the cinematic medium per se amid drastic social and technical changes. My approach to the films produced in the late 1980s is twofold: first, I will uncover the contradictory forces surrounding the liminal medium and underscore the role of cinema in redistributing the sensible and bringing out postsocialist subjectivities adaptive to the informationization of the social; second, as filmmakers and critics worked closely and filmmakers often wrote reflectively on their explorations of cinematic techniques and aesthetics, I regard the film works I analyze here not simply reflective of critical thoughts of film critics, but more important, as practices of theorization, in the sense that they constitute, in D. N. Rodowick's words, "a fluid metacritical space of epistemological and ethical self-examination that we may continue to call 'theory' should we wish to do so."[1] In other words, my cross-reading between critical discourses and film works draws them together and highlights the self-conscious theorization by filmmakers on the issue of mediation. Such an excavation recognizes practices and thoughts that are usually excluded from the conventional lineage of "theory" and sheds a new light on the issues of image and body, audience and market, power and technology, bringing a postsocialist perspective to rethink the much-debated question of cinema in the information age.

Away from Realism

As discussed in chapter 4, there had been efforts to redefine cinema since the late 1970s, when film critics started to champion the medium specificity of the cinema. Regarding the increasingly ossified form of socialist realism as evidence of the dominance of the dramatic tradition in Chinese film, they advocated "a divorce of cinema from drama." They opposed what they regarded as the Soviet tradition of montage in favor of long-shot and long take associated with "Bazinian realism."[2] The latter was believed to be free of dramatic manipulation and closer to the "nature" of cinema. The Bazinian question of "what is cinema?" was thus received as a question of medium specificity that validated the autonomy of cinema from political interventions. With this (mis)understanding of Bazinian realism, many fourth-generation directors discovered a "documentary aesthetic" (*jishi meixue* 纪实美学, literally "reportage aesthetics") in their works. Yuan Ying summarizes this transformation: "As cinema shifts to focus on an objective presentation of reality and a comprehensive representation of the external and internal world, with the maximum efforts of film makers to approximate what life is, it has to avoid the traditional mode of relying on dramatic conflicts to push forward the plot and establish typical characters."[3]

What Yuan Ying regarded as a pitfall to avoid was precisely the principle of socialist realism.[4] Typical characters and typical environment constructed through dramatic conflicts as developed by Marxist theorist Cai Yi and others, according to Peter Button, is a dialectic unity of the individual and the universal.[5] A typical character should both represent the universal characteristics of his or her class and show the peculiarity of the individual. But how to create such a typical character became ambiguous and controversial in the political environment of the 1950s.

This was tied to a big debate between 1955 and 1966 on the topic of "image-thinking" (形象思维). Chinese critics often traced the term back to Russian literary critic Vissarion Belinsky and Soviet writer Maxim Gorky, the latter credited as the founder of the literary tradition of socialist realism. This notion was promoted by Zhou Yang, who was in charge of the realm of literary and art works in the publicity department of the Party. The gist of "image thinking" was that the process of literary and artistic creation directly employed images rather than abstract concepts as in the logical reasoning process. This peculiar mode of thinking distinguished literary and artistic creation from other types of activities, such as theoretical and critical work. While the propagation of this notion generated heated discussions among literary theorists and critics, the publication of Zheng Jiqiao's essay in the journal *Red Flag* in 1966 terminated the discussion by announcing the political incorrectness of "image-thinking." Entitled "Wenyi lingyu li bixu jianchi makesizhuyi de renshilun" 文艺领域里必须坚持马克思注意的认识论 (We should hold onto Marxist epistemology in the realm of literature and arts), Zheng's essay criticized the argument of "image-thinking" as "intuitionism" (*zhijue zhuyi* 直觉主义), which mystified the process of literary and artistic creation.[6] This philosophical and aesthetic debate was highly politically charged, as the legitimacy of "image thinking" was directly related to the question of how much freedom and space that literary and artistic creation should enjoy beyond the regulation of the Party and the strictures of official Marxism.

After the official end of the Cultural Revolution (1966–76), in the critique of Mao's art policy, the issue of "image thinking" resurfaced. Although Zheng Jiqiao still tried to defend his argument, the literary and critical circle predominantly believed that the denial of "image thinking" should be held responsible for the ossified formulism of literary and artistic composition, especially the reduction of a character to the general and abstract characterization of his or her class in model operas and other works produced during the Cultural Revolution.[7] The key issue in question here was whether a concept separate from specific images should be developed before the writer creates a typical character/image. While Zheng insisted upon the formula of a cognitive process of moving from "appearances" (*biaoxiang* 表象) to "concepts" (*gainian* 概念) and then to newly created images, proponents of image thinking argued that Zheng's separation of concepts from concrete images laid the groundwork for the instrumentalization of literary and art works, which became merely illustrations of certain prescribed concepts and themes, and thus tools of political propaganda.[8] The reestablishment of the legitimacy of "image thinking" in effect endorsed an autonomous space of literary and art works from direct political interventions.

Similarly, the adoption of Bazinian realism released cinematic images from the principles of socialist realism. The excitement generated by *jishi meixue* derived from the fresh images that were no longer subject to types and the rule of continuity editing. Images were not required to convey one definite meaning, nor were they clustered around one single concept. Freeing images from overarching concepts was precisely what attracted Chinese film critics to Bazin, who is conventionally associated with what Daniel Morgan calls "perceptual realism," according to which, films provide an experience of the world of a film that replicates our habitual way of being in the world.[9] Associated with stylistic features such as deep focus, this version of realism supposedly allows the spectator to make a choice rather than being explicitly guided to what is important in the frame. Yet it would be simplistic to reduce this *jishi meixue* to a disinterested recording of profilmic objects. Yuan Ying sharply commented that cinematic images, by giving a form and thus a new order to concrete phenomena and appearances, were already refracted from the filmmakers' view of the world and injected with their experiences and emotions.[10] In other words, even when this *jishi meixue* flourished both in critical discourse and filmmaking practice, cinematic images were never understood as mechanic replica of reality.

More forceful moves to pull cinema away from the conventional understanding of realism came when a critique of Bazin, or of conventional understanding of Bazin, appeared in the mid-1980s. The translation of a chapter from George Wead and George Lellis's monograph *Film: Form and Function* became an important occasion for such discussions. The chapter was retitled "Movement" and published in the journal *Contemporary Cinema*. In a review entitled "Rethinking the Essential Nature of

Cinema," critic Kong Du was excited to announce how contemporary psychology had questioned Bazin's notion of "photorealism":

> Bazin accepted the hypothesis of the persistence of vision unquestioned in explaining the illusion of movement. According to Bazin, cinematic movement is as real as any movement in everyday life to the eyes. Thus he skipped the basic question and moved too fast into his psychological study of photorealism. . . . However, as Wead and Lellis point out, this basic question concerning the essential nature of cinema is not that simple.[11]

Kong further noted that the two authors had, by quoting Gestalt theory, which emphasized the active role of the human brain in cognitive activities, argued against the theory of vision persistence and instead contended that the illusion of movement was a psychological product: the brain is willing to be deceived. Concurrent with Western theorists' rediscovery of Hugo Münsterberg, who drew parallels between cinematic techniques such as close-up and editing, and cognitive activities such as attention, memory, and imagination, Wead and Lellis questioned the understanding of photorealism as a property of photographic images to replicate reality. Instead, the reality effects of cinema were believed to derive from the interaction between moving images and human beings. Kong thus shifted via Wead and Lellis the ontology of cinematic images from their relation to profilmic objects to their relation to human viewers.

The convenient association of long-shot realism with the medium specificity of cinema also came under question. As more of Bazin's works became available in Chinese translation, some theorists exclaimed that they had "misunderstood" Bazin. This generated a new round of discussion of "what is cinema?" In 1986, the established journal *Film Art* featured a special column titled "Discussion on the Essential Nature of Cinema." One of the essays, by Cai Shiyong, challenged the previous understanding of "documentary aesthetic" by disassociating it from long shot and deep focus. He also corrected the earlier assumption that Bazin had regarded drama as anticinematic. Instead of defending cinema as "one" "pure" medium, Cai argued, Bazin advocated that cinema should learn from other arts. Therefore, the specificity of the cinema was never about its "purity" from other media. Cai also advocated that, with the recent development of real-time television broadcasts, cinema should shift its pursuit from "authenticity" (*zhenshi xing* 真实性) to "suppositionality" (*jiading xing* 假定性).[12] What did Cai mean by "suppositionality"? As I shall argue below, Cai's term implied that the human mind and body would always respond to stimuli of the virtual environment beyond the question of authenticity.[13] This entailed a renewed relation of cinema to the human body in a transformed media environment.

Simulacra: Frameless Images and a Seamless Media Environment

This new relation of the image to the human body can be observed in a science fiction story entitled "Mysterious Waves." Zhang is a journalist who is sent to interview Professor Wang, an expert in wireless remote control and the chief designer of a national safety defense system called "Wave-45." However, he is baffled when he arrives at Professor Wang's house: the walls of the house are completely covered with lush vines and flowers. There is no entry to the house! Just as he freezes in confusion about what to do, a boy simply walks "through" the wall and leads him "through" the wall into the house. The rest of the story presents a string of similar surprises and attractions that dazzle Zhang: in Professor Wang's living room, the famous *Mona Lisa* hangs on a wall. Knowing that this painting is merely a copy, Zhang nonetheless believes that this one is "too real to be an imitation." However, when he reaches out his hand toward the painting, there is nothing on the wall! Instead of dispelling Zhang's puzzlement immediately, Professor Wang invites him to see the blooming daffodils around, which, in a blink of an eye, transform into roses. Even the scent has changed correspondingly! As he stands beside a fish tank, in the belief that what he sees is also an illusion, he puts his hand into the tank but immediately shrinks back—he "feels" water this time. Yet as he examines his hand, there are no water drops. After showing off these astounding tricks, Professor Wang finally explains to him that these are all the effects of waves: "According to the latest theory of 'waves,' everything uses different waves to express itself, and every bit of information we can sense is essentially waves. Though waves are originally emitted from different types of materials, we are now able to manufacture 'waves of pure information,' which can beguile our sensory organs—the visual, the olfactory, the hearing, and the tactile—into believing the signals are from a real material thing, even though the 'thing' is never present. All of this is achieved merely through the manipulation of electronic equipment."[14]

No doubt the waves are the "hero" of this story, which (discussed in chapter 1) are central to the imaginary of information media and cybernetic connections. Waves, attributed with the flexibility and convertibility usually associated with the digital today, magically interfaced human bodies into information environments. In this story, the celebratory (or devastating?) power of the waves is their blurring, if not erasure, of the boundary between the material and the immaterial. Waves are everywhere, transforming the environment in which people live into a magic field of metamorphosis, an ever-shifting phantasmagoric space that immediately changes the way people sense and know the world: Should people believe or disbelieve what they see, hear, smell, and touch? Yet the distinction between real and unreal, authentic and replica, seems irrelevant to this world of simulation. Just as the *Mona Lisa* in Professor Wang's living room matters less for its own authenticity than its effect, the "real" presence of something matters less than its effect on the sensorium. This indicates an important shift: media in this sense are neither for the representation of something "real," nor are they bound by rectangular screens that separate "represented space" from "real space." The disappearance of framing ensures the successful integration of media into the living environment: media constitute the very environment inhabited by human beings. More important, the human eyes, the brain, and the body become receptive surfaces onto which information waves are projected and displayed. Waves demand the human body not only to be part of but also to respond to the environment of metamorphosis.

Such an idea of wave-body interaction was by no means singular. One phenomenon that fascinated the popular imagination at the time was holographic technology—holographic photography (*quanxi sheying* 全息摄影), motion pictures, and holographic television. The idea of holography was initiated by the Hungarian electrical engineer and physicist

Denis Gabor and made commercially available in the 1960s.[15] It is a process of using lasers to create three-dimensional images. Briefly, a light beam from a single laser is split into a reference and an object beam. The object beam reflects off an object and the reference beam is directed to the recoding medium. The two light beams meet at the plane of the recording medium, resulting in a complex interference pattern imprinted on the recording medium. The interference pattern can thus be regarded as an encoded version of the scene. When reconstructing the scene, the reference beam is cast back through the hologram and diffracted into the object beam, creating a same wave front as when one's eyes look at the object. Instead of aiming at material reproduction of the object, holography simulates the way the viewer looks at the object by manipulating laser waves to reconstruct the wave front of light reflecting and refracting between objects and eyes.

Holography in this sense signaled a new understanding of human perception and consciousness as informed by information science. The writer Li Ming, who composed a series of essays on the impact of information science on contemporary philosophy and society, contended that we should abandon the orthodox Marxian understanding of consciousness as a reflection of the material world. Human consciousness did not passively receive information from the exterior world as conveyed by the clichéd metaphor of photography, he contended, but, instead, actively interfered with the exterior world by sending out its own information, the same way beams of different wavelengths interfered with one another as in holographic photography. Thus, perception arose from the interactions between the information sent out by humans and that which came from the exterior world.[16] The human body in this sense could be understood as an information sender and perception as deriving from the body's involvement in cybernetic exchanges of information.

Writing at the beginning of the 1980s, John Halas, an enthusiast of holography, admitted that there were still many technological difficulties to overcome in using holography for the production of motion pictures. Commenting on its visual effects, he added: "When developed on a small translucent film, the holographic film looks entirely inconspicuous. It only comes to life when placed in a cylinder and illuminated from within and below and rotated by means of a motor. By that motion the stereoscopic effect can be observed."[17] Presented as the deficiency of holography, Halas's description nonetheless showed the promise of holographic images to break down the two-dimensional frame. Despite the technological difficulties and special conditions necessary for three-dimensional images to appear, holographic technology fueled the imagination about a new, powerful medium in 1980s China. Laser technology, with its easy modifiability and flexibility, was listed by Qian Xuesen, along with computer technology, as providing possibilities for future new forms of art.[18] Qian also predicted that computers and optoelectronic technology would free film directors from the arduous processes of film shooting and enable them to produce images of nonexisting objects.[19] One article, entitled "Holographic Motion Pictures and Holographic TV of the Future," considered holographic photography as representing the future of media development, and an advanced technology that would be "able to capture all the information of the object." Speculating on these prospects, the article continues:

> In the future, with the holographic technology, the ordinary, flat screen of today will be replaced with the "holographic screen," which will enable the audience to see lifelike images. They will be surrounded by holographic signals and images, and immerse themselves into simulated situations the same as in life, feeling no separation from what surrounds them.
> If it is the ocean being projected, you will feel the gentle slapping of the waves, and see whales swimming around you, or ships sailing towards you.
> If it is a happy picture being projected, you will feel yourself sharing the happiness as well.
> If it is a grand gala, you will feel as if you were stepping into the luxurious dancehall.[20]

As in the story, this emphasis on the capacity of holography to create virtual but palpable simulations reorients the role of media from representation toward their effects on human sensorium. This imagination of the "holographic screen" gestures toward the dissolution of the boundaries of screens. Screens are everywhere, to the extent that even the very notion of "screen" becomes irrelevant. The full immersion annihilates the separation between screen space and physical space. As immersion implies much more than the engagement with visual signals, future media will have to be able to address different senses. A "pan-sensory cinema" (*quangan dianying* 全感电影) was also proposed as a future technology, not only providing visual and auditory stimuli but also activating tactile, olfactory, and other senses.

The dissolution of the screen means that the screen loses its particularity so that everything might serve as a screen. In one of the boldest imaginings of this sort of "screen-less cinema" (*wumu dianying* 无幕电影), the sky itself is made into a boundless screen: with a pair of special glasses, people can watch three-dimensional images projected into the sky even when they are on the beach, in the wilderness, or wherever. This idea dismantles the theater as the institutional locus for cinematic screening, but, more important, it transforms the natural landscape into a huge cinematic space. The landscape becomes a screen (or screens) onto which ever-shifting images can be projected. This seems to be close to the final step in creating an all-inclusive media environment in which nothing is left outside the information circuits: the mediascape would finally commingle with nature and render obsolete the distinction between reality and representation. The world becomes a cinematic theater.

Metamorphosis in *Flights of Fantasy*

This media environment of simulacra that envelops human beings is best captured by the 1986 film *Flights of Fantasy* (*Yixiang tiankai* 异想天开), directed by Wang Weiyi and adapted from a short story by the popular writer Zhang Xianliang, who later became a cultural entrepreneur and operated a film studio in Ningxia. The film begins in the morning of a regular workday of petty clerk Xu, who works in a corporate accounting department. Stuck in a crowded bus on his way to work, and anxious about being punished by his manager for being late, he fantasizes about his own metamorphosis into an animated character of supernatural flexibility. The cartoon character is "Astro Boy" (*Tetsuwan Atomu*, or "Mighty

Atom") from the eponymous Japanese anime (1963).[21] Atomu became a favorite character for Chinese audiences after China Central Television broadcast the Japanese anime series in the early 1980s. Having transformed into the guise of an anime, Xu's body flies free from gravity. He nimbly extricates himself from the packed carriage and soars swiftly across the skyline of the city, displaying the allure and pleasure of a weightless body. But the film soon cuts back to the live-action scene, featuring the human figure Xu running strenuously toward his office, his sweaty face and labored movements in no way resembling Atomu's effortless flight. The alternation between the animation and the live sequence exposes the discrepancy between the effortlessness of the metamorphosis and arduous heaviness of being, but it also reflects the interpenetration of the media world and real life.

Such media saturation brings forth a film richly layered with visual and audial effects, connecting different media through magical flows of energy. In fact, the film starts with a sequence that quite literally animates the dynamics between different media. The remarkable opening scene arrives with the clashing sound of sword on sword, as well as the sound of panting and the shouts of people fighting: a typical soundtrack for a martial arts movie. Yet these sounds are floating, their source unlocatable in the mise-en-scène. The disjunction between sound and image compels the camera to look for the source of the sounds, revealing items in the room, from graphic illustrations in tabloids to pulp martial arts fictions and popular film magazines, as well as film posters, a toy robot, and a small statuette of a martial arts hero. It is as if the camera is being taunted to discover the prankster from whom the sound comes, and whatever it touches becomes animated, brimming with energy for unexpected transformations. These opening shots self-consciously posit the film in a network of media culture, such as cassette tapes and pop music, popular print culture, and all sorts of movie culture tie-ins. The sequence also shows how various popular media saturate the world of our protagonist, whose own kicks and shouts seem to be a response to the free-floating soundtrack of martial arts film. The ambiguity of the location of the sounds blurs the boundary between the extradiegetic and diegetic space, almost dissolving the frame of the screen. Soon the soundtrack is

Figure 20. Metamorphosis in a crowded bus. Stills from *Flights of Fantasy*.

replaced by kinetic disco music, which animates the objects in the room in a fast montage. We see our protagonist squeezing himself into tight jeans, as if he cannot wait to get rid of the burden of physicality and prepare himself for a weightless flight.

The rest of the film showcases how cinema becomes a vehicle for the office-bound Xu's "flights of fantasy," bringing Xu into a mediated world of simulacra in which he constantly transforms himself in response to the metamorphosis of the environment. Sitting in his cagelike office, reluctant to start in on his boring, routine work, he is distracted by huge film posters across the street. All the characters and images on the posters begin to move of their own accord, overlapping and dissolving one after another. Xu falls into a daydream: sent out for a business trip, he finds himself to be the bearer of supernatural powers and is involved in an airborne fight against an invading alien. But this same Xu soon finds himself transformed into a martial arts hero at the Shaolin temple. After stealing a scroll of martial arts secrets from the abbot, he elopes with his lover. At this point, the film becomes a farcical game of chase: the abbot and another monk follow the couple into a kaleidoscopic urban landscape—an amusement park, a discotheque dancehall, a fashion show, and finally into a showroom displaying the latest innovations in robotics. In this process, our chameleon-like character immediately adapts himself to each environment and assumes a new identity. Immersed in the world of martial arts movies, he is quick to imitate the genre's characteristic stances and movements; in the fashion show, he becomes a denim-clad cowboy; more magically, as he presses himself into the body of a robot, he literally becomes "one" with the robot, and even defeats the abbot with this new shining, mechanical body; and when he puts on a woman's dress and makeup, he even speaks with a female voice. The discrepancy (or ostentatious display of fabricated congruity) between his physical body and the high-pitched woman's voice destabilizes the "natural" synchronization between sound and images, evoking an earlier historical moment when sound as a new medium was added to cinema.

Xu's transformation from a would-be film spectator to a self-fashioned actor in a string of genre films playfully conflates screen space and living space, echoing the fantasy in media discourses of seamless integration

Figure 21. The cowboy Xu. A still from *Flights of Fantasy*.

Figure 22. The female Xu. A still from *Flights of Fantasy*.

of screens into the living space. The surrounding world is now a live theater that invites the audience to be its actors and encourages them to travel across the cinematic world as in the real world. The vanishing boundary between living space and media space seemingly aspires to prevalent fantasies about a "pan-sensory" and "no-information-lost" holographic cinema. Vision, sound, smell, and touch, all senses of human beings, are susceptible to simulated media effects, to the extent that Yao Xiaomeng in the opening quotation of this chapter uses the Baudrillard term "hyperreality" to address the altered dynamics between the human body and the hypermediated environment.

The juxtaposition of live action and animation in this film converged with the rethinking of the question of "what cinema is." Kong Du in his review of the Wead and Lellis essay argued that their reexamination of cinematic images beyond the confines of photorealism would broaden the spectrum of cinemas, allowing the reincorporation of animation into cinema studies, which had long privileged a photorealistic understanding of cinema.[22] This is because, if cinematic images cannot be reduced into a replica of the world, and cinematic effects come from human interaction with the information environment, live-action footage and animation are no longer opposed to each other. To media theorist Lev Manovich, the affinity between animation and live-action footage precisely reveals the concealed ontology of cinema. In his *The Language of New Media*, Manovich raises the provocative idea that "digital cinema is a particular case of animation." Manovich argues that earlier techniques for creating and displaying moving images all relied on hand-painted or hand-drawn images. But once cinema was stabilized as a technology of machine vision, it "cut all references to its origins in artifice" and "pretends to be a simple recording of an already existing reality," denying that "the reality it shows often does not exist outside the film image, an image arrived at by photographing an already impossible space, itself put together with the use of models, mirrors, and matte paintings, and then combined with other images through optical painting."[23] But as cinema enters the digital age, live-action footage becomes "raw material for further compositing, animating, and morphing." Cinema obtains "a plasticity" to the extent that it is no longer clearly distinguished from animation.[24]

This plasticity Manovich sees as shared by animation and photographic images is also displayed in *Flights of Fantasy*. The film employs various optical tricks, such as stop tricks and matte shots, even incorporating found footage from *Shaolin Temple* to highlight Xu's elasticity. At the same time, the film metamorphosizes from science fiction, to martial arts, to a display of urban entertainments, and finally into a spy thriller. The dazzling generic transformations indicate that the film self-consciously positions itself in a network of media culture. Distancing itself from the representational mode that centers upon the relation of cinematic images to profilmic objects, the film invites its audience to suspend the question about authenticity and derive fun from its intertextual references.

Manovich designates the advent of the digital as the condition for the resurfacing of this different ontology of cinematic images. Yet if Manovich emphasizes more the technological manipulation of images, the renewed understanding of plasticity of cinematic images in 1980s China is predicated not necessarily upon the digital, but instead, upon the notion of the human body as the necessary "enframing" of information, which I elaborated in chapter 1 in my discussion of magic waves and cybernetic bodies. This brought about a new understanding of human perception. With "a transition from the classical optics to the information optics," an author named Song Feijun argued, "engineers of optics and engineers of electronics have found their work merged in the realm of informational sciences, as scientists of optics are dealing increasingly with the *frequencies of optical waves* just as informational scientists do with frequencies of electronic signals."[25] An adjustment of the frequencies of optical waves to human eyes would enable a fluid metamorphosis of images. One illustration from the book shows an old woman standing in front of a magic mirror, which reflects her image back as a beautiful, young lady.[26] This playful transformation was lauded as the magic of the new optical science.

However, if the plasticity of cinematic images invokes a liberating sense of freedom, these fantasized adventures are exquisitely framed in the structure of daydreaming. The fantasies of a flexible, spontaneous subject derive exactly from the opposite—the inability of the lackadaisical

Xu, trapped in his office, to free himself from his desk and the mechanical rhythms of daily routine. At the end of the film, the manager walks in and shakes Xu from his daydreams. Xu, lethargic, glimpses at the theater across the street, into which throngs of people are squeezing themselves, as if the cramped, boxlike theater could constrain their boundlessly unfolding fantasies. The tension between the endless unfolding of cinematic space and the delimiting walls of theaters is best captured in this metacinematic last shot. Cinema promises unprecedented mobility and possibility, but it also simultaneously traps and disciplines its audiences by turning them into information-sensitive workers under various contingent situations.[27]

"Flows" of Affectivity

The constant mutations in and of the film may remind us of Tom Gunning's notion of a "cinema of attractions" in his discussion of early cinema. Writing about the unique spectatorial address of the early cinema as distinguished from classical narrative films, Gunning points out that while the cinema of classic narrative is interested in building a diegetic world of fictional characters and places, the cinema of attractions addresses spectators by "arousing and satisfying visual curiosity through a direct and acknowledged act of display." In contrast to the "gathering of successive moments into a pattern" in order to create a "development in time" in classic narratives, attractions have one basic temporality "of the alternation of presence/absence" and a present immediacy of a "Here it is! Look at it." The cinema of attractions presents itself as "staccato jolts of surprise," as "a temporal irruption rather than a temporal development."[28] Gunning's characterization of the lack of "development in time" also applies to *Flights of Fantasy*. Metamorphosis in the film strings together discrete events, without providing cause-and-effect links between the transitions, nor resulting in a "development in time." The linear progression of narrative is abandoned for swift shifts between different scenes. If Gunning's insight on the "cinema of attractions" uncovers the "hybridity" of cinema, relating the aesthetic of early cinema to its historical connections with other forms of media and performance, the assemblage of optical photographic tricks in *Flights of the Fantasy* and its abandonment of linear classic narrative, by evoking an earlier moment of cinema, raises questions about the very nature of cinema in an era of electronic media.

Coincidently, with the end of the Classical-era Hollywood, there is a similar break of linear narrative and an aesthetic of display in American science fiction films of the late 1970s, as Vivian Sobchack observes:

> Most of today's SF films construct a generic field in which space is semantically described as a surface for play and dispersal, a surface across which existence and objects kinetically dis-place and dis-play their materiality.... It is filled with curious things and dynamized as a series of concatenated events rather than linearly pressured to stream forward by the teleology of the plot.[29]

Sobchack relates this surface for display to the emergent electronic space, which is "open only to 'pervasion'—a condition of kinetic accommodation and dispersal associated with the experience and representations of television, video games and computer terminals."[30] Astutely placing this new aesthetic in the intermedial relation of cinema to the pervasion of electronic media, Sobchack echoes Gunning by emphasizing the cinematic screen as a display of "curious things" and "concatenated events."

However, while in Gunning's argument it is the magician's whimsical performance that punctuates the moments of attractions, with the coming of the electronic age it is the audience's familiarity with and experience of various media forms and conventions that make it possible for the screen to become a surface for (dis-)play. *Flights of Fantasy* does not rely on "the delaying of resolution of that enigma"—as Gunning characterizes Classical Hollywood films—to absorb the audience psychologically into the diegetic world. Instead, the fun of watching the film derives from immediate recognition of generic conventions, from science fiction and martial arts films to the spy thriller. In other words, the narratives of these genre films are not simply absent as in early cinema, but randomly cut short, just like swift zapping among different television channels, or shifting from one videotape to another on a home media system. The random jump from one genre to another in *Flights of Fantasy* also echoes the audience's experience of sampling from a sea of information. By stringing together random excerpts of different narratives, *Flights of Fantasy* remediates the experience of using television and other electronic media, revealing the tension of cinema with other media in an era of expanding information networks.

Such remediation is also recognizable in other Chinese films of the late 1980s. Commenting on *The Perils of a Rich Boy* (*Shaoye de monan* 少爷的磨难), a comedy released in 1987, a critic describes the film as "a postcard film" that provides postcardlike glimpses into different places that the protagonist moves across. The development of the plot matters less to its audience than the tourist experience across different settings. Cause-and-effect temporality is also suspended. The critic highlights the "hybrid abundance" of information provided by postcards, in the sense that postcards often "mingle together different visual styles and contents" in order to enlarge the amount of information they can carry.[31] His comment is thought-provoking in several ways: first, cinema to him is less about the representation of the real than about the dissemination of information. The cinematic screen in this sense resembles the compact surface of a postcard that is maximized for information efficiency. Second, the ephemerality of postcards underlines the susceptibility of cinematic images to fast consumption. The fleeting images with their banal reproducibility, clearly distinguished from masterpieces of art, are made for sensorial stimulation and soon to be eclipsed by the successive emergence of new images. If Gunning's cinema of attractions accentuates the "staccato jolts of surprise," cinematic images in these films of the electronic age become flows of homogeneous images—"flows" in terms of continuous passing of images and events without a real ending or any linkage between.

"Flow," a critical term raised by Raymond Williams to describe both the transmission and reception of television, foregrounds the experience of "miscellaneous continuity." This is because, as Richard Dienst elaborates, narratives are cut up, and constant interruption has been transformed into something like its opposite—continuity. Flow also indicates the passage of a heterogeneous time bound together by abrupt shifts between levels of signification, the movement of multiplicity, and the mix of genres.

Richard Dienst, in addressing the ways that media images shape the experience of temporality, singles out television as the disruptive point when theoretical approaches drawn from film criticism are no longer adequate in understanding the images of the "after television" moment.[32] This is because, as Patricia Ticineto Clough elaborates, the image, "released from narrative and representative requisites," becomes "the image of time passing, the image of time's force, or its productivity in passing." By "producing value through socializing time—that is, time that has not already been socialized as labor time," television "points to the becoming of technologies that are productive of value through the modulation of subindividual bodily capacities or affect."[33]

Dienst's and Clough's insights on the role of flows of images in socializing time beyond labor time for the production of value is pertinent to our understanding of the conflation of working time and play time in *Flights of Fantasy*. The fluctuations of Xu between a versatile actor and a would-be spectator blur the boundary between work and play, production and consumption. The office-bound Xu, in his search for adventures and excitement to evade his boring work, inadvertently finds himself working to consume. This type of constantly mutating, zany character, who is "nothing but a series of adjustments and adaptations to one situation after another," as Sianne Ngai remarks, is actually a person who strives to find a job in "a precariousness created specifically by the capitalist organization of work," and who has to put into work affects and other human capacities when facing the politically ambiguous erosion of the distinction between play and work.[34] In late 1980s China, this zaniness speaks to the fantasies of self-fashioning and new possibilities of freedom allowed by the prospect of moving out from the shelter of state institutions, but it also anticipated the birth of a new postsocialist subject who has to constantly adapt themselves to the ever-changing market and deal with ever-shifting information flows of a marketized society.[35] By socializing the time previously beyond labor time, film viewing and television watching builds into the bodies of viewers a rhythm to match the rapid changes of the marketplace.

The embrace of zaniness in the film also suggests the increasing extraction of surplus value from affect and bodily capacities when the government started to leave individual businessmen and entrepreneurs to fill in the gaps of a society torn between market forces and state power. According to the statistics provided by the State Council, by the mid-1980s, there were about 17 million self-employed entrepreneurs (*getihu* 个体户), mostly in sales and service industry. They became a highly visible population for their putatively generous income compared to that of average state institution employers, and for their mixed constituents of job-awaiting youths, ex-convicts, and ambitious businessmen. New images of human types appeared on the screen by the mid-1980s. *Yamaha Fish Stall* (*Yamaha yudang* 雅马哈鱼档, 1984), directed by Zhang Liang, a veteran filmmaker from the Zhujiang film studio, for the first time made job-awaiting urban youths and self-employed businessmen (*getihu*) its main characters. Unlike Chen Kaige's and Zhang Yimou's focus on remote, barren areas, from the mid-1980s many films explored new social relations in the urban milieu and the possibilities of new identities in the new economic and cultural climate. One signal film that captures the new sentiments and anxieties is *Sunshine and Showers* (*Taiyang yu* 太阳雨, 1987) by Zhang Zeming. In this film, we see the emergence of new urban professionals, who no longer stick to the routines of a stable life but throw themselves into perpetual mobility and the endless pursuit of individual value. A young girl dissatisfied with her "too quiet" life remakes herself as a fashion model and busies herself with performance tours; an ambitious young man in the advertising business—which was indeed a new business in the 1980s—is always "on the road" and can seldom afford a few hours of leisure with his girlfriend. These new types of characters belonged to a chaotic world in transition that also promised unlimited possibilities. However, by forsaking the stable shelter of state institutions, these characters also throw themselves into unpredictable and precarious situations in their Faustian pursuit of unleashed freedom.[36] *Troubleshooters* (*Wanzhu* 顽主, 1988) is of particular interest here because it demonstrates the indispensability of affective labor in this simultaneously stimulating and unsettling social scenario. The film traces several young men who run a "Three

For" company that provides all sorts of odd services, such as replacing henpecked husbands to bear the scolding of their wives, dating girls on behalf of people who cannot afford to take the time themselves, comforting depressed losers, and pretending to be poets and writers on various gala occasions. Acting, playful mimicry, and role-playing are no longer the privileged province of film actors; they are part and parcel of their work. In this transformational postsocialist space, where the state can no longer encompass under its regulatory ambit all sorts of newly emergent social relations and sentiments, "Three For" company transforms the management of social relations and sentiments—previously the domain of the government—into profitable businesses. In this context, *Flights of Fantasy*, with its conflation of film acting and film viewing, working and playing, also indicates that cinema, under the new social conditions and amid the mediascape reshaped by television and other electronic media, works to modulate affectivity and bodily capacities and produce postsocialist subjectivities in synch with the constantly changing marketplace.

Television, Home Media, and the Crisis of Domestic Cinema

The close affinity between cinema and television as demonstrated in *Flights of Fantasy* is not merely a coincidence. Concurrent with the reinvention of cinema and the investment in cinema of new possibilities of postsocialist subjectivities was the crisis in the domestic film industry. The revival and flourishing of domestic cinema following the end of the Cultural Revolution lasted for only a short period. In 1979, film theater attendance in cities and towns was 9.2 billion individual visits. By the mid-1980s, the institutional authority of theaters waned as people discovered the new fun of television programs and home video players. The box office for domestically produced films dropped drastically. Urban film theater attendance in 1984 dropped by almost 30 percent compared with that in 1980. The statistics were even worse in 1985, with a decrease of 1.2 billion individual visits in that single year.[37] According to a survey, in eleven big cities, including Beijing, Shanghai, and Guangzhou, the cinema audience dropped more than 25 percent in the first half of 1985 compared with that in 1984. One reason was that television shows, especially martial arts series produced in Hong Kong, had diverted audiences from theaters. For example, two Hong Kong–produced television series, *The Legend of Condor Heroes* (*Shediao yingxiong zhuan* 射雕英雄传), adapted from Jin Yong's eponymous martial arts novel, and *Huo Yuanjia* 霍元甲, which features the story of a martial art hero in the late Qing dynasty, caused huge sensations in 1983.[38] In addition, 1983 also marked two significant moments in the development of Chinese television: first, the central government decided to allow local governments to start their own television broadcasts. Since then, television stations sponsored by local governments—not only provincial but also municipal and county-level governments—mushroomed across the country in both urban and rural areas. Second, the spring festival gala held by the China Central television station also started in this year, which began its nearly thirty-year run as the most popular television celebration in the nation. Videocassettes, as a new audiovisual medium, whether legally distributed or illegally pirated, brought with them the fad for Hong Kong and Taiwanese popular culture, further decentering regular film screening. Some film theaters even converted their space into video-screening parlors. Hollywood movies appeared not only on the list of television programs but also in local video-screening parlors. With this expanded realm of media, domestically produced cinema faced severe challenges. Many audience surveys and studies of audience psychology were conducted by film journals and related organizations with an aim to attract audiences back to the theater.

The distribution and production of Chinese film in the 1980s was also going through profound changes. In 1984, the Ministry of Culture initiated systematic reforms, redefining the film industry as an independent self-financing enterprise.[39] This was a significant step in changing the nature of film studios and distribution units from state-subsidized departments to market-oriented economic units. However, even before the details of reforms were finalized, film studios already began to seek distribution channels by themselves, circumventing the official distribution departments. Some studios, in order to sell their films at a better price, reserved their films solely for domestic cinema fairs, which resulted in a shortage of films for regular theater screening. Although these reforms aimed toward "self-production and self-marketing" (*zichan zixiao*

自产自销) were suspended by 1985, theater attendance dropped drastically as a result.[40]

With these deep anxieties about the future of the Chinese film industry, some film and media critics related this crisis to a global "death of cinema." One critic, noticing a parallel crisis in the Western world, saw the rise of home media as a challenge to theater attendance:

> Since 1984, videocassettes of foreign films have flooded the Chinese market. Because of this "videocassette fever," many theaters actually stopped film screening and got involved in the videocassette business instead. This is no small shock to the film industry. What has happened in the Western countries is also taking place in our country. It still remains unknown as to where this decrease of film audience will ultimately take the industry. However, an accelerating sense of crisis, perplexity and urgency has seized the industry.[41]

But the critic still preserved hope, seeing the proliferation of other media forms as opportunities for cinema to expand itself. The role of regular theaters as a venue for film screening may have diminished, yet "bigger screen, widescreen, 3-D and panorama cinema" were "playing increasingly important roles that cannot be replaced by TV." The author continued to argue that the recent "videocassette fever" in China confirmed the demand for rather than the redundancy of domestic cinema production.

The relation and tension of cinema with other media forms was central to the media discourse. Zhou Chuanji, in a 1988 interview, vehemently called for the development of a media theory that treated cinema as one among many other information media. Only in this way, he argued, could we understand the cause for the shift of the audience from theatrical screening to television. This is because, according to Zhou, their means of communication are different: "Television broadcasts rely on high-frequency electromagnetic waves, their signals can cover at least 100 kilometers; whereas film screening depend on visible light, which cannot cover a distance longer than 100 meters. The disparity in the two types of electromagnetic waves defines the differences between film and television, and their disparate sizes of audience."[42] Writing in 1989, Zhou traced a long history of the competition between the film industry and other media industries, from early television broadcasts, to cable television, and VCR and home media players, as well as the most recent electronic games. Instead of viewing this history simply as the competition between old and new media, he reminded readers of the different social agents behind various media platforms. He saw the recent increase of low-end Hollywood movies in Chinese television programming as a strategy of Hollywood to dump its out-of-date products on the Chinese audience, with the purpose of cultivating an audience for Hollywood and thus establishing its future business dominance.[43]

Following Zhou's argument about social agents behind different media, we may also ask: Did this transformed mediascape also entail shifting power relations in postsocialist China? What was the role of intellectuals in this tide of commercialization of cultural production and media? Interestingly, the journal *Popular Cinema* (*Dazhong dianying* 大众电影) published a series of investigations into the conditions of film theaters in Shanghai, Guangzhou, and other big cities, with an aim to finding out what kind of films most appealed to audiences. Some voices criticized the elitist aesthetic of "experimental films" (*tansuo pian* 探索片), such as *Yellow Earth*, for "scaring" the audience away from theaters. At the same time, a revaluation of "entertainment films" (*yule pian* 娱乐片)—the appearance of this neologism indicating the transformed milieu of film production and consumption in post-Mao China—entered the intellectual discourse. Some critics adopted Freudian language to confirm the legitimacy of entertainment films:

> We all admit that a "complete" human being has his own emotions and desires.... Once satisfied, the person reaches a state of psychological balance and harmony, and he feels pleasure. However, civilization forbids individuals from pursuing their desires freely.... The suppressed libido has to find an outlet. Cinema and art is the kingdom of freedom for the suppressed undercurrents.
>
> We've seen the popularity of *Shaolin Temple* and *Huo Yuanjia*, as well as the unprecedentedly high box office of *Thirty Nine Steps*, *The Cassandra Crossing*, and *Le Grande Vadrouille*.... The audiences are willing to

immerse themselves into fictive stories, and imagine themselves in the darkness of the theaters to be handsome cowboys, brave warriors, judges of justice, and couples in love. They are willing to lose control for a while and let themselves be driven by the intensive plot, tension-ridden chase, fierce combats and scenes of horror, and then recover their psychological balance through a happy ending.[44]

This critic related the entertainment function of films to a humanistic discourse of desires, which implied an assessment of the "inhuman," didactic tradition of socialist realism, and, therefore, strategically justifies the value of entertainment cinema by aligning it with the humanistic critique of the Mao era since the late 1970s. The "healthy" entertainment films he listed above included a Hong Kong–produced martial arts movie and a television show, and several popular thrillers, many of which appear as found footage or objects of parody in *Flight of Fantasy*. The playful role-playing cinematic experience of the audience described in this passage is explicated as the very content and structure of *Flights of Fantasy*, indicating a close feedback loop between audience studies and film production.

Film critics also eagerly advocated the development of entertainment films as a remedy to the crisis of domestic cinema. In this view, tensions between entertainment and experimental films were transformed into other binary terms. In a symposium on entertainment movies held by the journal *Contemporary Cinema* in 1986, Chen Xihe, differentiating contemporary cinema from the previous tradition of "art as the vehicle of ethical didacticism" (*zaidao* 載道), emphasized the indispensability of the enjoyment that films provided to the highly stressed nature of modern life. He related this entertainment function of films to a new understanding of "humans" not only as rational beings but also as possessing emotions and feelings. It was the latter, he argued, that Chinese cultural traditions repressed.[45] Li Tuo concurred, believing that "entertainment culture could be a powerful counterforce to the feudalist tradition of China."[46] To open a space for entertainment films against the dominant tradition of realism, Chen further elaborated: while realist works often address the logic of rationality, entertainment films follow irrational emotions. It was the aesthetic effects of entertainment films on the audience, Chen emphasized, that differentiated them from realist works. Li Tuo also advanced the notion of the "game" as a distinctive aesthetic feature of entertainment film. According to him, "chase scenes and suspense, both of which can be considered as close to the nature of games, essentially countervail the principle of realism."[47] In this sense, entertainment films were justified by their effects on the sensorium and the body of the audience, against the didactic rule of socialist realism.

In another essay, Chen Xihe confirmed the value of entertainment films: "[they] directly intervene in human issues on the *experiential level*" and "reasonably satisfy the *sensorial pleasures* of a 'complete' human being."[48] This notion of "a 'complete' human being" was proposed against the Mao era hero or heroine who sacrifices his or her "human" desires for the grand purposes of revolution. The adoption of a humanist discourse to justify entertainment films created a discursive space for the surge in the production of entertainment films in the late 1980s. But this humanist discourse, deeply inflected by a liberal intellectual discourse, obscured the increasing pressure of marketization and the transformations of cinema in relation to the emergent information economy. While on the surface it reconciled the liberal intellectual pursuits with the commercialization of cultural production, the humanist discourse would soon expose its own poverty when the dislocation of intellectuals became more acute amid the drastically changing social milieu.[49]

The Nightmare of *Dislocation*

Directed by Huang Jianxin, *Dislocation* (*Cuowei* 错位) is a sequel to *Black Cannon Incident*. It continues the story of Zhao, who, now the head of his department and stifled by his obligation to attend endlessly boring and time-consuming meetings, conferences, and banquets, makes a robot after his own image and sends the robot to these occasions in his place. While Zhao hides himself in his apartment/home lab to conduct his own scientific research, his robot double, with data input by Zhao, becomes a social animal, busying himself/itself with routine talks, drinking, and performing social functions. However, the robot begins to develop his own feelings and personality, which diverge from Zhao's initial intentions.

Liminal Mediation and the Cinema Redefined   225

These conflicts are exacerbated when Zhao finds out that the robot has even been secretly dating Zhao's girlfriend. Finally, afraid of losing control of the robot, Zhao destroys his own double.

Following the lineage of freak scientists in the science fiction tradition from *Dr. Jekyll and Mr. Hyde* on, in *Dislocation*, the workaholic Zhao often shuts himself in his lab, ignoring telephone calls and any outside contact. In one scene, Zhao's head, severed from the rest of his body, is shockingly placed on the workbench. The head is sandwiched between a pair of black-rimmed glasses and tubes for lab tests on the bench, his eyes staring upward at the ceiling, as if disdainfully refusing to communicate with the gaze of the camera. Later, the camera reveals that Zhao, sitting in front of the bench, is working on several tangled wires—he is making the head of his robot double. Surrounded by computer monitors, electronic instruments, and integrated circuit plates, the absorbed Zhao turns away from the camera to face the monitor, undisturbed by the existence of the identical head.

Disembodied heads haunt the screen of the late 1980s, not only in the crime scenes that pervaded genre films produced by film studios now eager to entertain their audiences, but also in science fiction-cum-horror genres. *Mistaken Identity* (*Hechengren* 合成人, or literally "synthetic man"), a film made by the Changchun Film Studio in 1988, tells the story of a

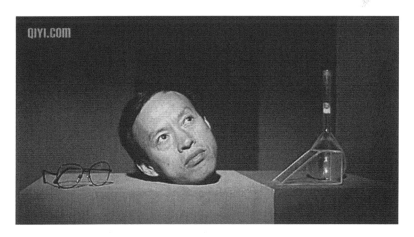

Figure 23. Disembodied head of Zhao. A still from *Dislocation*.

peasant's head being transplanted onto the body of the dying manager of a trade company. The human body is no longer considered to be an organic whole; rather, it is a set of parts that can be reassembled. In the 1989 film *A Beauty's Head in a Haunted House* (*Xiongzhai meirentou* 凶宅美人头), a freak scientist collects various heads in his lab and keeps them "alive" even though they are severed from their bodies. In order to obtain an ideal body for his experiments, he even plots murdering a dancing girl. Set in an isolated castlelike house, the film turns the lab, equipped with high-tech electronic devices, into a nightmarish site of horror.

This confusion between the organic and the mechanic, life forms and nonlife forms, reveals the deep uncertainties that lie beneath the understanding of human and life. What is humanity, after all, if human body parts can be dismantled and reassembled? What does it mean if a robot can be made to replace his/its human counterpart? What happens when human behaviors can be simulated through electronic and information technology? What if simulacra deny any origin, and simulation models cast aside any metaphysics of the real, as Baudrillard suggests?[50] In *Dislocation*, the human being and his double are often made to compete for "authenticity." In one scene, Zhao is putting his own watch onto the wrist of his robot double so that he/it can look exactly like him (Figure 24). However, from their identical images in the disconcerting scene, it is almost impossible to tell the two apart. The difference between a human being and a robot ironically rests upon the accessories they wear. The uncanny confusion between human beings and nonlife forms is replicated in other scenes: first in a sculpture gallery, the white, lifeless body of statues, shot in a series of montages, mimic human movements. Indeed, the art designer of the film intended to use live actors to play the lifeless sculptures of human forms.[51] Again, in a shopping mall, elegantly clad mannequins are posed in vivid human gestures and frozen in midmovement. Even more eerie is a moment in which the robot wanders aimlessly in the streets, staring at mannequins displayed in shop windows, as if to compete for "liveliness." In another scene, human actors are frozen into motionlessness and revealed to be no different from mannequins. The competition for authenticity does not affirm the real; it obliterates any difference between the real and its double.

Liminal Mediation and the Cinema Redefined 227

Figure 24. The uncanny double. A still from *Dislocation*.

This dislocation of human and nonhuman indicates the deep crisis underlying the very notion of "human." Zhao, subordinate to the bureaucratic machine, has no control over his own life and research. In continuity with the character in *Black Cannon Incident*, Zhao dares not raise his voice against the system. His robot double becomes the only means of silent resistance against a system of reification. On the surface, the director Huang Jianxin continues his critique in *Black Cannon* of the suppression of individual value and intellectuals by bureaucratic systems of the Party. Yet even after his liberation from his perfunctory obligation to attend boring meetings, Zhao is not more "human" than a frantic scientist who never has the time and patience to attend to the feelings and needs of people around him. By shifting his social responsibilities to the robot double, Zhao develops a specialization of labor: he focuses on intellectual research, while his robot double is tasked to maintaining social ties.

Once the cultivation and maintaining of social ties is relegated as a special form of labor, the intimacy of human relations becomes a professional performance. In contrast to Zhao's indifference to his girlfriend Yang, the robot behaves more like a lover toward her. The robot has learned how to perform like a lover by watching love films on videocassettes. Whether he has feelings toward Yang matters less than this performance of love behavior—it turns out that his simulation of a lover's behavior satisfies Yang more than the "real" Zhao does. Similarly, the difference between Zhao and the robot matters less than whether the robot functions smoothly to meet the expectations of performance at banquets and in conference rooms. Human affect and connections become a question of the operability of simulation models.

It is in this sense that the film captures the drastic dislocation of Chinese intellectuals and of their humanist discourse in the face of the intertwined processes of marketization and informationization. If the zany character in *Flights of Fantasy* capable of performing affective labor in varied situations introduces a new type of postsocialist subjectivity, *Dislocation* reveals the quandary of Chinese intellectuals between their humanist ideal and the demand of self-refashioning. Zhao eventually loses control of the robot whose zany performance displaces the existence of Zhao. In one shot, Zhao stares at his robotic double when talking to him, whereas on the wall there is a portrait in which he is looking in the opposite direction, as if there were another Zhao protesting the talking Zhao. This is followed by a countershot, in which another Zhao—the robot—with exactly the same solemn expression, looks back at the first Zhao. Here neither the portrait nor the robot image functions as a faithful representation of Zhao, but highlights the mediation or

Figure 25. Between different renditions of Zhao. A still from *Dislocation*.

externalization of Zhao at different interfaces with the other and the world, which in turn draws attention to the mediating role of cinema. The gaze and return gaze circulating between multiple renditions of Zhao eerily wind together, problematizing any association of the cinematic gaze with tenable subjective positions.

Images of Fluidity and Discrete Spaces

Instead of staging intense dramatic conflicts, the film conveys the deep tensions through the use of colors. As the cinematographer Wang Xinsheng explicates, the color design aims at "a radical experiment to break the balance of colors." Instead of graduated layers of colors, stark contrasts between red and blue, black and white, bright and dark, are used for conspicuous aesthetic effects. Linking the effects of color to the flow of psychological changes, he elaborates that red, blue, black, and white, all these colors "intersect and compete with each other, and disperse and disappear, along with the fluctuations of emotions," creating what he and the director call "a cloud of colors" (*secai tuan* 色彩团). The cloud never settles in one static state, and neither does the flow of emotions. While the colors are always mixed and nebulous, the "cloud" of emotions is not always distinctive and effable. In accordance, "the role of narration is reduced, and realistic design of the environment is avoided," so that the hallucinatory ambience fuses with emotions and feelings. Images stretch beyond the semantic level, for "a best approach to dreams," as Wang remarks, "should be sought in neither their content nor forms but instead through *the mutations of emotions* in the dreams."[52]

The film thus "frees itself completely from realistic conventions," as its art designer Qian Yunxuan affirms, to "create a mysterious, futurist ambience" that "breaks the boundary between the reality and the dream."[53] The film begins with just such a dream scene, in which Zhao, attired in a tight black suit, speaks agonizingly into a microphone. The camera zooms out, revealing him to be standing on a black podium, surrounded by oddly shaped sculptures. Instead of one microphone, a circle of microphones traps him inside. This red-lit space, divided by Cubist, geometrically irregular sculptures, is made more surrealistic by a bizarre, electronic pulsation on the soundtrack. As the sound accelerates into high-pitched hysterical squealing, snowflake-like documents fall from above, burying the panic-stricken Zhao in a white mountain of paper. A subsequent shot abruptly cuts to Zhao, buried under white bedcovers in a hospital, pulled by three black-robed men across a long, disturbingly white passage into an operating room, where Zhao's rigid, tiny body is laid among coldly shining scalpels and scissors, left to the ruthless hands of expressionless men. There is no logic or plot link between the two scenes, yet the white blankness of paper snowflakes and bedcovers are connected through a similar feeling of suffocation. The strong contrast between black and white, and bluish faces in red-tinged light, communicates an uncanniness, an intensity that envelops its audience into a nightmarish ambience through the defamiliarizing effects of sound and visual images.

Regarding cinema as "a form into which human thoughts and feelings take shape," the director Huang Jianxin mobilizes various elements of cinematic composition,[54] from colors and lighting to sound, as sensory stimuli on its audience, through the effects of which cinema becomes "a medium of communication."[55] This communication of thoughts and feelings relies less on concepts and words than on the ambience created by cinematic composition and the affective connection between images and audience. With this pursuit, every image breaks away from the gravity

Figure 26. The eerie opening scene. A still from *Dislocation*.

of realistic principle and follows the flows of psychological energy, as the cinematographer remarks:

> The composition might be balanced or imbalanced, but should always produce a shock. Movement of the images, as the basic feature of cinema, with its rhythm and regularity, and the relationship of one frame to another, should always follow the psychological trajectory, roaming along with the thought, and elicit a feeling of fluidity.[56]

Such fluidity defies the realistic principle of space-and-time coordinates, and thus cutting and editing between frames and scenes aims not at creating coherent space and time. Images roaming with thought in turn give thought a shock. Blurring the exterior and interior, the real and the fantastic, images jump across what Huang calls "discrete spaces."

In one scene, we are suddenly thrown with Zhao from his car into an airport terminal-like hall scattered with motionless human figures. Following the dream-walking Zhao out of the hall, we are soon engulfed in a golden desert that adjoins the high-modern architecture. Aimlessly wandering in the desert, Zhao is suddenly seized by blaring noises: amid the wilderness, a television set is emitting nonsensical foreign-language commercials. A close-up on the screen shows enlarged chewing mouths, swinging buttocks, and fragmented human bodies. A counter-shot reveals that in front of the television set sits an old scholar dressed in ancient Chinese attire, with an old-fashioned vertically printed book in hand. He stands up to turn off the television and recites to Zhao a quote from the ancient Daoist philosopher Laozi. The juxtaposition of discrete spaces from the modernist architectural space to the desolate desert, from the world of the vertical printed book and ancient philosopher to the consumerist, restless world of television commercials, demonstrates the effect of "irruption and accident" that Huang Jianxin pursues. The discrete spaces strung together also offer a metacomment on the experience of *asynchronous time and space* brought about by electronic media, especially television, as zapping among different television channels generates similar experiences of asynchronous time and space. The encounter with flows of television images is contingent and constantly mutable. Yet this

Figure 27. A television set in the desert. A still from *Dislocation*.

encounter is also a roaming of the thought when the sensory-motor linkage becomes loose, as Zhao acts little in response to the situation—neither his meditative silence in the car nor his aimless wandering in the wildness leads to any action of consequences. And the descriptions of the spaces are subordinate to the function of thought. The images, freed from linear causality, become questioning, puzzling, and probing. The screen therefore, in Deleuze's words, "constitutes a table of information, an opaque surface on which are inscribed 'data,' information replacing nature, and the brain-city, the third eye, replacing the eyes of nature."[57]

The film often draws our attention to the surfaces of various electronic devices: television screens, the displays of videocassette players, computer monitors, or the surface of some unknown futuristic devices (Figures 28–30). Abstract patterns on computer monitors often exceed the framing of the monitors and displays, overflowing to fill in the mise-en-scène, as if the cinematic screen now is not that different from a computer monitor. Placed at the interstices of scenes or sequences, these electronic patterns make the shift of scenes and settings as the change in patterns of information display. The camera, drawn to the nonanalogical images on monitors, pauses over the enigma of strange information patterns. If the electronic signals come from information circuits, the camera-mind also becomes part of the cybernetic loop.

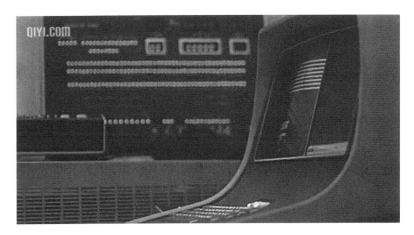

Figure 28. Abstract patterns on computer displays. A still from *Dislocation*.

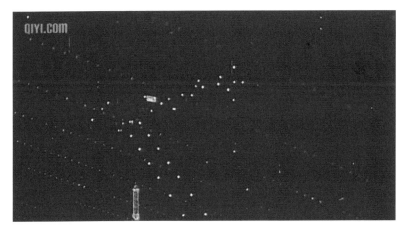

Figure 29. Abstract patterns of the city lights. A still from *Dislocation*.

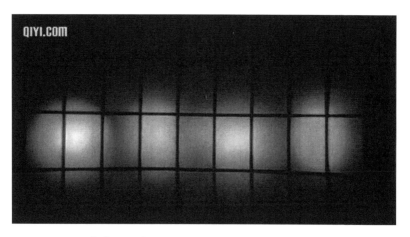

Figure 30. Signals from unknown sources. A still from *Dislocation*.

The Idea-Image as a Mode of Cinematic Aesthetic

The intersection of images, emotions, and thoughts and the indiscernibility between the exterior and the interior are not singular features of the film *Dislocation*, but were regarded as a distinctive mode of cinematic aesthetic by contemporary Chinese film theorists. Writing in 1986, Yao Xiaomeng argued that films such as *Yellow Earth* exposed the inadequacy of "realism" as a paradigm for the new developments in Chinese cinema, since they are irreducible to a simple "reduplication of the material world" and beyond the binary categorization of the montage aesthetics exemplified by the Hollywood and Soviet films and the long-shot aesthetic usually dubbed as "Bazinian realism." Converging with the rethinking of Bazin since the mid-1980s among Chinese film critics, Yao proposed the new cinematic aesthetic as a mode of "idea-image" (*yixiang* 意象).[58]

"Idea-image" is a term that derives from classical Chinese poetics. Although the formation of the term is closely related to early Confucian and Daoist views on the relationship between language, reality, and *Dao* (道, the way), its establishment as a poetic category is accomplished by two critics named Lu Ji (AD 261–303) and Liu Xie (AD 465–522). *Yi* 意 is a rich and ambiguous term, whose meaning shifts in different contexts and thus is not limited to a simplistic translation as an "idea." A superficial understanding may take *yi* as a conception to be expressed through an image (*xiang* 象). But a close reading of Lu's and Liu's critical works reveals a more complicated intertwinement of *yi* with emotions (*qing* 情), existing canons, and the formation of *xiang*. Lu Ji's *An Exposition on Literature* (*Wenfu* 文賦) depicts the mental process of literary creation as starting with the poet's emotional engagement with nature and sensitive responses to the shifting of seasons and changes of the universe. But the unmediated emotional response to external stimuli, as Zongqi Cai in his annotation of Lu's text points out, does not go directly into literary creation but has to be refined through the nourishment of classical canons.[59] This contemplation of emotions through the mediation of existing canons finally gives rise to *yi*, what Cai regards as an initial artistic conception. It is clear from this process that *yi* is neither an abstract concept or idea nor an unmediated, prediscursive affect. The existing forms of emotions from classical canons will "channel" or modulate the raw responses arising from stimuli, though the *yi* at this stage does not yet have a clear-cut form.

In order to develop the initial artistic conception into *yixiang*, both Lu and Liu proscribe a further-step contemplation, which borrows heavily from the Daoist practice of suspending all sense perception and emptying the mind that is close to a daimonic flight of spirit.[60] The flight frees the spirit of the poet from the constraints of time and space, which enables a refreshed encounter and experience of his spirit with both things and emotions, as Lu Ji describes: "Light gathers about moods (*qing* 情) and they grow in brightness; things (*wu* 物) become luminous and draw one another forward."[61] Zongqi Cai astutely reminds us that the *wu* (things) here are the insubstantial or virtual existence of objects that exist as images of mind, rather than real physical objects per se. Similarly, Liu Xie describes that the wandering spirit brings "the influx things from afar," creates a fusion of things and emotions through both perceptual and intellectual processes, and finally brings forth the "idea-image" (*yixiang*). Worth noting is that *yixiang* should be understood as an envisagement of the work-to-be, as Cai elucidates.[62] In other words, the work-to-be at this stage is an image work, rather than made of language and concepts, and more important, this idea-image has not been materialized and thus remains virtual. With this understanding of *yixiang* from classical Chinese poetics, Yao Xiaomeng's advancement of *yixiang* as a mode of cinematic aesthetic reshuffled the relation of cinematic images to objects, emotions, and thoughts. Yao elaborated on his argument:

> "Idea image" (*yixiang*) as an aesthetic category of a long history . . . is now under reconsideration as an artistic thinking mode in the circle of literary and art critics. The issue here is the unity of "thought-affect" (*yixu* 意绪) and "object images" (*wuxiang* 物象). In my opinion, *yixiang* is the qualitative transformation of the memory image into a creative imaginary image. . . . "Object images" are transformed by "thought-affect," whereas the actualization of "thought-affect" in a film relies on the accomplishment of image design. [In this sense,] the form has become the content *par excellence*. The cinematic "idea-image" is the perfect unity of the mind and the object, the emotions and the scene, and the thought and the image. . . . The cinematic aesthetic of "*yixiang*" is manifested in the first place as the governing of "images" by "*yi*." Such a deepening understanding of cinema is reached in the process of developing a critique of the Bazinian realism.[63]

The occasion for the renewed interest in *yixiang* Yao mentioned among the circle of literary and art critics was the resurfacing of the debate around image thinking (*xingxiang siwei* 形象思维) in the late 1970s and 1980s, which I discussed earlier in this chapter. In fact, this debate traveled beyond literature and art circles and captured the attention of Qian Xuesen. This scientist, intent on the development of artificial intelligence, was enthusiastic about the discussion on image thinking because he believed that the breakthrough of AI should be sought through an understanding of human thinking beyond logical deduction.[64] While the debate on image thinking in fact contended for the particularity of artistic creation and thus was not equivalent to or subject to the concepts of official Marxism, Qian argued for image thinking as a universal mode of thinking coexistent with logical thinking, and not necessarily restricted within the processes of artistic creation. A study of image thinking was indispensable to what he called "noetic science."[65] Qian's protégé, Yang Chunding, argued that *yixiang* was a basic unit for image thinking, and the relationship between *yi* and *xiang*, idea and image, was multifaceted, its transmission and effect relying on the deployment of artistic language.[66] Under this circumstance, *yixiang*, this term of classical poetics, engendered immense interest because it was seen as the best way to probe the secrets of artistic creation and image thinking. The reemergence of the term in the 1980s thus cut across both aesthetic debates and information sciences, and indicated the shift in political climate.

Several points can be ascertained from Yao's statement above:

First, similar to Lu Ji's and Liu Xie's understanding of the nature of objects in literary creation, Yao never defined the object-image as a replica of a real physical object. Instead, this object-image is saturated with emotions, sentiments, and thoughts, or what he called the "image in the heart" (*xinxiang* 心象) of filmmakers. Thus, the unfolding of time and space in cinema is "not so much about the development of the plot with the movement of object-images, but more about the continuous flows of thought-affect, to the extent that once the 'idea' is attained, the 'image' can be forgotten."[67] Yao here treated the image as a vehicle to communicate *yi*, its affective power more important than its references to objects and spaces.

Second, the effectiveness of communication of the image relies on the actualization of virtual images. This happens on both the filmmaker's and the audience's end. Filmmakers, not unlike the poet depicted by Lu and Liu, materialize their envisagement of work-to-be, or idea-image, into film signs—relying on what Yao called "the accomplishment of image design," which presumes no separation of the content and the form. The audience, on the other hand, draws from their memory images to turn the cinematic signs they encounter into their own images that are imbued with thought and emotions. With reference to Wead and Lellis, Yao proposed that "cinematic effects are indeed the creation of the audience, for it is the mind of the audience that creates cinematic movement, and gives deep-depth spatiality to the obviously two-dimensional images." Regarding the "idea-image" as "an imaginary image that is creatively developed from memory images," Yao argued that "a cinema of the idea-image mode" should not rely on dialogues and plot but instead on the combination of colors, lines, shapes (*zaoxing* 造型), sound and other elements of an image to create affectivity."[68]

But the emotions and feelings carried and invoked by idea-images are never unmediated and raw. Corresponding to Lu's and Liu's emphasis on the role of classical canons in nourishing and refining emotions, Yao called attention to the conventionality of cinematic signs. The 1980s witnessed the introduction of structuralism, semiotics and psychoanalysis into Chinese film studies, especially with American film scholar Nick Brown's visit and lectures in China. Saussure and Christian Metz were familiar names to Chinese critics. In his effort to negotiate between classical Chinese poetics and Western film theory, Yao saw the flows of *yixu* 意绪 as regulated by a deep structure of subconscious, which defies the constraints of time and space—an explanation he offered for discrete time and space in films. It is exactly this deep structure—not so much of myth, but more of collective social and cultural memories as evidenced by his use of the term "memory images"—and the conventionality of signs that make the communication from the filmmakers to the audience possible.

Finally, while acknowledging the conventionality of signs, Yao reserved the ambiguity and polysemousness of idea-images. Borrowing from classical poets terms such as "images beyond images" (*xiangwaizhixiang* 象外之象) and "ideas beyond images" (*xiangwaizhizhi* 象外之旨), Yao underscored that there would always be a tension between different forces inside a single shot and between different shots. This field of forces indicated that the "vitality" (*shen* 神) of a work extended beyond a simple replica of reality or a mechanical composition of different elements. This notion of "images beyond images" kept images open for varied paths of actualization. Yao thus reoriented the understanding of cinema toward the dynamics between the virtual and the actual and turned the Western semiotic and psychoanalytic critique of cinema into his theorization of a new cinematic mode—what he called "interpretative film." Not "seeing," but "interpretative," an intellectual process for understanding the world through signs that are simultaneously conventional and saturated with thoughts, sentiments, and feelings, signs that are in constant mutation in response to the changing environment. In this sense, cinematic images become the interfacing processes between the world and the human, and this interfacing goes beyond cinematic theaters and screening time.

So far we have seen that Yao Xiaomeng ingeniously developed a theory that not only addressed the new cinematic aesthetic that appeared since the mid-1980s but also offered a great insight on the affective power of cinema.[69] Yet, different from Western film scholars' recent articulations on this issue by Bergson, Yao never endorsed a realm of affect prior to and untouched by cultural discourses and conventions. Continuous with the richness of the *yi* of *yixiang* in classical Chinese poetics, the work of cinema on the audience is both perceptual and intellectual, involving thought, emotions, and bodily affect—yet neither emotions nor affect exists without the mediation of artistic conventions and cultural memories.

This also demands the competence of the audience to actualize cinematic images once the value of cinema shifts from a finished work of the filmmaker to the interpretative act of the audience. But when the audiences were increasingly surrounded by simulacra of no origin and of no history, what memories and cultural traditions could they draw from to accomplish this interpretative act?

Visions without Memories

Visions from a Jail Cell (*Moku zhongde huanxiang* 魔窟中的幻想), made in 1986, provides a precarious vision when memories and history are abruptly cut off. The film focuses on the longing of an eight-year-old boy for the world outside the high walls of a jail cell, in which he is confined with his mother as a "political prisoner." The boy on whom the story is based, nicknamed "Little Radish Head" (*Xiao luobotou* 小萝卜头), was called Song Zhengzhong in real life. The son of a Communist Party couple persecuted by the KMT, he was born in a jail cell. He became part of the Chinese Communist Party myth as a character and a revolutionary martyr in the novel *Red Cliff* (*Hongyan* 红岩). But the director Wang Jixing self-consciously distinguished his work from previous revolutionary narratives, as he remarked: "Who is the 'Little Radish Head'? He is neither Song Zhengzhong in real life, nor 'the youngest revolutionary martyr to sacrifice his life to the revolution' (as the official story goes). He is an ordinary, innocent life, who suffers extremely inhuman conditions in a Fascist prison."[70] Deliberately eschewing official narratives of revolution, Wang creates a generalized allegory of entrapment and freedom.

These transformations can be observed in the camerawork of the film. In one scene, when all the prisoners and warders are staged in a face-to-face confrontation, suddenly the little boy exclaims "butterfly!" The horizontal movement of shot and counter-shot between the two confrontational sides is subsequently replaced by an upward movement. Everyone, including the warders, looks toward the sky, at the butterfly fluttering across the high walls. The confrontational scene, well suited

Figure 31. The "butterfly effect." A still from *Visions from a Jail Cell*.

for staging the class struggle in a revolutionary story, is transcended by a moment of shared longing for liberty; a sequence of shot and reverse shot is replaced by the vertical movement of the camera.[71]

The vertical movement of the camera establishes the unique spatiality of the film. Contrary to the endlessly unfolding space in *Flights of Fantasy*, the restrictive high walls allow little space for the camera to explore. The camera is thus forced to move vertically in order to enlarge its horizon. The opening sequences begin with a close-up of a slowly crawling insect, which in a moment the camera reveals to be confined in a small matchbox. In the next shot, the camera continues to pull up, revealing a boy kneeling next to the matchbox, observing the insect. The camera moves up continuously to a high angle until it reveals the boy now as a tiny black dot confined in a high-walled courtyard, just like the insect in the matchbox. What the boy sees is a mirror image of himself. These shots call attention to the limits of vision framed by the camera. The word "vision" here is twofold: it refers to the visual perception of the world, but also, in accordance with the Chinese title *"huanxiang"* 幻想, to the formation of a view of the world in one's mind. The rest of the movie revolves around the possibility of a vision, and the mediality of cinema is placed at the center of this epistemological issue.

It is not hard to see that the jail cell in this movie is a rootless and timeless space. The director's deliberate dilution of historical details detaches the cell from temporal and spatial specifics. In this sense, the boy who was born and grows up in this closed system has no memories of the world outside the cell, nor does the passage of time have any impact on him. Staying out of historical time and cut off from cultural memories, the boy is never able to conjure up a vision of the world through the signifiers his teachers pass on to him. Several elder prisoners volunteer to teach him to read and write, in the hope that education will enable the boy to transcend the narrow cage. But the words and the characters he receives are just empty signifiers without the signifieds: a "horse" is no different from a "cow," and a "hill" and a "tree" to him are just signs without an origin. As he never sees a cow or a hill with his eyes, the words are just fragments, segmented from cultural traditions, and simulacra of the world that mask the absence of reality.

Figure 32. The prisonlike schoolyard, city, and street. Stills from *Visions from a Jail Cell*.

The visions the boy formulates become a short circuit of the floating signifiers and what he sees in the prison. In his dreams, the playground of a school is identical to the narrow yard of the prison, the city gate with a gigantic lock resembles the gate of the prison, and the houses along the street look exactly like little jail cells (Figure 32). The images of the film also become a closed system, generating simulacra of themselves, and simulacra of simulacra—the film becomes a self-reproductive machine with no reference to the external world.

Ironically, a failure of communication also haunted the reception of the film. A reviewer, casting the film as a children's film—probably because of its child protagonist—criticized it harshly for being too bleak and obscure: "Its cinematic design, ranging from the setting to the use of colors and others, does not simply present characters and things as they are. They become symbolic images. . . . However, are these images accessible to its children's audience? Enigmatic images pervade the whole film. . . . Even the adult audience will find the film hard to digest, let alone children. It would be unbearable to its young audience."[72]

This impossibility of cultivating a relevant vision of the world suggests a crisis in the diverging roles of media and cinema. While Yao Xiaomeng and other film critics entrusted an emancipatory potential and an affective power to cinema, the images and signs filmmakers dispatched did not necessarily generate the audience's interpretative acts when this audience was increasingly immersed in various simulacra of a commercial culture. In other words, film critics insisted upon film viewing as an intellectual process, whereas the marketization of cultural production carried film spectatorship toward sensorial stimuli and simulacra with no origins. This tension between different directions and understandings of cinema always erupted in film works of the late 1980s as an ambiguity toward the cinematic medium itself. Cinema became a haunted medium torn between different worlds.

Haunted Medium: The Liminality of Mediation

As the interrogation of cinema's relations to thought, affect, and memory in the 1980s radically reopened cinematic images to new dynamics between the actual and the virtual, the communicative efficacy of cinema went far beyond the visible. The cinematic medium was thus turned into a haunted site where the absent always accompanies the present and the visible indicates the invisible. Different from the mode of mediation given by cybernetics and information theory, which assumes communication between two points within a single, shared reality, haunted media suggests the coexistence of different epistemologies and realities.[73] To borrow Eugene Thacker's description of what he calls "dark media," haunted media "establishes a connection between two different ontological orders"—whether it is between natural and supernatural, earthly and divine, or life and afterlife.[74] In this sense, the cinematic medium mediates the invisible and the incommunicable, which in turn problematizes the notion of "communication" per se. This was further complicated by the fast-changing roles of cinema from a political and educational facility to an entertainment industry. Cinema as a medium could not be more ambiguous amid the competing and intertwined forces of state power, intellectual discourse, marketization, and audience expectation, to the extent that the self-references of the medium often dissolve its own communication efficacy in its ambivalent swing among different forces.

The film "haunted" by such contradictions of mediation is *The Lonely Spirit in a Dark Building* (*Heilou guhun* 黑楼孤魂), codirected by Liang Ming and Mu Deyuan and released in 1989. The film not only self-consciously reflects on the repositioning of cinema in the transformed social and media environments, but it also can be regarded as, I argue, a practice to theorize the liminality of mediation. By placing the process of filmmaking inside the film, the film develops an understanding of cinema, rather than simply as "one" medium, but as modes of mediation that bestride boundaries.

As the title indicates, the film is set in a desolate building that is soon to be torn down in the tides of urbanization of the late 1980s. The building happens to be a residential building for the staff of a state-owned film studio. One day, Huo Feng, the sound engineer of a film crew, unsatisfied with the outcome of on-location recording, takes the leading actress, Yu Hong, to this building for the purpose of recording some sound effects. Incidentally, his recorder captures some eerie sounds of unidentifiable source. Yu Hong, allegedly possessing extrasensory powers, claims to see a little girl in the basement of the building, even though the basement has been vacant and locked for almost ten years. Determined to find out the secret buried in this haunted building, Huo Feng breaks into the basement, only to find at the end of the long, dark passage an apartment with traces buried under the dust of the people who had lived there before. A series of bizarre incidents continue to happen in the building, causing the death of two other residents. Tracking down all sources of information, Huo starts to gather fragmentary information about the basement apartment: the residents of the apartment were a family of three. During the Cultural Revolution, the father was sentenced to death after the suicide of the humiliated mother. Before his death, the father left his only daughter, named Xiaoju, and all his savings to the care of his best friend. But not long after that, the girl was curiously hanged to death in that apartment. The cause of her death remains unclear, with the case finally closed as a suicide.

Suspicious that there is something wrong with this case, Huo Feng decides that the eerie sounds come from the ghost spirit of the little girl, whose manner of death is unclear. In one scene, Huo pulls out his sound recorder, holding in his hands a long shotgun microphone, as if he were a cowboy about to fight for justice. Equipped with a powerful sound sensor, he goes down to the basement, pointing his "gun" in the air and telling the ghost: "Xiaoju, tell me what you want to say, I am listening!" (Figure 33). Up to this point, the film invokes a tradition from *The Conversation* by Francis Ford Coppola (1974) to *Blow Out* by Brian De Palma (1981), which features the use of sound equipment as an investigation into the "real," or what Fredric Jameson calls "the conspiratorial allegory of late capitalist totality."[75] Sound recording in this film tradition becomes a site for preserving the ultimate truth, an infallible tool of documentation and exposure.

However, the film invokes this tradition only to disavow the testimony of the sound recorder, because what Huo's recorder captures are just indecipherable noises. However powerful his equipment is, there persists the threshold of communication, which raises questions concerning the ethics of communicability: What can be communicated and

Liminal Mediation and the Cinema Redefined   247

Figure 33. Huo's shotgun microphone. Stills from *The Lonely Spirit in a Dark Building*.

in whose language? In this sense, noises reveal the very limit for the mode of communication that assumes equal parties of rational human subjects.

In the film, Xiaoju's own story never comes through as legible information. It is filtered as nonsensical gibberish, nonsensical not only because of the line separating humans and ghosts, but also because Xiaoju was a child who never mastered an adult language. The cries of children are often dismissed as silly gibberish, and thus children and ghosts are similarly excluded from the realm of human rationality. Huo Feng's self-appointment as the voice representing Xiaoju fulfills the enlightenment schema that only a mature man can objectively state the truth and establish justice. But the impenetrability of the gibberish noises on his recorder exposes the coding process inherent to any production of "truth." The persistence of noises indicates the unassimilability of Xiaoju's voice into his version of truth.

If the microphone fails to "record" intelligible sounds, the camera is neither useful in capturing any visible evidence of the spirit. Xiaoju's spirit never materializes into a perceptible shape in front of the camera. Eventually, it is Yu Hong's extrasensory powers that enable her to "see" the past as psychic images: the murderer of Xiaoju is no one but her father's best friend, the director named Zheng Lei, with whom Huo Feng and Yu Hong are collaborating in making a film that boasts realistic long takes and on-location sound recording. In one scene at the shooting location, the director Zheng is lost in thoughts about his illegal deal with an antiquity smuggler so that he forgets to say "cut." This inadvertently produces an extremely long take, which, ironically, is commended for its "innovative" and "profound" camerawork. This reference about the "birth" of a long take becomes a black-humor mockery of the abuse of long takes in filmmaking, which is the stylist mark of earlier "exploratory films." The ironic juxtaposition of the realist pursuit of the film-within-the film with the "avisual" invokes reflections on the nature of cinematic images and questions the representational capacity of the medium: What are beyond the scope of the camera and the microphone? The "avisual" resistant to the mechanic eye of the camera disrupts the economy of visuality and its role in producing "reality."[76]

Yet the film's interrogation of the medium does not stop simply on the level of disavowal, precisely because the unrepresentable has to be acknowledged by the cinematic medium. It is the shotgun microphone and the Nagra IV-S recorder that capture the sounds beyond the range of everyday hearing, while the audio electronics such as amplifiers and headphones enable Huo to hear the otherwise imperceptible sounds. In one scene, we see Huo Feng trying repeatedly to tune his devices in order to hear more, and more. In this sense, it is not that the medium is inadequate; it is too sensitive to the extent that it provides more than what is expected.[77] The contingent mediation brings in what is beyond expectation. On the shooting location, the director Zheng sits in front of a set of audio recording devices, wearing a pair of headphones to oversee the sound production. He, however, accidently overhears through the microphone Huo Feng and Yu Hong's secret conversation at the other end of the room. As he focuses all his attention on what they are saying, banging sounds on-location, casual chatting sounds of other staff also fill in the channel, in competition with the sounds that Zheng is dying to comprehend at this moment. The conversation is transmitted through a sound boom held by a sound engineer who happens to stand in an attic right above Huo and Yu. As the engineer casually swings the boom when chatting with a coworker, the conversation of Huo and Yu is transmitted on and off to Zheng's headphone. The profusion of sounds almost drowns the channel with noises. Never intended to be listened to, the conversation between Yu and Huo is merely noise to other people, yet incidentally it becomes key information to Zheng. The unexpectedness accompanies the "excess" of the medium, and the aleatory formation of "information" is also subject to the precariousness of mediation. However, it is this precariousness of mediation that reveals the liminality of the medium at the interface of different epistemologies, realities, and temporalities.

This liminality of mediation is demonstrated by the recorder, which exceeds the simple function of "recording" in the sense of registering what has happened in the past. This notion of recording is tied to an irreversible, linear temporality, and thus testifies to an incident in the past, the singularity of one ironclad reality. For example, in Brian De Palma's *Blow Out*, what has happened is already there, registered by the tapes, only waiting to be rediscovered. Yet *The Lonely Spirit* defies such a logic of recording, because there is nothing left on the tape as the trace of the past. Even more curious, the recorder invokes a different temporality: What if the recorder "records" something to happen in the future? This is what the Nagra IV-S recorder does in the film. Every time before the ghost punishes a concealed criminal who has in the past taken advantages of her family, the Nagra IV-S recorder plays the "soundtrack" of the process of vengeance: the criminal being lured by the illusion of an acquaintance's call into a trap, his panic screaming upon death, and so on. A recorder that "records" sounds of the future troubles the linear temporality and becomes a haunted medium of different worlds—human and nonhuman, life and afterlife, and a liminal site of competing worldviews, value system, and modes of justice. This competition of different views and modes of justice becomes viscerally inscribed onto the body of Huo Feng—when he tries to stop the ghost from taking revenge, he is attacked by an electric shock passing through the headphones, his ears bleeding with flesh cut open, as if being forced open to the way in which he has refused to hear (Figure 34).

At the intersection of different worldviews and value systems, the signification of the haunted media become ambiguous and diffusive. In the film, sound equipment is ostentatiously displayed as an object of curiosity. Huo Feng's shotgun microphone, his sound amplifier and headphones, and his Nagra IV-S recorder, all of these are presented in

Figure 34. Revenge through sound. A still from *The Lonely Spirit in a Dark Building*.

constant close-up shots and exude an aura of technological superiority (Figure 35). To a certain degree, the devices are masculinized. In the scene where Huo pulls out his shotgun microphone and walks down to the basement, Richard Strauss's tone poem *Also Sprach Zarathustra* rises from the soundtrack, reminding its audience of the epic opening of Stanley Kubrick's *2001: A Space Odyssey*. Huo's daring adventure in the basement becomes analogous to a voyage into outer space to explore the unknown. The devices are attributed with a sense of sublimity, accompanying Huo's heroic explorations into nonhuman realms. Yet, in other scenes, the display of the sleek-looking devices takes place in Huo's simple but cozy and modernly equipped apartment. In one scene, Huo pours himself a glass of foreign wine, adds several ice cubes from his refrigerator—which was still a luxury home appliance to ordinary consumers in 1980s China—and throws himself onto a couch before he puts on the headphones, as if to say the sound experience provided by his devices is just as sensuous as the wine with ice (Figure 36). The framing of the devices in a private living space rather than in public space indicates an emergent consumer culture in post-Mao China that domesticates the audio electronics for private consumption. The sublime and the quotidian, the unknown and the domestic, these contradictions cloud the devices with uncertainties and ambiguities. There is always more about them, more than what can be neatly incorporated into one singular epistemological and ethical order.

Indeed, since the early 1980s, film sound had become a concentrated concern of both filmmakers and critics. *Wild Mountain* (*Yeshan* 野山, directed by Yan Xueshu), made in 1985, was the first film that adopted synchronous on-location sound recording after the Cultural Revolution. The film won the Golden Rooster award of that year for its groundbreaking experiment in sound recording. According to Tao Jing, the sound designer and engineer of *The Lonely Spirit*, on-location sound recording became indispensable to a new aesthetic and cinematic authenticity around the turn of 1980s when he was studying at Beijing Film Academy. When collaborating with Chen Kaige in the shooting of *King of the Children* (1987), Tao himself experimented with using synchronous on-location sound recording to replicate the spatiality of the place.[78] In other

Figure 35. The shining Nagra IV-S recorder. A still from *The Lonely Spirit in a Dark Building*.

Figure 36. Wine and headphones. A still from *The Lonely Spirit in a Dark Building*.

words, on-location sounds were associated with the new-wave "exploratory cinema" and the intellectual ambitions of artistic innovation and authenticity.

However, this was also a time when sound and new sound technologies were commercialized as a new selling point. In the same year as *Wild Mountain*'s release, the Grand Theater (*Da guangming dianyingyuan* 大光明电影院) in Shanghai adopted imported Dolby Stereo systems for the screening of a Hollywood science fiction film, *Superman III*. Film sound became a new attraction to lure audiences back into film theaters when attendance was suffering a drastic decline. Obviously well aware of these developments, *Lonely Spirit* advertised itself as a film made with Dolby Stereo technology, which was newly available in post-Mao China. This selling of stereo sound is also embedded inside the film, with repeated close-ups on the Nagra IV-S recorder, a new generation of the famous portable professional audio recorder, which features two-track stereo and was thus marketed as Stereo Nagra. The shots of the recorder even clearly display the words "Nagra IV-S recorder" on the shiny surface of the device, almost like a product placement of the recorder.

The Lonely Spirit pulls together this constellation of different forces, invoking a dialogue with the new aesthetic pursuit by new-wave directors such as Chen Kaige, but also addressing the fast commercialization of filmmaking. The first film made with private funding in post-Mao China, with the investment from a township entrepreneur, *The Lonely Spirit* was also among the first movies rated as "unfit for children" after the implementation of a rudimentary rating system in May 1989. This rating system divided films into only two categories: the ordinary and the ones "unfit for children." But the system was soon aborted, partly because the label of "unfit for children" ironically became a best promotion for films to attract curious audiences. A huge commercial success with a box-office five times of its investment, *The Lonely Spirit*, however, was banned from public screening not long after its release, because a woman in Beijing allegedly died of heart attack during the screening of the film. This incident uncannily resembled Ma-Xu Weibang's planting of a false story about a girl's death for the promotion of *Song at Midnight* more than fifty years ago.[79]

Figure 37. Ensnared by a haunted audiotape. A still from *The Lonely Spirit in a Dark Building*.

In the final scenes of the film, the director is trapped in a high-speed car by a reel of a haunted audiotape, his body ensnared in entangled tape stripes (Figure 37). What would be a better image than this for filmmakers who were struggling in the whirlpool of contradictions, divided between their enlightenment ambitions and the frenzy of commercialization and an emergent consumer culture in 1980s China? The film provides the best elaboration on the liminality of precarious mediation at the threshold of drastic historical, technological, and ethical change.

EPILOGUE

The Virtual Past(s) of the Future(s)

From the late 1980s on, China began actively to seek to connect local networks to the burgeoning international network of the World Wide Web. In 1989, the China Research Net (CRN) was set up, linking research institutes in Beijing, Chengdu, Shijiazhuang, Shanghai, and Nanjing, allowing them the use of email and indirect links to the internet. Full internet connectivity was achieved in 1994. By 2012 there were 564 million internet users in China, among which 420 million had access to broadband internet services.[1] Various online forums and activities became an integral part of contemporary life and culture in China. Testifying to this new socioeconomic phenomenon, Shanda Interactive Entertainment Limited, one of China's largest purveyors of online games, internet literature, and book publications was listed on the NASDAQ stock exchange in 2004. Its internet literature websites, including the popular platform for aspiring writers, *Qidian*, developed a system that recruited talents from its mass users, which challenged the prerogatives of the book publishing industry and rapidly changed the scene of cultural production and consumption in contemporary China. Shanda is just the most successful of many emergent operators who were tapping into the market of online literature and cross-media cultural economy.

In 2006, Jin Hezai 今何在 (an internet writer whose pen name is Zeng Yu and whose *nom-de-plume* literally means "whereabout now") started serializing the second installment of a fantasy story entitled "Youth,

Chinese-style" (*Zhongguoshi qingchun* 中国式青春) on his blog. Born in the post-Mao late 1970s, Jin Hezai is known for his novel that he adapted from Stephen Chow's film series *Chinese Odysseus* (*Dahua xiyou* 大话西游), which itself is an adaptation from the classic vernacular fiction *Journey to the West*. He later became a high-level manager of the Jiuzhou Fantasy Media and Culture Company. Set in the 1980s, the story "Youth, Chinese-style" is about a six-year-old boy named He Jing, who is told by his mother that he is destined to be the savior of humanity in a future world dominated by robots and the internet. The empire of robots, in order to nip in the bud any human rebellion against its dominion, has sent back from the future world a robot to kill our hero—the future leader of the insurgency—before he can grow up. This story becomes a running joke among his classmates, especially when it becomes known that his mother has been institutionalized for mental illness. Yet one day a little girl named Yue Xiaoshan claims herself to be a robot terminator, proclaiming to her classmates that her mission is to end the life of He Jing. A rewriting of the 1984 Hollywood sci-fi film *Terminator*, the story deliberately sets up a temporal "strange loop," in which the cause-and-effect linearity between the present and the future is disrupted. The effect is heightened when the boy is told that his father was sent back alone from the future as his bodyguard and met his mother in the process of fighting against the robot terminators. Their accidental encounter, in turn, led to the birth of our protagonist, that is, the future leader of the rebels. Such nonlogical logic conflates the present and the future, setting the future-oriented adults surrounding the boy for ridicule as they insist on convincing the boy to prepare for a future that is allegedly already cast in stone. These responsible adults, who zealously claim to devote themselves to the cause of humanity, are revealed as being no different than task-oriented robots in their lack of free will.

The task that his instructor from the future assigns He Jing is simple: to kill the seemingly harmless girl Yue Xiaoshan, who claims to be the terminator. He Jing, incredulous, asks his terminator when she plans to kill him. Yue Xiaoshan replies without any hesitation that she is programmed to kill him on the very day that he becomes the savior. The problem is that the boy can only become the savior on the day he is to kill the terminator. Tortured by this convoluted logic, our hero loses himself in these irreconcilably strange loops:

> My brain starts running fast in order to compute the strange loops. If I don't kill Yue Xiaoshan, she won't kill me and thus she won't become the terminator. If she doesn't become the terminator, why should I kill her? If I don't kill her, I won't become the savior and thus the world is doomed to come to an end. So I have to kill her. But if I kill her, I will become the savior, and then the world is doomed to be destroyed—otherwise, how would I become the savior? If the world is doomed, that's because of the Sky Net [Sky Net is the fictive prototype of the internet in the story]. So I have to get rid of the Sky Net. But if I destroy the Sky Net, the world will continue as it is now, and then I will have to continue to go to high school and on to college, to look for a job, to marry some woman and raise a kid, and then send the boy to high school and college, and then he will have to find a job, marry some woman and raise a kid of his own.... In short, I won't become a savior. If I don't become a savior, Yue Xiaoshan will remain here. And as long as she is here, the Sky Net will continue working, and the world will be doomed to come to an end. So to prevent the end of the world, I must kill Yue Xiaoshan. But once I kill her, she becomes the terminator, and I the savior.

Trapped in the strange loops of procedures no matter what he chooses to do, it seems that everything about the boy's life has been preprogrammed, albeit by way of a ridiculous and redundant computational logic. This preprogrammed future does not resemble in the least the brilliant, utopian future prescribed by Alvin Toffler and others. Ironically, Yue Xiaoshan's home address in the realm of the future is registered as "Luck and Beauty Street in Brilliance New Village." Yet following her home one day after school, He Jing discovers that the future is but a wasteland "no different from the ruins left by a gigantic earthquake hundreds of years ago, in which everything solid is disintegrating into ashes, a pall of gray-white ashes that covers the earth." This bleak future, ironically, is precisely the result of the idealistic desire to "save" the world through preprogrammed actions that He Jing had been taught by the adults. For at the very moment that He Jing kills Yue Xiaoshan, the Sky Net is activated, forming a sprawling network that takes control of every machine and turns them into weapons of a frenzied mass destruction. The moment he becomes the savior, then, is also the moment when the future itself ends, and the world is trapped in a permanently recursive hell. As He Jing witnesses the destruction of the world he has unwittingly initiated by killing Yue Xiaoshan, a building falls into ruin in front of him, "leaving only a few flights of a staircase on leveled ground, like an origami sculpture (that could fall anytime)." This staircase that goes nowhere spatializes a temporality that does not flow forward, but is instead trapped in continuous repetition.

Such a narrative of the future by no means resembles the futuristic imaginations of a coming information society as envisioned by Alvin Toffler and propagated by the official ideology, which assumed the advancement of science and technology as the single most important driving force for social progress and linear development. The information fantasies fade out, and the anxieties and unsettled indeterminacy associated with information and cybernetic technology in the science fiction stories of the 1980s now drown out any utopian optimism, leaving a doomed sense of temporality that goes nowhere, as well as an antagonistic opposition between machines and networks and humans. Yet, the war humanity wages against the networked machines shows no promise for the end of their enslavement, as they are trapped in the endless recursive structure of strange loops. The strange loops, no longer tied to the "backwardness" of Chinese culture and the "persistence of feudalism" in China as understood in the intellectual discourse of the 1980s, now appear as the very logic of computational programmability: every being in the story is entangled in loops of programmed temporality. The terminator Yue Xiaoshan, for instance, is programmed for a single purpose: to kill the future savior. Strangely enough, the wicked robot terminator is not so different from an ordinary human girl, who is always a victim of He Jing's pranks, and lives a regulated life as other school girls do. Her everyday life is programmed as a repetitive round of going to school, going "home" to a windowless, dilapidated building, and doing assigned homework. Her human enemies live no better, as they are similarly "programmed" to "go to high school and college, marry some woman and raise a kid." Life is subsumed into the programmability of these strange loops. Even "leisure" time is organized around programs, for the sole hobby of the task-oriented Yue Xiaoshan is programmed to watch *Hana no Ko Lunlun* (The flower child Lunlun), a 1980s Japanese anime broadcast on television, on a precise schedule every day.

Here the story calls attention to the role of media technologies, especially television—the most powerful "new media" information platform in the 1980s—in inscribing into the body a temporality of programmability. The recursion is inscribed into the body per se, now attuned to the rhythm of a highly mediated society. The body becomes a cybernetic body that is integrated into ceaseless information flows. If, as I discussed in chapter 3, recursion is hardly a hard-wired neurological feature or a particular cultural trait of a "backward" society, but rather is inextricably tied to modernization and bureaucratization, here in the story the temporality of strange loops indicates the further pervasiveness of this recursion into everyday life in the form of algorithmic computation. Yet humans are in no way external to this algorithmic dominance, for their very strategy of resistance and mode of social organization, as shown in the story, are already penetrated with algorithmic logic, to the extent that even their proclaimed opposition to the machines becomes destabilized and problematic. While the discussion of "recursive structure" and "ultrastable system" of the 1980s was tied to a developmentalist discourse that posited science and technology, particularly information technology, as the remedy for "backwardness" and "stagnancy," now with the high-speed economic growth in China in the past decades, this temporality of recursion and stagnancy, ironically, grips even more tightly the everyday experience of the "net-born generation" (*wangshengdai* 网生代). Growing up under the "information fantasies" and witnessing China's ensuing drastic changes, Jin Hezai and his fellows, who are probably stuck in front of their computers and chained to their digital devices daily, no longer regard information technologies as a sublime object, nor as a liberating force that would free people from labor. Rather, the internet and digital devices have become the media environment, the habitat for their daily life, and the very realm where their work and life, labor and play, become interpenetrated and indistinguishable from each other.

An entrepreneur of the digital/information economy, Jin Hezai successfully reinvented himself from a fan/consumer of popular media culture and an amateur writer to a best-selling internet writer, game developer, screenwriter, and high-level executive of a media corporation. Mixing the theme of bildungsroman with science fiction and fantasy genres, his internet writings and creations resonate with his followers particularly for their evocation of common experience and sentiments based on shared references to popular media culture, which demonstrates again, as we have seen in the earlier moments of marketization of the 1980s, the intertwinement of affect and market in the information economy. To an extent, it is not exaggerating to say that the rapidly expanding digital economy today is operating precisely with enormous affective investment and power, which recycles previous media culture for renewed affective connections.

In fact, the whole story of "Youth, Chinese Style" is made up of pastiches of popular cultural references: the Hollywood blockbuster *Terminator* (1984); *Kyōryū Sentai Koseidon* (Dinosaur Corps Koseidon), a Japanese science fiction TV series that was made in 1978 and attracted fandoms among youths in mainland China especially for its eye-dazzling special effects; *Transformers*, a cartoon franchise coproduced by Japanese and American toy companies; *Paprika* (2006), a Japanese science fiction anime film directed by Satoshi Kon and based on a 1993 eponymous novel; as well as stories by Zheng Wenguang, Ye Yonglie, and other sci-fi writers active in the 1980s. The recursive structure thus established between the present and the future resembles that of *Chinese Odysseus*, a series directed by Stephen Chow, the films for which the author Jin Hezai proves his fandom by his own act of novelization. In other words, not only the narrative, but the very production of the story as well, is caught in the repetitious cycle of multimedia networked popular culture, a culture in which consumers have come to play the roles of disseminators and producers, and work and play to continuously recycle cultural icons and generate affective connections.

Curiously, with such an array of references to popular culture of the 1980s, postsocialist histories and politics are absent in the story, and even its theme of "resistance" and "revolution" appears deflated and dehistoricized. Reduced to a simplistic opposition between humans and machines, the struggle against "enslavement" becomes an aimless and hopeless battle, guided by no explicit political vision or strategy. The absence of socialist histories and memories symptomatically underlines the postsocialist politics of depoliticization in the understanding and imaginations of information technology. The brutality of information capitalism is presented as the conquering of humans by machines, although such an opposition is latently problematized in the story. This simplification of social contradictions as the competition between different species and the struggle between humans and nonhumans is a common symptom of science fiction narrative that explores the anxiety over the ubiquity of information technologies. Missing from this antagonistic scenario are specific human relations that mediate and are mediated by information technologies. However, despite the absence of socialist histories in the story, it is precisely the almost trivial details in its depiction of human relations and the materiality of everyday life, from the setting of public education and public school to schoolteacher Xiaochu's *Danwei* 单位 ("socialist work-unit-style") dormitory, that indicate the faded but indelible memories of socialist experiences.

Such lived experience of late socialist China of the 1980s is transformed in the story into a nostalgia for the bygone times when technology has not yet turned into a devilish power against humans. The story ends with He Jing, now the leader of humanity's rebellion against the robots, engaging in a series of endless, desperate battles against the machines. In this "gloomy and silent future" dominated by the internet and robots, He Jing harks back to a past in which Sky Net was still a crude nothing, a toy for a good-for-nothing little boy.

> I bend down to have my ears closer to that thing, and one moment later, I hear the rustling sound of electric currents.
> I become excited instantly, continuing to twist the buttons around.
> Then I heard some incredible sounds emitted by the gadget, its rhythm as punctual as a time-keeper.

This is Sky Net One, a "failed" internet project made by the little boy. Of no other use, Sky Net One is pressed into service as a toy radio. It is eventually replaced by a more ambitious project—Sky Net Two:

Wires, bulbs, and electrodes are like moss sprawling across the whole wall now. Everyday Xiaochu has to lower her head to get through the net of wires, carefully crossing the minefield formed of electrical resistance, then tiptoeing among the electric circuits as if she is doing rubber band skipping, and finally jumping into bed. But she doesn't stop my experiments. As the weather gets cold, the wires beneath the bed serve to heat the bed like an electric blanket.

This scene, set in the schoolteacher Xiaochu's dormitory, comically exposes the materiality of the network. With the rustling sound of electric currents and the spider's web of wires, the invisible and often dematerialized flows of information become palpable. Such crude, primitive versions of the internet also debunk the myth of information, revealing the continuity between the "new" media and the "archaic" media. Moreover, the appropriation of Sky Net for other uses (such as heating) diverges from a teleological, task-oriented narrative of the development of technology, opening up a space for ludic play. The depiction of Xiaochu's almost acrobatics-like movement among wires and bulbs removes her from the goal-oriented adult world dominated by the stringent rationality of capitalism. Her interaction with the Sky Nets is a bodily engagement that never becomes constrained by a single predetermined purpose. It is the excess, or the "waste" of technology beyond programmability, that allows for the (re)appropriation of technology, and for imagining new relationships between humans and technology other than the mode of exploitative extraction. Unlike the evil internet that eventually enslaves humankind in the future, this Sky Net refuses to be annexed into the programmed strange loops of repetition. Like the boy who refuses to live for the predetermined and programmed future, it resides in the present, leaving its future(s) open to possibilities.

This reinvented story of the internet exists only in the virtual realm, just as the reconstructed histories of the 1980s are ultimately speculative. Among the virtual past(s), there nestle the underdeveloped, unmaterialized future(s).

Acknowledgments

The intellectual journey and encounters that this book took me to are beautiful and fulfilling to a scholar who thinks and writes. I am grateful to my teachers, colleagues, fellow travelers, friends, and family, who have given me inspiration, support, and encouragement, without which this book could not have come to this current shape. Andrew Jones is the best mentor I could have had. My graduate school years at Berkeley could not have been so intellectually rewarding and enjoyable without his guidance. Kristen Whissel read and commented on earlier versions of this book. Her intellectual generosity and her enthusiasm for cinema assured me of the fun of ideas and images. I also express my gratitude to Paula Varsano, Linda Williams, Martin Jay, D. Cuong O'Neill, Robert Ashmore, Anne Nesbet, Sophie Volpp, William Schaefer, Abigail De Kosnik, Weihong Bao, and Linghon Lam.

In the process of research and writing, I participated in several interdisciplinary working groups and seminars sponsored by a number of institutions: the "Imperial Legacies, Postsocialist Contexts" working group funded by UC Humanities Research Institute, "Socialism and Postsocialism" seminar hosted by Pembroke Center for Teaching and Research on Women at Brown University, and a year-long seminar at the Center for Humanities and Information at Penn State University. I thank the seminar participants for their invigorating conversations and their feedback, which helped me better frame my work for a larger, interdisciplinary audience. At the final stage of this book project, I had the chance to participate in a weeklong workshop, "Social and Political Imaginations of Digital Media," where I benefited from lively discussions with brilliant minds. I sincerely thank the organizers Bingchun Meng and Wu Jing for inviting me.

My colleagues and friends at McGill University have provided the most intellectually stimulating environment for my research and writing. I especially thank Thomas Lamarre, Grace Fong, Robin Yates, Yuriko Furuhata, Philips Buckley, and Griet Vankeerberghen for their invaluable support, help, and suggestions. Beyond McGill, I thank Dudley Andrew, Yomi Braester, Briankle Chang, Anatoly Detwyler, Xuefeng Feng, Gang Yue, Erin Huang, Paola Iovene, Jie Li, Fan Lin, Jason McGrath, Jack Linchuan Qiu, Paul Roquet, Shuang Shen, Kalindi Vora, and Alexander Zahlten for inspiring conversations, offering feedback on my chapters, and giving me the opportunities to present my work. I am especially grateful to Margaret Hillenbrand, who read and commented on my manuscript and warmly offered advice and help. I am grateful for her generosity.

A number of grants and fellowships were instrumental to the completion of this project, including Luce/ACLS Postdoctoral Fellowships in China Studies, Franklin Research Grant of American Philosophical Society, Senior Visiting Fellowship at the Center for Humanities and Information at Penn State University, Insight Development Grant of Social Sciences and Humanities Research Council, and Chiang Ching-kuo Foundation's Publication Subsidies Grant. I thank He Jianye at the East Asian Library of UC Berkeley and Macy Zheng at McGill library for their assistance with archives and materials. My experience working with the University of Minnesota Press has been pleasant and rewarding, and I thank my editor Danielle Kasprzak for her guidance.

I could not have survived without the friendship of Neda Atanasoski and Julietta Hua. I cannot thank them enough for sharing happy times, helping me through difficult times, and assuring me of the meaningfulness of what we have chosen to do. Neda not only read through the manuscript and offered advice instrumental to the revision, but also continuously reminds me of the intellectual and political commitment of academic writing. Julie taught me to cope with stress with wisdom and good humor, and she always shares with me the pure fun of reading.

Finally, I thank my parents and Guo Yu. Their unconditional love has given me the strength to travel thus far. I know that I always have their support, whatever path I choose.

This book is for Alfred. He takes me to see the world anew.

Notes

Introduction

1. See Nathan Sivin, "State, Cosmos, and Body in the Last Three Centuries B.C.," *Harvard Journal of Asiatic Studies* 55, no. 1 (June 1995): 5–37; John Hay, "The Human Body as a Microcosmic Source of Macrocosmic Values in Calligraphy," in *Theories of the Arts in China*, ed. Susan Bush and Christian F. Murck (Princeton: Princeton University Press, 1983): 74–102; and Robin D. S. Yates, "Body, Space, Time, and Bureaucracy: Boundary Creation and Control Mechanisms in Early China," in *Boundaries in China*, ed. John Hay (London: Reaktion Books, 1994), 56–81.

2. Of course, the sky and outer space constantly occupy the imagination of communication and give rise to many of what John Peters calls "sky-born" media. Rather than being empty, the sky is often conceived as the environment for the interactions between the human and the other. The development of communication technologies, from telegraph to wireless communication and radio and television networks, has also fueled all sorts of paranormal and spiritual imaginations and discourses to define the sky and the atmosphere as the active space and agent for the encounter and mediation of different forces. See John Durham Peters, *The Marvelous Clouds: Toward a Philosophy of Elemental Media* (Chicago: University of Chicago Press, 2016); and Jeffrey Sconce, *Haunted Media: Electronic Presence from Telegraphy to Television* (Durham: Duke University Press 2000).

3. Shu Ting, "Huanghun Xing" 黄昏星 [Stars in twilight], *Shanghai Wenxue*, no. 7 (1982): 44–45.

4. Li Xiaoying and Wang Yu, "Chengshi fengqi yugutianxian, Gangfeng beijian" 城市疯起鱼骨天线，港风北渐 [Fishbone antennas sweep across cities, and fashion of Hong Kong move northward], http://culture.ycwb.com/2013-06/18/content_4547051_5.htm.

5. See Alexander Ornella, Stefanie Knauss, and Anna-Katharina Hopflinger, eds., *Commun(icat)ing Bodies: Body as Medium in Religious Symbol Systems* (Zurich: Pano Verlag, 2014); Jeffrey Sconce, *Haunted Media: Electronic Presence from Telegraphy to Television.*

6. To give a few examples: Mark B. N. Hansen, *New Philosophy for New Media* (Cambridge, Mass.: MIT Press, 2004); and *Bodies in Code: Interface with New Media* (New York: Routledge, 2006); Bernadette Wegenstein, *Getting Under the Skin: The Body and Media Theory* (Cambridge, Mass.: MIT Press, 2006).

7. About the representation of laboring bodies in the Mao era and the elevation of mental labor over physical labor in post-Mao China, see Paola Iovene, *Tales of Futures Past: Anticipation and the Ends of Literature in Contemporary China* (Stanford: Stanford University Press, 2014), chap. 1, 19–49. Lisa Rofel regards the production of various desires and the creation of "desiring subjects" as crucial to China's reconfiguration of its relationships to a postsocialist neoliberal world. Although she focuses on the post-Tiananmen world of 1990s China, this process of producing "desiring subjects" started as early as the 1980s with the start of marketization and especially the commercialization of culture in the mid- to late 1980s. See Lisa Rofel, *Desiring China: Experiments in Neoliberalism, Sexuality, and Public Culture* (Durham: Duke University Press, 2007).

8. Mark B. N. Hansen, *New Philosophy for New Media.*

9. Mark B. N. Hansen, *New Philosophy for New Media*, 2.

10. The celebration of prediscursive affect in recent media studies often ignores the fact that the affective capacity of the body is increasingly subject to the value extraction of information capitalism. Autonomist feminists and Marxists such as Michael Hardt and Kathi Weeks use the term "affective labor" to refer to labor for "the creation and manipulation of affects." Steven Shaviro adopts this line of Marxist critique in his recent discussion on media and affect economy. See Steven Shaviro, *Post-Cinematic Affect* (Winchester, UK: Zero Books, 2010). See also Luciana Parisi and Steve Goodman, "Mnemonic Control," in *Beyond Biopolitics: Essays on the Governance of Life and Death*, ed. Patricia Clough and Craig Willse (Durham: Duke University Press, 2011), 163–76. Weihong Bao in her book also questions the understanding of affect as prediscursive. Instead, affect itself should be examined historically as a discursive construction and understood as susceptible to political and economic manipulation. See Bao, *Fiery Cinema: The Emergence of an Affective Medium in China, 1915–1945* (Minneapolis: University of Minnesota Press, 2015), 14–17.

11. Alexander Galloway, Eugene Thacker, and McKenzie Wark, *Excommunication: Three Inquiries in Media and Mediation* (Chicago: University of Chicago Press, 2014), 7–10.

12. N. Katherine Hayles, *How We Became Posthuman: Virtual Bodies in Cybernetics, Literature, and Informatics* (Chicago: University of Chicago Press,

1999); and "Cybernetics," *Critical Terms for Media Studies*, ed. W. J. T. Mitchell and Mark B. N. Hansen (Chicago: University of Chicago Press, 2010), 145–56.

13. Hayles, *How We Became Posthuman*, mainly focuses on the development of cybernetics in North America. Andrew Pickering explores another genealogy among a group of British thinkers from 1940s to the present. See Andrew Pickering, *The Cybernetic Brain: Sketches of Another Future* (Chicago: University of Chicago Press, 2010). Slava Gerovitch traces the history of cybernetics in the Soviet Union and how cybernetics was conceived as a universal method of problem solving and a language of objectivity and truth. See Gerovitch, *From Newspeak to Cyberspeak: A History of Soviet Cybernetics* (Cambridge, Mass.: MIT Press, 2002). Benjamin Peters provides a fascinating history of the rise of economic cybernetics in the Soviet Union, the attempts to build a "unified information network" to manage the national economy, and its unfortunate failure. See Peters, *How Not to Network a Nation: The Uneasy History of the Soviet Internet* (Cambridge, Mass.: MIT Press, 2016). Eden Medina uncovers the history of short-lived socialist experiments in Chile under Salvador Allende by adopting a cybernetic system for economic management. See Medina, *Cybernetic Revolutions: Technology and Politics in Allende's Chile* (Cambridge, Mass.: MIT Press, 2011). Yuriko Furuhata explores the interconnections of cybernetics, architectural design, and multimedia environment in the case of Expo '70 held in Osaka. Furuhata, "Multimedia Environments and Security Operations: Expo '70 as a Laboratory of Governance," *Grey Room*, no. 54 (Winter 2014): 55–79. In general, scholarship on cybernetic histories in the non-Western and Asian context has been limited, and even less has been written on the historical connections between the advent of postsocialism and the sudden pervasive discourse about a coming information society around the turn of the 1980s.

14. Yuezhi Zhao and Dan Schiller, "Dancing with Wolves? China's Integration into Digital Capitalism," *Info* 3, no. 2:137–51.

15. Alexander Galloway, *The Interface Effect* (Cambridge: Polity, 2012), 17.

16. Galloway, *The Interface Effect*, 16.

17. Jussi Parikka, "Postscript: Of Disappearances and the Ontology of Media (Studies)," in *Media after Kittler*, ed. Eleni Ikoniadou and Scott Wilson (New York: Rowman & Littlefield International, 2015).

18. John Guillory, "Genesis of the Media Concept," *Critical Inquiry* 36, no. 2 (2010): 321–62.

19. Guillory, "Genesis of the Media Concept," 343.

20. Guillory, "Genesis of the Media Concept," 344.

21. Guillory, "Genesis of the Media Concept."

22. Raymond Williams, *Marxism and Literature* (Oxford: Oxford University Press, 1977), 97.

23. Williams, *Marxism and Literature*, 99.

24. Williams, *Marxism and Literature*, 98.

25. Eva Horn, "Editor's Introduction: 'There Are No Media,'" *Grey Room* 1, vol. 29 (2007): 6–13.
26. See, for example, John D. Peters, *The Marvelous Clouds: Toward a Philosophy of Elemental Media*; Ned Rossiter, *Software, Infrastructure, Labor: A Media Theory of Logistical Nightmares* (New York: Routledge, 2016).
27. Horn, "Editor's Introduction: 'There Are No Media,'" 8.
28. Vincent Mosco, *The Digital Sublime: Myth, Power, and Cyberspace* (Cambridge, Mass.: MIT Press, 2004).
29. Mosco, *The Digital Sublime*.
30. James Beniger, *The Control Revolution: Technological and Economic Origins of the Information Society* (Cambridge, Mass.: Harvard University Press, 1986), 427.
31. Beniger, *The Control Revolution*, 25.
32. For the convergence of the media, see Henry Jenkins, *Convergence Culture: Where Old and New Media Collide* (New York: New York University Press, 2006).
33. Beniger, *The Control Revolution*, 8.
34. For a concentrated discussion of this in the digital setting, see Trebor Scholz, *Digital Labor: The Internet as Playground and Factory* (New York: Routledge, 2013).
35. Branden Hookway, *Interface* (Cambridge, Mass.: MIT Press, 2014).
36. Hookway, *Interface*, 64.
37. N. Katherine Hayles, "Cybernetics," in *Critical Terms for Media Studies*, 148.
38. Johanna Drucker, "Humanist Approaches to Interface Theory," in *Cultural Machine* 12 (2011): 1–20.
39. Brushing aside the notion of "user-friendly interface," in his recent book Galloway argues that all interfaces are fundamentally unworkable. See Alexander Galloway, *The Interface Effect* (Malden, Mass.: Polity, 2012).
40. See, for example, Lev Manovich, "On Totalitarian Interactivity," http://manovich.net/index.php/projects/on-totalitarian-interactivity.
41. John Harwood, *The Interface: IBM and the Transformation of Corporate Design, 1945–1976* (Minneapolis: University of Minnesota Press, 2011), 81.
42. See Xudong Zhang, *Chinese Modernism in the Era of Reforms, Cultural Fever, Avant-garde Fiction, and the New Chinese Cinema* (Durham: Duke University Press, 1997); Jing Wang, *High Culture Fever: Politics, Aesthetics, and Ideology in Deng's China* (Berkeley: University of California Press, 1996); Arif Dirlik and Xudong Zhang, eds., *Postmodernism and China* (Durham: Duke University Press, 2000).
43. Jason McGrath finds that both Zhou Yang and Mao in their elaboration of socialist realism did not reject revolutionary romanticism. See Jason McGrath, "Cultural Revolution Model Opera Films and the Realist Tradition in Chinese Cinema," *Opera Quarterly* 26, no. 2–3 (2010): 343–76. For the transformation

of folklores and folk culture into revolutionary culture in the case of the model operas such as *The White-Haired Girl*, see Duan Baolin, Meng Yue, and Li Yang, *Baimaonv qishinian* 白毛女十七年 [The seventy years of the white-haired girl] (Shanghai: Shanghai renmin chubanshe, 2015).

44. Peter Button, *Configurations of the Real in Chinese Literary and Aesthetic Modernity* (Boston: Brill, 2009), 183.

45. McGrath, "Cultural Revolution Model Opera Films," 356.

46. McGrath, "Cultural Revolution Model Opera Films," 368.

47. Chris Berry, *Postsocialist Cinema in Post-Mao China: The Cultural Revolution after the Cultural Revolution* (New York: Routledge, 2004), 18.

48. Arif Dirlik, "Postsocialism? Reflections on 'Socialism with Chinese Characteristics,'" in *Marxism and Chinese Experience*, ed. Arif Dirlik et al. (New York: M. E. Sharpe, 1989), 364.

49. Sharad Chari and Katherine Verdery, "Thinking between the Posts: Postcolonialism, Postsocialism, and Ethnography after the Cold War," *Comparative Studies in Society and History* 51, no. 1 (2009): 6–34.

50. Michael Latham, *Modernization as Ideology: American Social Science and "Nation Building" in the Kennedy Era* (Chapel Hill: University of North Carolina Press, 2000), 41–44.

51. Chari and Verdery, "Thinking between the Posts," 19–20.

52. Jason McGrath, *Postsocialist Modernity: Chinese Cinema, Literature, and Criticism in the Market Age* (Stanford: Stanford University Press, 2008).

53. Richard Barbrook, *Imaginary Futures: From Thinking Machines to the Global Village* (London: Pluto, 2007).

54. Barbrook, *Imaginary Futures*, 102.

55. Barbrook, *Imaginary Futures*, 109–69.

56. Zhang Xudong and Zhu Yu, "Cong 'xiandai zhuyi' dao 'wenhua zhengzhi': Fangtan Zhang Xudong jiaoshou" 从"现代主义"到"文化政治"：访谈张旭东教授 [From "modernism" to "cultural politics": An interview with Prof. Zhang Xudong], *Xiandai zhongwen xuekan* [Journal of modern Chinese studies], no. 3 (2010): 4–27.

57. Paola Iovene discusses such continuity in futuristic imaginations in *Tales of Futures Past* (Stanford: Stanford University Press, 2014), especially chap. 1.

58. Neda Atanasoski and Kalindi Vora, "Surrogate Humanity: Posthuman Networks and the (Racialized) Obsolescence of Labor," *Catalyst: Feminism, Theory, Technoscience* 1, no. 1 (2015): 1–40.

59. Steven Shaviro, *No Speed Limit: Three Essays on Acceleration* (Minneapolis: University of Minnesota Press, 2015), 2.

60. Shaviro, *No Speed Limit*.

61. Zhang Xudong and Zhu Yu, "Cong 'xiandai zhuyi' dao 'wenhua zhengzhi.'"

1. Extrasensory Powers, Magic Waves, and Information Explosion

1. "*Dazu xian faxian yige nengyong erduo bianzi de ertong*" 大足县发现一个能用耳朵辨字的儿童 [A child in dazu county discovered to be capable of reading with ears], in *Chuangjian renti kexue* 创建人体科学 [Establishing somatological science], ed. Qian Xuesen et al. (Chengdu: Sichuan jiaoyu chubanshe, 1989), 1–2.

2. He Chongyin, "*Tansuo shengming kexue de aomi*" 探索生命科学的奥秘 [Exploring the secrets of the life sciences], *Ziran zazhi* 4 (1980): 289–93.

3. Sheila Murphy also makes the argument that television played an important role in the emergence of digital interactive devices in the Euro-American context. See Murphy, *How Television Invented New Media* (New Brunswick: Rutgers University Press, 2011).

4. Qian Xuesen, "*Yingjie di'erci wenyi fuxing de daolai*" 迎接第二次文艺复兴 [Welcome the second renaissance], in *Chuangjian renti kexue* 开创人体科学 [Establishing somatological science], 273–82.

5. Qian Xuesen, "*Renti kexue de youling zai paihuai*" 人体科学的幽灵在徘徊 [The specter of somatological science is haunting us], in *Chuangjian renti kexue*, 256–67.

6. The term, coined by Raymond Williams, enables us to talk about lived and unfixed experience, which is "emergent or pre-emergent" and does not "have to await definition, classification or rationalization before they exert palpable pressures and set effective limits on experience and on action." While affirming the sociality of feelings, this term also leaves space for the experiences that have not yet hardened into ideologies. See Raymond Williams, *Marxism and Literature* (New York: Oxford University Press, 1977), 128–35. Especially relevant to my project here is the "emergent or preemergent" nature of the "structure of feeling," which registers the discontents toward information capitalism at a moment when the dominant discourses were information utopianism.

7. Chen Xin, "*Ren, Ji, Huanjing Xitong Gongchengxue Gailun*" 人，机，环境系统工程学概论 [A brief introduction to Human-Machine-Environment Engineering], in *Lun ren, ji, huanjing xitong gongcheng* 论人，机，环境系统工程 [On Human-Machine-Environment System Engineering], ed. Chen Xin et al. (Beijing: Renmin junyi chubanshe, 1988), 1–9.

8. Chen Xin, "*Ren, Ji, Huanjing Xitong Gongchengxue Gailun*."

9. Qian Xuesen, "*Kaizhan renti kexue de jichu yanjiu*" 开展人体科学的基础研究 [Starting the Basic Research of Somatolgoical Science], in *Chuangjian renti kexue*, 41–57.

10. David Palmer, *Qigong Fever: Body, Science, and Utopia in China* (New York: Columbia University Press, 2007), 29–45.

11. Qian Xuesen, "*Kaizhan renti kexue de jichu yanjiu*," in *Chuangjian renti kexue*, 41–57.

12. Qian Xuesen, "*Jianli weixiang qigongxue*" 建立唯象气功学 [Establishing a phenomenological study of *qigong*], in *Chuangjian renti kexue*, 246–55.

13. He Chongyin et al., "*Zhongguo de qigong kexue yanjiu*" 中国的气功科学研究 [Scientific studies of qigong in China], in *Chuangjian renti kexue*, 300–313.
14. Zhu Runlong and Zhu Yiyi, "*Zhongguo de renti teyi gongneng yanjiu*" 中国的人体特异功能研究 [The research into extrasensory powers in China], in *Chuangjian renti kexue*, 314–55.
15. "*Zhongguo kexue yu wei kexue douzheng dashiji*" 中国科学与伪科学大事记 [A chronicle of the struggles between science and pseudoscience], http://www.uua.cn/article/show-201-2.html.
16. Liu Xiaohe, *Zhonghua qigong* 中华奇功 [Legendary art of China] (Beijing: Xueyuan chubanshe, 1988), 95–100.
17. Yin Zhiguo, "Ganjue ji'e yu xinxi baoza" 感觉饥饿与信息爆炸 [The hunger of the senses and the explosion of information], *Jiefangjun shenghuo* [The journal of PLA life], no. 3 (1987): 35.
18. Jin Kemu, "Dushu, duren, duwu" 读书，读人，读物 [Reading books, reading people and things], *Dushu* [Reading], no. 4 (1984): 7–12.
19. Xiang Jiang, "Renti teyigongneng caixiang" 人体特异功能猜想 [Speculations on extrasensory powers], *Huashi*, no. 3 (1980): 11–13.
20. Xiao Jianheng, *Meng* 梦 [Dreams] (Nanjing: Jiangsu renmin chubanshe, 1979), 1.
21. He Chongyin et al., "*Zhongguo de qigong kexue yanjiu*" 中国的气功科学研究 [The study of *qigong* science in China], *Chuangjian renti kexue*, 300–313.
22. Liu Ronghan, "Wuxiandian ye ganbushang" 无线电也赶不上 [Even telegrams are not fast enough], in *Wuxiandian ye ganbushang* (Shanghai: Shanghai wenyi chubanshe, 1959), 1–6.
23. For a discussion on the overcoming of sleep during Mao's era, see Paola Iovene, *Tales of Futures Past: Anticipation and the Ends of Literature in Contemporary China* (Stanford: Stanford University Press, 2014), 20–24.
24. *Zhongguo guangbo dianshi nianjian: 1986* 中国广播电视年鉴：1986 [The 1986 China TV and Broadcast Yearbook] (Beijing: Zhongguo guangbo dianshi chubanshe, 1986), 857–59.
25. Chen Gang, *Dangdai zhongguo guanggaoshi: 1979–1991* 当代中国广告史：1979–1991 [A history of contemporary Chinese advertising] (Beiijng: Peking University Press, 2010), 169.
26. Andrew Jones, "Quotation Songs: Portable Media and the Maoist Pop Song," in *Mao's Little Red Book: A Global History*, ed. Alexander C. Cook (Cambridge: Cambridge University Press, 2014), 43–60.
27. Nicole Huang, "Sun-Facing Courtyards: Urban Communal Culture in Mid-1970s' Shanghai," *East Asian History*, no. 25/26 (2003): 161–82.
28. See Xiao Kechang, *Shuzi dianshi qianshuo* 数字电视浅说 [Preliminary introduction to digital TV] (Beijing: Kexue chubanshe, 1987).
29. Liu Zhong'en, *Weichuliji zai caisedianshi jishu zhong de yingyong* 微处理机在彩色电视技术中的应用 [The application of microprocessors in color TV] (Beijing: Guofang gongye chubanshe, 1987), 68–80.

30. Liu Zhong'en, *Weichuliji zai caisedianshi jishu zhong de yingyong*, 81–90.
31. Xiao Kechang, *Shuzidianshi qianshuo*, 147.
32. Liu Zhong'en, *Weichuliji zai caisedianshi jishu zhong de yingyong*, 91.
33. John H. Maier, "Thirty Years of Computer Science Developments in the People's Republic of China: 1956–1985," *IEEE Annals of the History of Computing* 10, no. 1 (1988): 19–34.
34. Xue Hong, "Mangren de fuyin: Wei mangren yinlu de dianzi zhuangzhi" 盲人的福音：为盲人引路的电子装置 [Gospel for the blind: Direction-guiding electronic resource for the blind], *Dazhong dianshi* [Mass TV], no. 3 (1982): 25.
35. See Institute of Scientific & Technical Information under the Ministry of Electronics Industry, *Dianshichangpian, changpian de fazhanqianjing* 电视唱片，长篇的发展前景 [The future of videodiscs and disc] (Beijing: Dianzi gongyebu kejiqingbao yanjiusuo, 1985). See also E. Segal, *Dianshichangpian yuanli, yingyong yu qianjing* [The principle, application, and future of videodiscs], trans. Wang Zhihua (Beijing: Kexue chubanshe, 1988).
36. The use of technical media for education has a long history in China and includes the official establishment of a "film education committee" at Jinling University in the early 1930s and the building of a mobile film-projection team and the production of "science-education films" (*kejiao pian* 科教片). The idea of building a network of education around television was also implemented in Western countries. See John Harwood, "TV University ca. 1964," *Art Papers* (January–February 2015): 24–31.
37. Wang Yishan, "Zhongguo de guangbodianshi daxue" 中国的广播电视大学 [The radio and TV universities in China], *Jiaoyu zhanwang* [Education outlook], no. 1 (1984): 127–32.
38. *Zhongguo jiaoyu tongji nianjian: 1988* 中国教育统计年鉴 [China statistical yearbook of education: 1988] (Beijing: Renminjiaoyu chubanshe, 1989), 104.
39. Yu Wenzhao, "Cong renji xitong lun dianhua jiaoyu" 从人机系统论电化教育 [Electrified education from the perspective of human–machine systems] (pt. 1), *Waiyu dianjiao* [Electrified education of foreign languages], no. 1 (1983): 30–32; and Yu Wenzhao, "Cong renji xitong lun dianhua jiaoyu" (pt. 2), *Waiyu dianjiao*, no. 2 (1983): 24–26.
40. Yu, "Cong renji xitong lun dianhua jiaoyu" (pt. 1), 30–32; and Yu, "Cong renji xitong lun dianhua jiaoyu" (pt. 2), 24–26.
41. Hu Yongguang, "Dianhua jiaoyu" 电化教育 [Electrified education], *Dianzi shijie* [Electronics world] 1 (1979): 8.
42. He Chongyin, "*Tansuo shengming kexue de aomi*" 探索生命科学的奥秘 [Exploring the secrets of the life sciences], *Ziran zazhi*, no. 4 (1980): 289–93.
43. Wang Boyang, "*Siwei chuangan zhong 'pingmu xiaoying' xianxiang de fenxi*" 思维传感中的"屏幕效应"现象的分析 [An analysis on the "screen effects" of parapsychological transference], *Chinese Journal of Somatic Science*, no. 1 (1992): 12–14.

44. Friedrich A. Kittler, *Grammophone, Film, Typewriter* (Stanford: Stanford University Press, 1999), 1–2.
45. Mark Hansen, *New Philosophy for New Media* (Cambridge, Mass.: MIT Press, 2004), 7.
46. Mark Paterson, *Senses of Touch: Haptics, Affects, and Technologies* (Oxford: Berg, 2007), 37–48.
47. Oliver Sacks, "A Neurologist's Notebook: The Mind's Eye—What the Blind See," *The New Yorker* (July 28, 2003), 48–59. See also Paterson's discussion of Sacks in *Senses of Touch*.
48. Zhang Chongqi et al., eds., *Renti teyigongneng yanjiu zhuantibaogao* 人体科学研究专题报告 [Special reports on the studies of extrasensory powers] (Beijing: Beijing Normal University, 1980).
49. Friedrich Kittler, "The History of Communication Media," *Ctheory* 114 (1996), http://www.ctheory.net/articles.aspx?id=45.
50. Qian Xuesen, "Letter to Chen Xin" on September 11, 1988, in *Qian Xuesen shuxin* 钱学森书信 [Correspondences of Qian Xuesen] (Beijing: Guofang gongye chubanshe), vol. 4, 267.
51. N. Katherine Hayles, *How We Became Posthuman: Virtual Bodies in Cybernetics, Literature, and Informatics* (Chicago: University of Chicago Press, 2008): 85–112.
52. Qian Xuesen, "Letter to Kuang Diaoyuan" on April 30, 1988, in *Qian Xuesen shuxin* [Correspondences of Qian Xuesen] (Beijing: Guofang gongye chubanshe), vol. 4, 190–91.
53. Elizabeth Dunn in her study of socialist factories in Poland and their transformations into postsocialism, drawing upon Katherine Verdery's study on central planning, resources allocation, and power in the Soviet Union, argues that although Henry Ford's system of industrial management was embraced enthusiastically by the Soviet and other socialist production systems, the central planning and resource-allocation systems in fact spawned "radically different experiences of labor and the construction of workers as different types of persons" (18). Thus in order to transform the former socialist workers into flexible workers in the 1990s, the first thing is to instill in the body a different rhythm. See Dunn, *Privatizing Poland: Baby Food, Big Business, and the Remaking of Labor* (Ithaca: Cornell University Press, 2004), 8–22.
54. Chen Gong, "Xinxi, jiezhou, weilai—Fang meiguo zhuming weilaixuejia Tuofule fufu" 信息，节奏，未来 —访美国著名未来学家托夫勒夫妇 [Information, rhythm, and the future: An interview with the famous American futurists the Tofflers], *Renmin ribao* [People's daily], September 20, 1988.
55. One of the most remarkable observations on the class politics of the body came from Mao Zedong's "Talk at the Yenan Forum on Literature and Art," in which he told his own story of once wrongly believing as a student that "intellectuals were the only clean people in the world, while in comparison

workers and peasants were dirty." Later, when he became a revolutionary, he came to realize that such feelings belonged to the petty-bourgeois, and that "the workers and peasants were the cleanest people," even though "their hands were soiled and their feet smeared with cow-dung." See Mao, "Talks at the Yenan Forum on Literature and Art," https://www.marxists.org/reference/archive/mao/selected-works/volume-3/mswv3_08.htm.

56. Wei Yahua, "*Diushi de meng*" 丢失的梦 [The lost dream], *Xiaoshuo lin* 小说林 [Forest of stories] 3 (1983): 35.

57. Wei Yahua, "*Diushi de meng.*"

58. N. Katherine Hayles, *How We Became Posthuman*, 91–112.

59. Wei Yahua, "*Diushi de meng*," 42.

60. Wei Yahua, "*Diushi de meng*," 43.

61. Claude E. Shannon, "A Mathematical Theory of Communication," reprinted with corrections from the *Bell System Technical Journal* 27, no. 3 (July 1948): 379–423, and 27, no. 4 (October 1948): 623–56, http://cm.bell-labs.com/cm/ms/what/shannonday/shannon1948.pdf.

Norbert Wieners's *Cybernetics* was partially translated into Chinese as early as the 1950s (as *kongzhi lun* 控制论 "the theory of control"), and the first full translation was published in 1961. See Hao Jiren, *Kongzhi lun* 控制论 [Cybernetics] (Beijing: Kexue chubanshe, 1961). The reception of cybernetics from the 1950s to 1966 (before the break of the Cultural Revolution) followed two relatively separate paths. In philosophy, cybernetics was discussed in relation to Marxist philosophy. Introductions to and translations of articles on cybernetics (most originally authored in the Soviet Union and Eastern Europe) often appeared in such journals as *Studies on Dialectics of Nature*. In the area of science and engineering, cybernetics was closely related to the development of national defense systems and military weapons during the Cold War, in which Qian Xuesen played an important role. It was not until the late 1970s that cybernetics gained much broader social influences, and cybernetics was adopted as a method to analyze human society and social problems, such as population control and the one-child policy.

62. Han Shaogong, "*Wenxue de 'gen'*" 文学的根 [The roots of literature], *Zuojia zazhi*, no. 4 (1985): 2–69.

63. Important scholarship on Chinese science fiction includes: David Wang, *Fin-de-siècle Splendor: Repressed Modernities of Late Qing Fiction, 1849–1911* (Stanford: Stanford University Press, 1997), chap. 4; Andrew Jones, *Developmental Fairy Tales* (Cambridge, Mass.: Harvard University Press, 2011), chap. 1; Paola Iovene, *Tales of Futures Past*, chap. 1; Mingwei Song, "Variations on Utopia in Contemporary Chinese Science Fiction," *Science Fiction Studies* 40, no. 1 (March 2013): 86–102.

64. Merle Goldman and Denis Simon, "Introduction: The Onset of China's New Technological Revolution," in *Science and Technology in Post-Mao China*,

ed. Denis Simon and Merle Goldman (Cambridge, Mass., Harvard University Press, 1989), 3–4.

65. Chen Jie, "27tian jueding kehua mingyun qifu" 27 天决定科幻命运起伏 [The fate of science fictions fixed in 27 days], http://blog.sina.com.cn/s/blog_484a22af0100d2sr.html.

66. Cai Xiang, "1970: Modai huiyi" 1970: 末代回忆 [1970: Memoirs of the end of an era], www.wyzusx.com/Article/Class14/200812/62971.html. For other references to Deng's popularity in mainland China in the early 1980s, see Nimrod Baranovitch, *China's New Voices: Popular Music, Ethnicity, Gender, and Politics, 1978–1997* (Berkeley: University of California Press, 2003), 10–13.

67. Zheng Wenguang, "Mingyun yezonghui" 命运夜总会 [Destiny club], *Xiaoshuo jie*, no. 2 (1981): 212.

68. Acoustic weaponry is not merely a science fiction fabrication. According to Steve Goodman, as early as the 1960s a French robotics researcher, Vladimir Gavreau, discovered strange physiological anomalies in the human body caused by inaudible vibrations, which led to the increasing adoption of acoustic weaponry. See Steve Goodman, *Sonic Warfare: Sound, Affect, and the Ecology of Fear* (Cambridge, Mass.: MIT Press, 2010), 15–25. According to Branden Joseph, the techniques of acoustical bombardment used at the US detention center in Guantanamo Bay can date back to the CIA-sponsored experiments during the Cold War on "no touch" torture. Joseph also revealingly shows that the development of sonic weapons was closely tied to the experiments and theory of digital musical composition, especially to a researcher named Manford L. Eaton. See Branden W. Joseph, "Biomusic," *Grey Room*, no. 45 (Fall 2011): 128–50. See also Suzanne G. Cusick and Branden W. Joseph, "Across an Invisible Line: A Conversation about Music and Torture," *Grey Room*, no. 42 (Winter 2011): 6–21.

2. The Curious Case of a Robot Doctor

1. Dai Ruwei 戴汝为, "'Renji jiehe' de Dacheng zhihui" "人机结合"的大成智慧 [Metasynthetic wisdom of human–machine systems], *Moshishibie yu rengongzhineng* (PR&AI) 7, no. 3 (1994): 181–90.

2. Dai Ruwei, "Qian Xuesen lun Dacheng zhihui gongcheng" 钱学森论大成智慧工程 [Qian Xuesen's view on metasynthetic engineering], *Zhongguo gongcheng kexue* [Engineering science] 3, no. 12 (2001): 14–20.

3. Alexander Galloway, *The Interface Effect* (Cambridge: Polity Press), 18.

4. Edward Feigenbaum, "Knowledge Engineering: The Applied Side of Artificial Intelligence," *Annals of the New York Academy of Sciences* 426, no. 1 (November 1984): 91–107.

5. Paul Edwards, *The Closed World: Computers and the Politics of Discourse in Cold War America* (Cambridge, Mass: MIT Press, 1997), 240–44.

6. Edwards, *The Closed World*, 256.

7. Hubert Dreyfus, *What Computers Still Can't Do: A Critique of Artificial Intelligence* (Cambridge, Mass.: MIT Press, 1972, 1979, 1992).

8. Edward Feigenbaum and Pamela McCorduck, *The Fifth Generation: Artificial Intelligence and Japan's Computer Challenge to the World* (Boston: Addison-Wesley Publishing Company), 17.

9. Feigenbaum and McCorduck, *The Fifth Generation*.

10. Chen Gong 陈功, "Xinxi, jiezhou, weilai—fang meiguo zhuming weilaixuejia Tuofule fufu" 信息，节奏，未来—访美国著名未来学家托夫勒夫妇 [Information, rhythm, and the future: An interview with the famous American futurists the Tofflers], *People's Daily*, September 20, 1988.

11. Zhao Ziyang 赵紫阳, "*Yingdang zhuyi yanjiu shijie xin de jishu geming he womende duice*" 应当注意研究世界新的技术革命和我们的对策 [A worldwide new technological revolution and our strategies], *zhongguo jingji daokan* 中国经济导刊 [Journal of Chinese economy] 1 (1984): 3–9.

12. Huang Keming 黄可鸣, *Zhuanjia xitong daolun* 专家系统导论 [Introduction to expert systems] (Nanjing: Dongnan daxue chubanshe, 1988), 15–16.

13. Edward Feigenbaum, "Interviewed for Expert Systems by Kenneth Owen," *Expert Systems* 6, no. 2 (April 1989): 112–15.

14. Feigenbaum, "Interviewed for Expert Systems by Kenneth Owen."

15. Huang Keming, "Zhuanjia xitong ershi nian" 专家系统二十年 [The development of expert systems in the past twenty years], in *Jisuanji kexue* 0 [Computer science] 4 (1986): 26–37.

16. Feigenbaum and McCorduck, *The Fifth Generation*, 76–77.

17. Feigenbaum and McCorduck, *The Fifth Generation*.

18. Feigenbaum, McCorduck, and Nii, *The Rise of the Expert Company: How Visionary Companies Are Using Artificial Intelligence to Achieve Higher Productivity and Profits* (Boston: Addison-Wesley Publishing Company, 1983), 251.

19. Agnes Kukulska-Hulme, *Language and Communication: Essential Concepts for User-Interface and Documentation Design* (New York: Oxford University Press, 1999).

20. Jin Zhi 金芝, Liu Fengqi 刘凤岐, and Yu Xianyi 俞咸宜, "Zhongyi zhuanjia xitong gongju YHW-CTMEST" 中医专家系统工具 YHW-CTMEST [Traditional Chinese medicine expert system tool YHW-CTMEST], *Jisuanji gongcheng yu yingyong* 计算机工程与应用 [Computer engineering and application], no. 6 (1988): 61–65.

21. Anthony Giddens, *The Consequences of Modernity* (Stanford: Stanford University Press, 1990), 23–29. See also Sianne Ngai, *Our Aesthetic Categories: Zany, Cute, Interesting* (Cambridge, Mass.: Harvard University Press, 2012), 197–98.

22. Giddens, *The Consequences of Modernity*, 88.

23. Giddens, *The Consequences of Modernity*.

24. Mao Zedong 毛泽东, "Ji'nian Bai Qiu'en" 纪念白求恩 [In memory of Norman Bethune], in *Mao Zedong Zhuzuo Xuandu* 毛泽东著作选读 [Selected

Notes to Chapter 2 279

writings of Mao Zedong], (Beijing: Beijing renmin chubanshe, 1966), 130–31. English translation at https://www.marxists.org/reference/archive/mao/selected-works/volume-2/mswv2_25.htm.

25. For a detailed reading of this story, see Cai Xiang 蔡翔, *Geming, xushu: Zhongguo shehuizhuyi wenxue, wenhua xiangxiang* 革命，叙述：中国社会主义文学·文化想象 [Revolution and narrative: The literary and cultural imaginations of socialism in China] (Beijing: Beijing daxue chubanshe, 2010), 302–6.

26. Zhang Zhengxian 张正宪, "Cong 'Rendao Zhongnian' Lu Wenting de xingxiang kan shehuizhuyi xinren de suzao" 从《人到中年》陆文婷的形象看社会主义新人的塑造 [The image of Lu Wenting in "At Middle Age" as a new socialist person], *Nanjing daxue xuebao* 4 (1984): 34–38.

27. Xu Chunqiao 许春樵, "Yibu you yanzhong quexuan de yingpian" 一部有严重缺陷的影片 [A severely defective film], *Wenyi bao* 6 (1983): 57–80.

28. Zhang Zhengxian, "Cong 'Rendao Zhongnian' Lu Wenting de xingxiang kan shehuizhuyi xinren de suzao," 37.

29. Wang Ruoshui 王若水, "Ren shi Makesi zhuyi de chufadian" 人是马克思主义的起点 [Human beings are the starting point of Marxism], in *Wei Rendaozhuyi bianhu* 为人道主义辩护 [Defending humanism], (Beijing: Shenghuo dushu xinzhi sanlian shudian), 200–216. For a more in-depth analysis of Marxist Humanism and Wang Ruoshui in 1980s China, see Wang Jing, *High Culture Fever: Politics, Aesthetics, and Ideology in Deng's China* (Berkeley: University of California Press, 1996), esp. 12–13.

30. In 1980 the journal *Zhongguo Qingnian* 中国青年 [Chinese youth] published a letter from a twenty-three-year-old factory worker named Pan Xiao, who claimed that as a kid she had modeled herself on Pavel Korchagin, the hero in the Soviet novel *How the Steel Was Tempered*, and Lei Feng, a selfless, socialist hero whom Chairman Mao asked the whole country to emulate. Like most of her generation, she was indoctrinated with the belief that her individual value should be realized through her sacrifice for the interests of the Party and people. However, the distress she suffered throughout the Cultural Revolution had made her rebel against this education: "I know what I am doing is no longer for the service of the people, nor for the modernization of this country. It is for myself, for my own satisfaction. . . . I realize that one's life and work has to serve one's own interest." See Pan Xiao 潘晓, "*Rensheng de lu he, zenme yuezou yuezhai*" 人生的路呵，怎么越走越窄 [Why did the road of life become narrower and narrower?], *Zhongguo Qingnian* [Chinese youth] 5 (1980): 3–5. Young readers reacted enthusiastically to the letter and voiced support for Pan Xiao. It was later revealed that Pan Xiao is not a real person but a fictive character based on a female factory worker named Huang Xiaoju and a college student named Pan Wei who had earlier attempted suicide. The editors of *Zhongguo Qingnian* combined the two's accounts of life experiences and the language they used in their letters, and decided to publish their accounts under one fictive character named Pan Xiao. For more details of the

Pan Xiao case, see http://news.xinhuanet.com/theory/200812/11/content_10 486877_1.htm.

31. Yan Hairong 严海蓉, "'Zhishi fenzi fudan' yu jiawu laodong" 知识分子负担与家务劳动 ["The Burden of Intelligentsia" and domestic duties], *Kaifang shidai* 6 (2010): 103–20.

32. For a detailed reading of the story, see Yan Hairong, "'Zhishi fenzi fudan' yu jiawu laodong."

33. Qin Dulie and Bao Yiwan, eds., *Zhongyi jisuanji moni ji zhuanjia xitong gailun* 中医计算机模拟及专家系统概论 [Computer simulation of traditional medicine and introduction to expert systems], (Beijing: Renmin weisheng chubanshe, 1989), 370.

34. Kevin Kelly, "The Three Breakthroughs That Have Finally Unleashed AI on the World," *Wired*, October 27, 2014, https://www.wired.com/2014/10/future-of-artificial-intelligence/.

35. Jean-François Lyotard, *The Postmodern Condition: A Report on Knowledge* (Minneapolis: University of Minnesota Press, 1979), 23–27.

36. Michael Hardt, "Affective Labor," *Boundary 2* 2 (1999): 89–100.

37. Paola Iovene discusses a different story by Wei Yahua about a robot wife, entitled "Conjugal Happiness in the Arms of Morpheus," with a particular focus on gendered labor and the commercialization of "care labor" in 1980s China. See Iovene, *Tales of Futures Past: Anticipation and the Ends of Literature in Contemporary China*.

38. Translation of passages from the story are adopted from *At Middle Age*, trans. Yu Fanqin (Beijing: Panda Books, distributed by China International Book Trading Corp., 1987), with my modifications.

39. Zhang An, "Zhishi fenzi fenlei wenti suotan" 知识分子分类问题琐谈 [Cursive notes on the categorization of intellectuals], *Beijing shehui kexue* 2 (1989): 20–27.

40. Zhao Yifan 赵一凡, "Bailing, Quanli jingying, Xinjieji" 白领，权力精英，新阶级 [White collar, elite, and the new class], *Dushu zazhi* 12 (1987): 115–25.

41. Gu Xin 顾昕, "Zhishi fenzi, Zhuanjia zhiguo yu minzhu" 知识分子、专家治国与民主 [Meritocracy and democracy], *Shehui Kexue Yanjiu Cankao Ziliao* 29 (1988): 11–19.

42. Nina P. Halpern, "Scientific Decision Making: The Organization of Expert Advice in Post-Mao China," in *Science and Technology in Post-Mao China*, ed. Denis Simon and Merle Goldman (Cambridge, Mass.: Harvard University Press, 1989), 157–74.

43. Cai Xiang, *Geming, xushu: Zhongguo shehuizhuyi wenxue, wenhua xiangxiang*, 273–323.

44. Chunjuan Nancy Wei, "Barefoot Doctors: The Legacy of Chairman Mao's Healthcare," in *Mr. Science and Chairman Mao's Cultural Revolution: Science and Technology in Modern China*, ed. Chunjuan Nancy Wei and Darryl E.

Brock (New York: Lexington Books, 2013), 327. About the barefoot doctor and its cultural representations, also see Laikwan Pang, "The Visual Representations of the Barefoot Doctor: Between Medical Policy and Political Struggles," *Positions: East Asia Cultures Critique* 22, no. 4 (Fall 2014): 809–36.

45. See Wei and Brock, eds., *Chairman Mao's Cultural Revolution*, esp. chap. 2, "The People's Landscape: Mr. Science and the Mass Line" by Darryl E. Brock. See also Sigrid Schmalzer, *The People's Peking Man: Popular Science and Human Identity in Twentieth-Century China* (Chicago: University of Chicago Press, 2008); and Fa-ti Fan, "'Collective Monitoring, Collective Defense': Science, Earthquakes, and Politics in Communist China," *Science in Context* 25, no. 1 (2012): DOI: 10.1017/S0269889711000329.

46. Wang Hongzhe 王洪喆, "Cong chijiao diangong dao dianzibaogong: Zhongguo dianzi xinxi chanyede jishu yu laodong zhengzhi" 从赤脚电工到电子包公：中国电子信息产业的技术与劳动政治 [From barefoot electrician to electronic judge. Bao: The politics of technology and labor in China's electronic and information industry], *Kaifang shidai*, no. 3 (2015), http://www.opentimes.cn/bencandy.php?fid=397&aid=1886.

47. Sigrid Schmalzer, "Speaking about China, Learning from China: Amateur China Experts in 1970s America," *Journal of American-East Asian Relations* 16, no. 4 (2009): 326.

48. Schmalzer, "Speaking about China, Learning from China," 329–30. For more about Science for the People, see the website maintained by the SFTP research collective, http://science-for-the-people.org.

49. Fa-ti Fan, "Redrawing the Map: Science in Twentieth-Century China," *Isis* 98 (2007): 534.

50. Wang Hui 汪晖, "*Quzhengzhihua de zhengzhi, baquan de duochonggoucheng yu liushi niandai de xiaoshi*" 去政治化的政治，霸权的多重构成 与 六十年代的消逝 [Depoliticized politics, multiple components of hegemony, and the eclipse of the sixties], *Kaifang shidai* 2 (2007): 5–41. For two different versions of the English translation, see "Depoliticized Politics, from East to West," trans. Chris Connery, *New Left Review* 41 (2006): 29–45, and "Depoliticized Politics, Multiple Components of Hegemony, and the Eclipse of the Sixties," trans. Christopher Connery, *Inter-Asia Cultural Studies* 4 (2006): 683–99.

51. Johanna Drucker, "Humanist Approaches to Interface Theory," *Cultural Machine* 12 (2011): 1–20.

52. Lydia Liu, *The Freudian Robot: Digital Media and the Future of the Unconscious* (Chicago: University of Chicago Press, 2010), 1–14.

53. Nick Dyer-Witheford, *Cyber-Marx: Cycles and Circuits of Struggle in High-Technology Capitalism* (Champaign: University of Illinois Press, 1999), 219–21.

54. Feigenbaum and McCorduck, *The Fifth Generation*, 84.

55. Kelly, "The Three Breakthroughs That Have Finally Unleashed AI on the World."
56. Kelly, "The Three Breakthroughs."
57. "Baidu Danao: Zouzai Rengong Zhineng Yanjiu Zuiqianyan" 百度大脑：走在人工智能研究最前沿 [Baidu brain: Cutting-edge research on artificial intelligence], http://news.xinhuanet.com/tech/2014-09/10/c_1269691 09.htm.
58. Kelly, "The Three Breakthroughs."
59. Lilly Irani, "The Cultural Work of Microwork," *New Media & Society* 17, no. 5 (2015): 720–39, first published online, November 21, 2013, https://doi.org/10.1177/1461444813511926.
60. Paolo Virno, "General Intellect," *Historical Materialism* 15, no. 3 (2007): 3–8. For a critique of the autonomist take of Marx's notion of the "general intellect," see Tony Smith, "The General Intellect in the *Grundrisse* and Beyond," http://www.slashdocs.com/mtwkrw/tony-smith-the-general-intellect-in-the-grundrisse-and-beyond.html. See also Carlo Vercellone, "From Formal Subsumption to General Intellect: Elements for a Marxist Reading of the Thesis of Cognitive Capitalism," *Historical Materialism* 15, no. 1 (2007): 13–36.
61. Maurizio Lazzarato, "Immaterial Labor," in *Radical Thought in Italy: A Potential Politics*, ed. Paolo Virno and Michael Hardt (Minneapolis: University of Minnesota Press, 1996), 133–47.
62. Michael Hardt and Antonio Negri, *Multitude: War and Democracy in the Age of Empire* (New York: Penguin, 2004), 148.
63. Hardt and Negri, *Multitude*.
64. Hubert L. Dreyfus, *What Computers Still Can't Do: A Critique of Artificial Intelligence*, esp. 231–55.
65. Qian Xuesen 钱学森, "Zhi Ma Xiwen" 致马希文 [Letter to Ma Xiwen], October 8, 1988, *Qian Xuesen shuxin* 钱学森书信 [Correspondence of Qian Xuesen] (Beijing: Guofang gongye chubanshe), vol. 4, 275.
66. Qian Xuesen, "Zhi Ma Xiwen," July 13, 1988, *Qian Xuesen shuxin* 钱学森书信 [Correspondence of Qian Xuesen], vol. 4, 240–41.
67. Qian Xuesen, "*Guanyu siwei kexue*" 关于思维科学 [About noetic science], in *Guanyu Siwei Kexue*, ed. Qian Xuesen (Shanghai: Shanghai renmin chubanshe, 1986), 13–27.
68. Qian Xuesen, "Zhi Ma Xiwen," July 13, 1988.
69. Irani, "The Cultural Work of Microwork."
70. "Machine" here no longer means "mechanical" but refers to what John Johnston describes as "an ensemble of heterogeneous parts and processes whose connections work together to enable flows of matter, energy, and signs (and consequently desire)." See Johnston, *The Allure of Machinic Life: Cybernetics, Artificial Life, and the New AI* (Cambridge, Mass.: MIT Press, 2008), 111.

3. The "Ultrastable System" and the New Cinema

1. Cui Wenhua 崔文华, ed, *Heshang lun* 《河殇》论 [On *River Elegy*], (Beijing: Wenhua yishi chubanshe), 1988. Also quoted in Chen Fong-ching and Jin Guantao, *From Youthful Manuscripts to River Elegy: The Chinese Popular Cultural Movement and Political Transformation, 1979–1989* (Hong Kong: Chinese University Press, 1997), 218.
2. Wenhua, *Heshang lun*, 56.
3. It is not hard to see the similarity with Jin's argument. Worth noting here is that Hegel attributes this lack of historical movement to the inability of substance to "arrive at reflection on itself—at subjectivity." For Hegel's account, see Georg Wilhelm Friedrich Hegel, *The Philosophy of History*, trans. J. Sibree (New York: Dover Publications, 1956), 132–33.
4. Qian Xuesen 钱学森, Xu Guozhi 许国志, and Wang Shouyun 王寿云, "*Zuzhiguanli de jishu: Xitong gongcheng*" 组织管理的技术：系统工程 [The technics of management and organization: Systems engineering], *Wenhui bao*, September 27, 1978.
5. Qian Xuesen, Xu Guozhi, and Wang Shouyun, "*Zuzhiguanli de jishu: Xitong gongcheng*."
6. Qian Xuesen and Wu Jiapei 乌家培, "*Zuzhi guanli shehuizhuyi jianshe de jishu*: shehui gongcheng" 组织管理社会主义建设的技术 [The technics of organizing and managing socialist construction: Social engineering], *Jingji Guanli*, no. 1 (1979): 5–9.
7. Alvin W. Gouldner, *The Coming Crisis of Western Sociology* (New York: Avon, 1970), 145.
8. Gouldner, *The Coming Crisis of Western Sociology*.
9. Gouldner, *The Coming Crisis of Western Sociology*, 227.
10. Wang Jing, *High Culture Fever: Politics, Aesthetics, and Ideology in Deng's China*, 58.
11. He Guimei 贺桂梅, "*Xin Qimeng*" *zhishi dang'an: 80 niandai zhongguo wenhua yanjiu* "新启蒙"知识档案：80 年代中国文化研究 [The Archival of the "New Enlightenment": Studies on 1980s Chinese Culture] (Beijing: Bejing daxue chubanshe, 2010), 250–59.
12. Latham, *Modernization as Ideology*, 5.
13. Latham, *Modernization as Ideology*.
14. Chen Fong-Ching and Jin Guantao, *From Youthful Manuscripts to River Elegy*, 105.
15. Chen Fong-Ching and Jin Guantao, *From Youthful Manuscripts to River Elegy*.
16. Jin Guantao 金观涛, *Wo de zhexue tansuo* 我的哲学探索 [My philosophical explorations] (Shanghai: Shanghai Renmin chubanshe, 1988), 19.
17. Jin Fan, *Gongkai de qingshu* 公开的情书 [Open love letters] (Beijing: Beijing chubanshe, 1981), 43.
18. Jin Guantao, *Wo de zhexue tan suo*, 30.

19. Jin Guantao, *Wo de zhexue tan suo*, 31 (italics mine).
20. Jin Guantao, "Bashi niandai de yige hongda sixiang yundong" 八十年代的一个宏大思想运动 [A magnificent intellectual movement in the 80s], in *Wo yu bashi niandai* 我与八十年代 [The eighties and me], ed. Ma Guochuan (Beijing: Shenghuo dushu xinzhi sanlian shudian, 2011), 167.
21. Liu Hong 柳红 ed., *Baling niandai: Zhongguo Jingjixueren de guangrong yu mengxiang* 八零年代：中国经济学人的光荣与梦想 [1980s: An age of glories and dreams for Chinese economists], (Guilin: Guangxi shifan daxue chubanshe, 2010), http://book.ifeng.com/lianzai/detail_2010_11/03/2989011_25.shtml.
22. The group, after conducting extensive field surveys of rural areas all over the country, argued strongly in their report for a general policy of total privatization, which influenced the CCP's policy of "the responsibility system of farm production." See Chen Fong-Ching and Jin Guantao, *From Youthful Manuscripts to River Elegy*, 84–86.
23. Pan Jing, "Guanyu wenge de sifengxin" 关于文革的四封信 [Four letters on the Cultural Revolution], http://beijingspring.com/bj2/1995/240/2003129133951.htm.
24. Liu Hong, *Baling niandai*.
25. Interview with Gan Yang 甘阳, in *Bashi niandai fangtan lu* 八十年代访谈录 [Interviews and conversations about the eighties], ed. Zha Jianying 查建英 (Beijing: Shenghuo dushu xinzhi sanlian shudian, 2006), 196–97.
26. Chen Lai 陈来, "*Sixiang chulu de san dongxiang*" 思想出路的三动向 [Three directions of thoughts], in *Zhongguo Dangdai Wenhua Yishi* [Cultural consciousness in contemporary China], ed. Gan Yang (Xianggang: Sanlian shudian, 1989), 581–87.
27. Wang Jing, *High Culture Fever*, 58–72.
28. Chen Lai, "*Sixiang chulu de san dongxiang*," 585.
29. Zhang Yimou 张艺谋, "*Wo pai Huangtudi*" 我拍《黄土地》 [My experience filming *Yellow Earth*], in *Huashuo Huangtudi* 话说《黄土地》 [On *Yellow Earth*], ed. Zhongguo Dianying Yishi (Beijing: Zhongguo dianying chubanshe, 1986), 285.
30. Zheng Dongtian 郑洞天, "*Huangtudi* suixiangqu" 《黄土地》随想曲 [Some thoughts on *Yellow Earth*], in *Huashuo Huangtudi*, 37–47.
31. Ni Zhen 倪震, "Qitiao de gaodu" 起跳的高度 [The height of the first jump], in *Huashuo Huangtudi*, 67–81.
32. Luo Ka, "Huangtudi de zhigan yu lianxiang" 《黄土地》的直感与联想 [First impressions and some thoughts on *Yellow Earth*], in *Huashuo Huangtudi*, 117.
33. Chen Xihe, "*Zhongguo dianying meixue de zairenshi*" 中国电影美学的再认识 [Rethinking the film aesthetics of China], in *Dangdai dianying* [Contemporary film] 1 (1986): 82–90.

34. Li Tuo 李陀 et al., "*Dianying, ke xue de duixiang: Chongti 'dianying shi shenme'*" 电影，科学的对象：重提 "电影是什么" [Film as an object of scientific examination: Rethinking the question of "what is cinema"], *Dianying yishu* [Film art] 5 (1988): 3–14.
35. Wang Jing, *High Culture Fever*, 61.
36. Zhang Xudong, *Chinese Modernism in the Era of Reforms: Cultural Fever, Avant-Garde Fiction, and the New Chinese Cinema* (Durham: Duke University Press, 1997), 241.
37. Chen Xihe 陈犀禾, "*Zhongguo dianying de xinshijiao*" 中国电影的新视角 [A new perspective on Chinese film], in *Huashuo Huangtudi*, 247–48. Interestingly, Peter Brooks argues that melodrama "comes into being in a world where the traditional imperatives of truth and ethics have been violently thrown into question, yet where their promulgation of truth and ethics, their instauration as a way of life, is of immediate, daily, political concern." The Manichean terms of melodrama are to compensate such loss of traditional truth and ethics by inventing "a regime of virtue" of a new world. Brooks also regarded melodrama as the product of the French Revolution, as a mode of excess to produce "incessant struggle against enemies, without and within, branded as villains, suborners of morality, who must be confronted and expunged, over and over to assure the triumph of virtue." See Peter Brooks, *The Melodramatic Imagination: Balzac, Henry James, Melodrama, and the Mode of Excess* (New Haven: Yale University Press, 1976), 15. This manichaeistic logic of melodrama is also pervasive in revolutionary films of the Mao era. Chen Xihe's objection to "cheap, melodramatic gimmicks" should be understood as a repulsion toward the manipulation of the audience's reaction for the purpose of revolutionary didacticism.
38. Zhang Xudong, *Chinese Modernism in the Era of Reforms*, 251.
39. Stephanie Donald, "Landscape and Agency: *Yellow Earth* and the Demon Lover," *Theory, Culture & Society* 14, no. 1 (1997): 97–112.
40. Donald, "Landscape and Agency," 104.
41. Donald, "Landscape and Agency," 111.
42. N. Katherine Hayles, *How We Became Posthuman: Virtual Bodies in Cybernetics, Literature, and Informatics* (Chicago: University of Chicago Press, 1999), 136.
43. Hayles, *How We Became Posthuman*.
44. Jin Guantao, *Ren de zhexue: Lun kexue yu lixing de jichu* 人的哲学：论科学与理性的基础 [The philosophy of the human: The foundation of science and rationality] (Chengdu: Sichuan renmin chubanshe, 1988).
45. Douglas R. Hofstadter, *Gödel, Escher, Bach: An Eternal Golden Braid* (New York: Vintage Books, 1979), 149.
46. Hofstadter, *Gödel, Escher, Bach*, 15.
47. Hofstadter, *Gödel, Escher, Bach*.
48. Hofstadter, *Gödel, Escher, Bach*.

49. Jin Guantao, "*Luoji beilun he zizuzhi xitong*" 逻辑悖论和自组织系统 [Logical paradox and self-organizing systems], *Ziran bianzhengfa tongxun* [Journal of dialectics of nature] 2 (1985): 7–15.

50. Li Tuo, "'Huang Tudi' *gei women dailaile shenme?*" 《黄土地》给我们带来了什么？[What has *Yellow Earth* brought to us?], in *Huashuo Huangtidi*, 52.

51. Paolo Totaro and Domenico Ninno, "The Concept of Algorithm as an Interpretative Key of Modern Rationality," *Theory, Culture & Society* 31, no. 4 (2014): 29–49.

52. Totaro and Ninno, "The Concept of Algorithm as an Interpretative Key of Modern Rationality," 33.

53. Huang Jianxin 黄建新, "*Daoyan chanshu*" 导演阐述 [Director's notes], *Dangdai dianying* 2 (1986): 62.

54. Yuan Ying 远婴, "You yiwei de xingshi" 有意味的形式 [A significant form], in *Dangdai dianying* 3 (1986): 65–66.

55. Xu Chi 徐迟, "Xiandaihua yu xiandaipai" 现代化与现代派 [Modernization and modernism], *Waiguo wenxu yanjiu* [Studies of foreign literatures] 1 (1982): 115–17.

56. Xu Chi, "Xiandaihua yu xiandaipai."

57. Li Tuo, "'Xiandai xiaoshuo' budeng yu 'Xiandai pai'" "现代小说"不等于"现代派" [Modern fiction is not identical with modernism], in *Shanghai wenxue* [Shanghai literature] 8 (1982): 92–94.

58. Chen Chong 陈冲, "Xiandai yishi he wenxue de modenghua" 现代意识和文学的摩登化 [Modern consciousness and the literary modern], *Pinglun xuankan* [Selected review] 4 (1987): 14–20.

59. Li Tuo, "*Yetan 'wei xiandaipai' jiqi piping*" 也谈"伪现代派"及其批评 [Further words on "pseudo-modernism" and related criticism], *Beijing wenxue* [Beijing literature] 4 (1988): 4–10.

60. Huang Ziping 黄子平, "*Guanyu 'wei xiandaipai' jiqi piping*" 关于"伪现代派"及其批评 [On "pseudo-modernism" and related criticism], *Beijing Wenxue* 2 (1988): 4–9.

61. Miriam Hansen, "The Mass Production of the Senses: Classical Cinema as Vernacular Modernism," *Modernism/Modernity* 6, no. 2 (1992): 59–77.

62. Zhang Xudong, *Chinese Modernism in the Era of Reforms*, 23.

63. Zhang Xudong, *Chinese Modernism in the Era of Reforms*, 22.

64. Yuan Yunfu 袁运甫, "Di'er ziran de geshou: Yao Qingzhang" 第二自然的歌手：姚庆章 [The lyric poet of second nature: Yao Qingzhang], *Meishu zashi* [Arts magazine] 11 (1983): 52–54.

65. Ke Nan 柯南, "Yao Qingzhang de huihua: 'yingying'" 姚庆章的绘画："映影" [Paintings of C. J. Yao: Reflections and shadows], *Xin Jianzhu* [New architecture] 1 (1986): 41–42.

66. Ke Nan, "Yao Qingzhang de huihua: 'yingying.'"

67. Ke Nan, "Yao Qingzhang de huihua: 'yingying.'"

68. Huang Jianxin, "*Curen shensi de heipao shijian*: 1985 nian gushipian chuangzuo huigu zuotan" 促人深思的《黑炮事件》：1985年故事片创作回顾座谈 [Thought-provoking *Black Canon Incident*: A symposium on features produced in 1985], *Dianying yishu* 4 (1986): 10.
69. Yuan Ying, "You yiwei de xiangshi," 64.
70. Yuan Ying, "You yiwei de xiangshi," 65.
71. Hofstadter, *Gödel, Escher, Bach*, 258.
72. For a reading of the film as a rehearsal and disruption of the genre, see Jason McGrath, "*Black Cannon Incident*: Countering the Counter-Espionage Fantasy," in *Chinese Films in Focus*, ed. Chris Berry (London: BFI, 2008), 25–31.
73. Huang Jianxin, "*Daoyan chanshu*."

4. Affective Form

1. Wang Meng 王蒙, "Ling de shan" 铃的闪 [The Blinking of the Bell], originally published in *Beijing wenxue*, no. 2 (1986): 31–34, trans. Zhu Hong and others, *The Stubborn Porridge and Other Stories*, 177–83. English translations of Wang Meng's stories quoted in this essay are based on the version in Wang Meng, *The Stubborn Porridge and Other Stories*, trans. Zhu Hong and others (New York: George Braziller, 1994), with slight modifications of mine.
2. Avital Ronell, *The Telephone Book: Technology, Schizophrenia, Electric Speech* (Lincoln: University of Nebraska Press, 1989), 3.
3. Wang Meng, "The Blinking of the Bell," 183.
4. Wang Meng, "Laijin" 来劲 [Thrilling], originally published in 小说选刊, no. 4 (1989): 4–17, trans. Zhu Hong and others, in *The Stubborn Porridge and Other Stories*, 159.
5. Quoted and highlighted by Lydia Liu, *The Freudian Robot: Digital Media and the Future of the Unconscious* (Chicago: University of Chicago Press, 2010), 80–81.
6. Lydia Liu, *The Freudian Robot*.
7. Wang Meng, "The Blinking of the Bell," 178.
8. *Zhongguo guangbo dianshi nianjian: 1986* 中国广播电视年鉴: 1986 [The 1986 China TV and broadcast yearbook] (Beijing: Zhongguo guangbo dianshi chubanshe, 1986), 857–59.
9. Wang Jing argues for "the stubbornness of the Chinese socialist legacy" that is present in the many cases of corporate culture and marketing strategies in post-Mao China, despite the discontinuity often perceived between Mao's China and the Reform era. She also gives examples of Hai'er and Lenovo, the CEOs of which were both erstwhile sent-down youths during the Cultural Revolution. See Wang Jing, *Brand New China: Advertising, Media, and Commercial Culture* (Cambridge, Mass.: Harvard University Press, 2008), 1–2 and 144–79.
10. Katherine Hayles, *Writing Machines* (Cambridge, Mass.: MIT Press, 2002), 25.

11. Karl Gerth, "Compromising with Consumerism in Socialist China: Transnational Flows and Internal Tensions in 'Socialist Advertising,'" *Past & Present* 218, suppl. 8 (2013): 203–32.

12. Gerth, "Compromising with Consumerism in Socialist China." See also Anne Kaminsky, "'True Advertising Means Promoting a Good Thing through a Good Form': Advertising in the German Democratic Republic," in *Selling Modernity: Advertising Twentieth-Century Germany*, ed. Pamela E. Swett, S. Jonathan Wiesen, and Jonathan R. Zatlin (Durham: Duke University Press, 2007), for a comparative view and the international intersections of "socialist advertising."

13. Gerth, "Compromising with Consumerism in Socialist China."

14. Wang Zhongming 王忠明, "Jianchi shehui zhuyi fangxiang" 坚持社会主义方向 [Adhering to the socialist direction], *Zhongguo Guanggao* 中国广告 [China advertising], no. 5 (1983): 2–3.

15. Wang Zhongming, "Jianchi shehui zhuyi fangxiang," 3.

16. Wang Zhongming, "Jianchi shehui zhuyi fangxiang."

17. Zhang Shuping 张庶平, "Lun shehuizhuyi guanggao xinxi huodong de jige lilun wenti" 论社会主义广告信息活动的几个理论问题 [Several theoretical issues on the function of information management through socialist advertising], *Zhongguo Guanggao*, no. 1 (1984): 5–7.

18. Ding Yunpeng 丁允朋, "Wei Guanggao Zhengming" 为广告正名 [Rectifying the name of advertising], originally in *Wenhui bao* 文汇报, February 1979, reprinted in Xu Zhenglin and Zhang Huixin, eds., *Zhongguo guanggaoxue yanjiu 30nian wenxuan: 1978–2008* 中国广告学研究30年文选: 1978–2008 [Selected essays of advertising studies from 1978 to 2008] (Shanghai: Shanghai jiaotong daxue chubanshe, 2009), 3–4.

19. Ding Yunpeng, "Wei Guanggao Zhengming."

20. For example, it was reported that the head of Yong Kang Wireless Equipment Factory was successful in using advertising to promote its new microprocessors. See Tian Wang 天望, "Tadein pu zai dakai chanpinxiaolu shang" 他的心扑在打开产品销路上 [His efforts to promote the products of his factory], *Zhongguo Guanggao*, no. 4 (1984): 44–45.

21. Chen Ran 陈然, "Kexue de yuce guanggao xiaoguo" 科学地预测广告效果 [To scientifically predict the effects of advertising], *Zhongguo Guanggao*, no. 5 (1983): 32.

22. This idea of measuring media effects through physiological reactions has a long history in communication and media studies. Brenton J. Malin calls this tradition "media physicalism," which understands human experience as reducible to a set of physiological traits. Malin shows how the rise of "media physicalism" overlapped with the growth of advertising, as well as the growth of public relations in the United States in the twentieth century. See Brenton J. Malin, *Feeling Mediated: A History of Media Technology and Emotion in America* (New York: New York University Press, 2016).

23. Wang Shouzhi 王受之, "Xinxi, canxiang, chengxiao" 信息, 残象, 成效 [Information, fraction, effects], *Zhongguo Guanggao*, no. 2 (1984): 13–14.

24. Gao Caiming 高才明, "Ruhe jiaqiang guanggao de jiyidu," 如何加强广告的记忆度 [How to improve the memorability of an advertisement], *Zhongguo Guanggao*, no. 4 (1984): 3–4.

25. Tian Ping 天平, "Guanggao yuyan wenzi manhua" 广告语言文字漫话 [Cursory notes on the language of advertising], *Zhongguo Guanggao*, no. 2 (1988): 32.

26. Wang Jing argues that in the United States and other Western countries it was not until the 1960s that ad agencies began to work on "brand" as advertising entered the "image era," leaving behind the "product era" with its "straightforward focus on product features and customer benefits." "Brand management" and "brand positioning" use icons and images to sell consumers "an emotional attachment to objects as nonsensical as an eye patch." See Wang, *Brand New China*, 23–25.

27. Liu Kangsheng and Hu Yaowu, "Guanggao de shehui yiyi he jiazhi" 广告的社会意义和价值 [Social significance and value of advertising], *Zhongguo Guanggao*, no. 1 (1986): 14.

28. Interestingly, Wang Meng at the beginning of his short story "Fengzheng piaodai" [Kite streamers] compares the manipulative power of the mushrooming billboard advertising in the post-Mao urban space to that of revolutionary slogans repeatedly stressing class struggles during the Cultural Revolution. See Wang, *The Butterfly and Other Stories* (Beijing: China Publication Center, 1983), 155–56. In his autobiography, Wang Meng particularly noted this detail as a mockery of the indoctrinations imposed by Lin Biao, as the "Little Red Book" of Mao's quotations was compiled by Lin. He also noted that the opening of the story generated discussion among German scholars of contemporary Chinese literature as to whether the metaphor indicates that Wang was already alarmed by the market economy as early as the 1980s. See Wang Meng, *Wang Meng Zizhuan* 王蒙自传 [Autobiography of Wang Meng], vol. 2 (Guangzhou: Huacheng Press, 2007), 76. For an illuminating account of the "little red book," the memorability of Mao's quotations, and their ritual repetition in everyday practices in relation to the media culture, especially the new portable media technology in the global 1960s, see Andrew Jones, "Quotation Songs: Portable Media and the Maoist Pop Song," in *Mao's Little Red Book: A Global History*, ed. Alexander Cook (Cambridge: Cambridge University Press, 2014), 43–60.

29. Er Sheng 尔盛, "Wufabao de guanggaozhan guanhougan" 乌发宝的广告战观后感 [Thoughts on the advertising war of hair-dye products], *Xinwen shijian*, no. 2 (1986): 17–18.

30. Hong Yilong 洪一龙, "Guanggao yu xinwen buying hunxiao" 广告与新闻不应混淆 [Advertising and news should not be mixed up], *Xinwen yu xiezuo zazhi*, no. 5 (1985): 40.

31. Wei Lin 魏林, "Xinwen yu guanggao buneng hunxiao" 新闻与广告不能混淆 [News should not be confused with advertising], *Xinwen Jie*, no. 5 (1986): 11.

32. Wu Liang 吴亮, "Guanggaoshen he tade xintumen" 广告神和它的信徒们 [The god of advertising and its disciples], *Nanfang Wentan* 南方文坛, no. 6 (1988): 24–26.

33. Yang Xiaosheng 杨晓升, "Guanggao damofang" 广告大魔方 [The magic cube of advertising], *Zhongguo Qingnian*, no. 11 (1988): 12–15.

34. Wang Meng, "Tiaoshi" 调试 [Fine tuning], *Xiaoshuo yuebao*, no. 11 (1992): 36–41; for the English translation, see "Fine Tuning," in *The Stubborn Porridge and Other Stories*, 125–38.

35. Wang Meng, "Tiaoshi."

36. Huang Aihe 黄艾禾, "Dubukai libuliao de dianshiguanggao" 躲不开、离不了的电视广告 [Unavoidable and indispensable TV commercials], *Zhongguo guangbo yingshi*, no. 5 (1987): 24.

37. Zhu Jinghe 朱景和, "Manhua dianshi guanggao jiemu" 漫话电视广告节目 [Cursory talk on TV commercials], *Beijing guangbo xueyuan xuebao*, no. 3 (1985): 34–39.

38. Ni Feng 倪峰, "Rang guanzhong zai shierbujian zhong jianshou guanggao" 让观众在视而不见中接受广告 [Make audiences accept advertising in oblivion], *Shangye yanjiu*, no. 2 (1985): 36.

39. For a detailed history of and the discourse of subliminal control in popular culture, see Charles Acland, *Swift Viewing: The Popular Life of Subliminal Influence* (Durham: Duke University Press, 2012).

40. Ni Feng, "Rang guanzhong zai shierbujian zhong jianshou guanggao," 36.

41. Charles Acland, *Swift Viewing: The Popular Life of Subliminal Influence*, 19.

42. Wu Liang, "Guanggaoshen he tade xintumen," 24.

43. Wu Liang, "Guanggaoshen he tade xintumen," 25.

44. Ding Xinmin 丁新民, "Jiedai, lianxiang, qingli" 借代,联想,情理 [Metonymy, association, and sensibility], *Zhongguo Guanggao*, no. 2 (1987): 33–34.

45. Fan Wenjiang 樊文江, "Chuqi zhisheng he lianxiang" 出奇制胜和联想 [Novelty and association], *Zhongguo Guanggao*, no. 2 (1987): 32.

46. Ma Yongliang 马永良, "Leibi lianjue xinli he guanggao yishu" 类比联觉心理和广告艺术 [Associative, analogical psychology, and advertising art], *Xinjiang Yishu* 新疆艺术, no. 5 (1988): 31–33.

47. He Zhengxiong 何震雄, "Rujin, Guanggao yao biaoshu lianxiang" 如今,广告要表述联想 [Nowadays, advertising should evoke associations], *Zhongguo Guanggao*, no. 4 (1988): 47–48.

48. Wu Liang, "Guanggaoshen he tade xintumen," 26.

49. Wu Liang, "Guanggaoshen he tade xintumen."

50. Wang Meng, "The Blinking of the Bell," 181.

51. Wang Meng, *Wang Meng Zizhuan*, 91.
52. Wang Meng, "Guanyu yishiliu de tongxin" 关于"意识流"的通信 [Correspondences about the "Stream of Consciousness"], in *Wang Meng Yanjiu Ziliao* 王蒙研究资料 [A compendium of Wang Meng studies], ed. Song Binghui and Zhang Yi (Tianjin: Tianjin renmin chubanshe, 2009).
53. Wang Meng, "*Zhi Ailisi*" 致爱丽丝 [To Alice], *Zhuomuniao*, no. 2 (1986): 89–91, trans. Zhu Hong and others, in *The Stubborn Porridge and Other Stories*, 154.
54. Wang Meng, "*Zhi Ailisi.*"
55. Wu Liang, "Guanggaoshen he tade xintumen," 25.
56. This new trend can be observed in the publication of several monographs as well as compiled anthologies of representative essays that used "scientific methods" to analyze literary classics: Ping Lun, *Wenyi kongzhilun chutan* 文艺控制论初探 [Tentative explorations into literary cybernetics] (Shenyang: Liaoning daxue chubanshe, 1986); Wen Zao, *Xitong kexue yu wenxue* 系统科学与文学 [Systems science and literature] (Shenyang: Liaoning daxue chubanshe, 1986); Sun Ziwei, ed., *Wenyi yanjiu xinfangfa tansuo* 文艺研究新方法探索 [Explorations into new methods of literary research] (Wuhan: Huazhong shifan daxue chubanshe, 1985); Liu Zaifu, Qian Xuesen et al., *Wenyixue, meixue yu xiandai kexue* 文艺学，美学与现代科学 [Literary studies, aesthetic studies, and modern science] (Beijing: Zhongguo shehui kexue chubanshe, 1986).
57. Jiang Qingguo 姜庆国, "Xinxilun meixue chutan" 信息论美学初探 [Tentative explorations into information aesthetics], in Liu Zaifu, Qian Xuesen et al., *Wenyixue, meixue yu xiandai kexue* 文艺学,美学与现代科学 [Literary theory, aesthetics, and modern science] (Beijing: Zhongguo shehui kexue chubanshe, 1986), 486–501.
58. Jiang Qingguo, "Xinxilun meisue chutan."
59. Jin Kemu 金克木, *Yishu kexue luncong* 艺术科学论丛 [Monograph series on arts and sciences] (Beijing: Shenghuo,dushu,xinzhi sanlianshudian,1986), 8–25.
60. Abraham Moles, *Information Theory and Esthetic Perception*, trans. Joel E. Cohen (Urbana: University of Illinois Press, 1966), 1.
61. Moles, *Information Theory and Esthetic Perception*, 2.
62. Moles, *Information Theory and Esthetic Perception*, 100.
63. Li Yanzu 李砚祖, "Guanggao wenhua yu guangao yishu" 广告文化与广告艺术 [Advertising culture and advertising art], originally in *Wenyi yanjiu* 文艺研究 [Literature studies], no. 5 (1988), reprinted in Xu ZhengLin 许正林 etc., eds., *Zhongguo guanggaoxue yanjiu sanshinian wenxuan: 1978–2008* 中国广告学研究30年文选 [Selected writings on Chinese advertising studies in the last thirty years] (Shanghai: Shanghai jiaotong daxue chubanshe, 2009), 27–38.
64. Moles, *Information Theory and Esthetic Perception*, 129.

65. Moles, *Information Theory and Esthetic Perception*, 167.

66. Rudolf Arnheim, "Review of *Information Theory and Esthetic Perception* by Abraham Moles," *Journal of Aesthetics and Art Criticism* 26, no. 4 (Summer 1968): 553.

67. Lydia Liu, *The Freudian Robot: Digital Media and the Future of the Unconscious* (Chicago: University of Chicago Press, 2010), 74.

68. Lydia Liu, *The Freudian Robot*, 39–98.

69. Li Tuo 李陀 and Li Jie 李劼, "Yuyan, wenhua, wenxue" 语言,文化,文学 [Language, culture, and literature], *Wenxue jiao* 文学角 [Literature stand], no. 3 (1988): 8–16.

70. Li Tuo 李陀 etc., "*Yuyan de fanpan*" 语言的反叛 [The rebellion in the realm of language], *Wenyi yanjiu*, no. 2 (1989): 75–80.

71. Li Tuo and Li Jie, "Yuyan, wenhua, wenxue."

72. Yang Qingxiang 杨庆祥, Wu Liang 吴亮, and Li Tuo 李陀, "Bashi niandai de xianfengwenxue he xianfengpiping" 八十年代的先锋文学和先锋批评 [The avant-garde literature and avant-garde critique of the 1980s], *Nanfang Wentan* 南方文坛 [Literary forum of the south], no. 6 (2008), http://www.chinesepen.org/Article/sxsy/200903/Article_20090308014935.shtml.

73. Xu Zidong 许子东, "Xinshiqi de sanzhong wenxue" 新时期的三种文学 [Three types of literature in the new era], *Wenxue pinglun* 文学评论 [Literature comments], no. 2 (1987): 64–78.

74. Li Tuo etc., "*Yuyan de fanpan*."

75. Meng Yue 孟悦, "*Yuyan fengxi zaojiude xushi*" 语言缝隙造就的叙事 [Narrative between the interstices of language], *Dangdai zuojia pinglun* [Comments on contemporary writers], no. 2 (1988): 84–90.

76. Meng Yue, "Yuyan fengxi zaojiude xushi."

77. Meng Yue, "Yuyan fengxi zaojiude xushi."

78. Meng Yue, "Yuyan fengxi zaojiude xushi."

79. Xudong Zhang, *Chinese Modernism in the Era of Reforms: Cultural Fever, Avant-Garde Fiction, and the New Chinese Cinema* (Durham: Duke University Press, 1997), 179. Zhang astutely points out: "The image of the female in Ge Fei also reveals the allegorical substation of social interests, which is based on a narrative of seduction.... Ultimately, it foretells the commercial relationship between a producer and a buyer in the literary marketplace, a situation that was not clear until after the bloody ending of the New Era. In this respect, meta-fiction can be considered the result of a stylistic negotiation between its prehistory and its posthistory. The post-socialist world of the early years of the New era and the consumer society in the post-Tiananmen phase are both addressed symbolically in meta-fiction." See Zhang, *Chinese Modernism in the Era of Reforms*, 178.

80. Qiu Yun 秋耘, "Guanggao wenxue" 广告文学 [Advertising literature], *Xin guancha* 新观察 [New observations], no. 5 (1988): 19.

81. Qiu Yun, "Guanggao wenxue."
82. Wu Liang 吴亮, Chen Cun 陈村, etc., "Chunwenxue yu 1988 nian" 纯文学与1988年 [Pure literature and the year of 1988], *Wenxue ziyoutan* 文学自由谈 [Free speech on literature], no. 2 (1989): 10–19. Interestingly, Chen Cun is also one of first and most prominent avant-garde writers who actively participated in internet literature since the late 1990s. Chen fiercely defended against commercialization the niche of web literature as a realm of literary freedom and experiments when he moderated for the well-known literary website Under the Banyan Tree. For an interesting account of Chen Cun's internet writing activities as well as their relationship to the literary experiments of the 1980s, see Michel Hockx, *Internet Literature in China* (New York: Columbia University Press, 2015), 59–84.
83. Fang Lin 方林, "Wenyijie jiu chunwenxue de duzhe riyi jianshao zhankaitaolun" 文艺界就"纯文学"的读者日益减少展开讨论 [The literary circle discussed the issue of shrinking readership of "pure literature"], *Zuopin yu Zhengming* 作品与争鸣 [Works and discussions], no. 8 (1988): 66–68.
84. Wu Liang and Chen Cun et al., "Chunwenxue yu 1988 nian."
85. For a description of the role of this socialist system in the emergence of avant-garde writing, see Shao Yanjun 邵燕君, "Chuantong wenxue shengchan jizhi de weiji he xinxing jizhi de shengcheng" 传统文学生产机制的危机和新兴机制的生成 [The crisis in the traditional literary production mechanism and the emergence of a new-style mechanism], *Wenyi zhengming*, no. 12 (2009): 13–14. A particular passage from Shao's essay is worth quoting here: "From the postal system that allowed the free sending of manuscripts for submission, to the patronage of and generous instruction to writers by the editors of the big magazines; from the formal establishment of culture bureaus at prefecture level to the assistance with revising manuscripts, free travel and lodgings provided by the big magazines, the whole emergence and development of the avant-garde movement relied on the latent continuity of the traditional literary mechanism." Quoted and translated by Michel Hockx, in *Internet Literature in China*, 26.
86. Shao Yanjun, "Chuantong wenxue shengchan jizhi de weiji he xinxing jizhi de shengcheng."
87. Wang Meng, "*Zhi Ailisi*,"

5. Liminal Mediation and the Cinema Redefined

1. D. N. Rodowick, "An Elegy for Theory," *October* 1, no. 122 (2007): 91–109.
2. Recent scholarship has contributed new insights into Bazin's notion of "realism." First, there is an effort to complicate Bazin's understanding of realism beyond the mechanical replica of the material world; second, some scholars, especially Daniel Morgan, redefine Bazin's "realism" as a plural set of styles

not confined to Italian neorealism. See *Opening Bazin: Postwar Film Theory and Its Afterlife*, ed. Dudley Andrew and Herve Joubert-Laurencin (Oxford: Oxford University Press, 2011); Dudley Andrew, *What Cinema Is! Bazin's Quest and Its Charge* (Hoboken, N.J.: Wiley-Blackwell, 2010); Daniel Morgan, "Rethinking Bazin: Ontology and Realist Aesthetics," *Critical Inquiry* 32, no. 3 (Spring 2006): 443–81.

3. Yuan Ying 远婴, "*Dianying de zijue: Xin shiqi dianying chuangzuo huigui*" 电影的自觉：新时期电影创作回顾 [The self-consciousness of cinema: A retrospective on the film production of the new period], *Dangdai dianying* 6 (1986): 13–21.

4. For an in-depth discussion of the term "realism" in the film theory of the Republican era, see Victor Fan, *Cinema Approaching Reality: Locating Chinese Film Theory* (Minneapolis: University of Minnesota Press, 2015).

5. Peter Button, *Configurations of the Real in Chinese Literary and Aesthetic Modernity* (Boston: Brill, 2009), chap. 4.

6. Hua Jia and Feng Baoxing, "Zheng Jiqiao pipan xingxiang siwei shimo (1)" 郑季翘批判形象思维始末 [Tracing the story of Zheng Jiqiao's critique of image thinking], *Dangdai wenxue yanjiu ziliao yu xinxi* 当代文学研究资料与信息 [Sources and information on contemporary literature studies], no. 3 (2006): 36–44; "Zheng Jiqiao pipan xingxiang siwei shimo (2)," *Dangdai wenxue yanjiu ziliao yu xinxi*, no. 4 (2006): 36–47.

7. See Huo Songlin 霍松林, "Chongtan xingxiang siwei: Yu Zheng Jiqiao tongzhi Shangque" 重谈形象思维：与郑季翘同志商榷 [Back to the topic of image thinking: A discussion with comrade Zheng Jiqaio], originally published in *Shanxi shida xuebao*, no. 4 (1979), reprinted in Huo Songlin, *Wenyi Sanlun* [Cursory discussion on arts] (Beijing: Zhongguo shehui kexue chubanshe, 1981), 217–60.

8. Peng Zhiping, "Guanyu 'xingxiang siwei wenti' lunzheng de nuogan lishi qingkuang" 关于"形象思维问题"论争的若干历史情况 [Several historical records of the debates on "image-thinking"], *Wenyi lilun yu piping*, no. 5 (2010); "Guanyu 'xingxiang siwei wenti' lunzheng de nuogan lishi qingkuang (2)," *Wenyi lilun yu piping*, no. 6 (2010).

9. Morgan, "Rethinking Bazin." Morgan points out that this version of perceptual realism reduces the richness and complexity in Bazin's use of "realism," as Bazin not only rejects verisimilitude as an essential component of realism but also believes that perceptual realism is an inadequate criterion for realism.

10. Yuan Ying, "*Dianying de zijue: Xin shiqi dianying chuangzuo huigui.*"

11. Kong Du 孔都, "*Dianying benxing de zairenshi*" 电影本性的再认识 [Rethinking the nature of cinema], *Dangdai dianying* 5 (1986): 33–38.

12. Cai Shiyong, "*Manlun dianying jiluxing*" 漫论电影记录性 [A causerie on "documentaryness"], *Film Art*, no. 4 (1986): 19–28.

13. Although scholars have previously discussed the notion of "suppositionality" in relation to the Chinese opera tradition as the translation for the Chinese term "jiading xing" 假定性 in the context of opera, here Cai Shiyong's use of this term does not directly invoke this operatic tradition. Yet it is fair to say that the new technical possibilities generated reflections on the interrelations and interactions between the human body and the environment, which renders the "authenticity" of images no longer a central concern. For a discussion of "suppositionality" in terms of acting, especially the actor's performing body and its highly stylized mimic movement in Chinese opera and opera films, see Bao Weihong, "The Politics of Remediation: Mise-En-Scène and the Subjunctive Body in Chinese Opera Film," *Opera Quarterly* 26, no. 2 (2010): 256–90. Jason McGrath argues that Chinese opera performance tends toward semiosis, "the inscription of symbolic meaning by convention," which was pitted against "realist acting" in the 1920s. See McGrath, "Acting Real: Cinema, Stage, and the Modernity of Performance in Chinese Silent Film," in *The Oxford Handbook of Chinese Cinemas* (Oxford: Oxford University Press, 2013), 401–20.

14. Wang Xiaoda, "*Bo*" 波 [Waves], in *Kexue huanxiang xiaoshuoxuan* 科学幻想小说选 [A selection of science fantasy stories] (Beijing: Zhongguo qingnian chubanshe, 1980), 248–82.

15. Denis Gabor was also considered a key figure whose communication theory laid the earlier foundations for information technology and theory, although in later official histories his name is obscured by more iconic names, such as Claude E. Shannon. In 1953, in the inaugural issue of *IEEE Transactions on Information Theory*, Gabor, along with Donald Mackay and Shannon, offered competing theories of "information." For different origins and histories of "information," see Bernard Geoghegan, "The Historiographic Conception of Information: A Critical Survey," *EEE Annals on the History of Computing* 30, no. 1 (January–March 2008): 66–81.

16. Li Ming, *Kongzhi lun yu shehui gaige* 控制论与社会改革 [Cybernetics and social reforms] (Beijing: Guangming ribao chubanshe, 1988), 62–75.

17. John Halas, *Graphics in Motion: From the Special Effects Film to Holographics* (New York: Van Nostrand Reinhold, 1981), 159.

18. Qian Xuesen, "Kexue jishu xiandaihua yiding yao daidong wenhua yishu xiandaihua" 科学技术现代化一定要带动文化艺术现代化 [Modernizing literature and arts through the modernization of science and technology], *Xinhua wenzhai*, no. 8 (1980): 144–46.

19. Qian Xuesen, "Kexue jishu xiandaihua yiding yao daidong wenhua yishu xiandaihua."

20. "*Weilai de quanxi dianying he dianshi*" 未来的全息电影和电视 [Holographic motion pictures and holographic television of the future], *Guowai shengxiang jishu* [Sound and image technologies abroad] 3 (1980): 61–62.

21. "Astro Boy" played an important role in the transmedia practice of character merchandising in Japan. See Marc Steinberg, *Anime's Media Mix: Franchising Toys and Characters in Japan* (Minneapolis: University of Minnesota Press, 2012).
22. Kong Du, "*Dianying benxing de zairenshi*," 33–38.
23. Lev Manovich, *The Language of New Media* (Cambridge, Mass.: MIT Press, 2001), 287–333.
24. Manovich, *The Language of New Media*.
25. Song Feijun, *Cong bodong guangxue dao xinxi guangxue* 从波动光学到信息光学 [From classic optics to information optics] (Beijing: Kexue chubanshe, 1987), 3 (italics mine).
26. Song Feijun, *Cong bodong guangxue dao xinxi guangxue*.
27. Kristen Whissel argues that metamorphosis brought by digital special effects is always related to the theme of imprisonment and freedom in films. She traces the precursors of digital "morph" to overlapping dissolves, time-lapse photography, and animation. Taking further Eisenstein's observations about the "protean power" of animation in mobilizing "the fantasy of transcending any type of categorization or boundary," she examines "the struggle between an ossified, standardized existence that imprisons and enslaves and the dynamic freedom implied by metamorphosis," which is displayed in early 1990s and recent films that employ the technique of digital morph. See Kristen Whissel, *Spectacular Digital Effects: CGI and Contemporary Cinema* (Durham: Duke University Press, 2014), chap. 4.
28. Tom Gunning, "'Now You See It, Now You Don't': The Temporality of the Cinema of Attractions," in *Silent Cinema Reader*, ed. Lee Grieveson and Peter Kramer (New York: Routledge, 2004), 41–50.
29. Vivian Sobchack, *Screening Space: The American Science Fiction Film* (New York: Ungar, 1987), 227–28.
30. Sobchack, *Screening Space*, 229.
31. Qian Haiyi, "*Xiandai mingxinpian xiju*" 现代明信片喜剧 [Modern postcard comedy], *Dianying xinzuo* [New film works] 6 (1987): 71–73.
32. Richard Dienst, *Still Life in Real Time: Theory after Television* (Durham: Duke University Press, 1994).
33. Patricia Clough, "Future Matters: Technoscience, Global Politics, and Cultural Criticism," *Social Text* 3 (Fall 2004): 1–23.
34. Sianne Ngai, *Our Aesthetic Categories: Any, Cute, Interesting* (Cambridge, Mass.: Harvard University Press, 2012), 197–210.
35. In the privatization and marketization processes of former state socialist countries, socialism and its centrally planned economy were often associated with the rigidity and mass production of Fordism, portrayed as "stagnant" and incapable of changing without collapsing. Former workers of socialist work units amid the new developments of the market economy were thus required to reinvent themselves as agile, flexible individuals. Elizabeth Dunn's study of this production of flexible bodies and the remaking of persons in the context

of Poland provides insightful observations on how white-collar managers and businessmen were faced with particular pressure to demonstrate their own flexibility and adaptability in order to prove their membership in the imagined community of the transnational market economy and severed ties with socialist systems and social networks. See Dunn, *Privatizing Poland*, esp. chap. 3, 58–93.

36. See Wang Hui, "*Dangdai dianying zhong de xiangtu yu dushi: Xunzhao lishi de jieshi yu shengming de guisu*" 当代电影中的乡土与都市：寻找历史的解释与生命的归宿 [The urban and the rural in contemporary films: In search of historical explanations and the significance of life], *Dianying yishu* 2 (1989): 12–19. Wang read the film and its new restless characters in relation to the society and economy in transformation.

37. Yang Ke, "*1985 nian dianying faxing fangying gongzuo huigu*" 1985 年电影发行放映工作回顾 [A review of film distribution and screening in 1985], *Zhongguo dianying nianjian* (Beijing: Zhongguo dianying chubanshe, 1986), 11.1–11.5.

38. "*Jing, jin, hu deng shiyige chengshi 1985nian shangbannian dianying shichang qingkuang*" 京、津、沪等十一个城市1985年上半年电影市场情况 [The conditions of the film market in eleven cities, including Beijing, Tianjin, and Shanghai] (Beijing: Zhongguo dianying nianjian, 1986), 11.5–11.7.

39. Ni Zhen, *Gaige yu Zhongguo Dianying* 改革与中国电影 [Reforms and Chinese cinema] (Beijing: Zhongguo dianying chubanshe, 1994), 47.

40. Yang Ke, "*1985 nian dianying faxing fangying gongzuo huigu*."

41. Qi Fang, "*Dianying mianlin tiaozhan haishi binling siwang?*" 电影面临挑战还是濒临死亡 [Is cinema facing challenges or about to die?], *Dangdai dianying* 2 (1986): 34–44.

42. Zhou Chuanji and Shao Mujun, "Zhou Chuanji and Shao Mujun tan zhongguo dianying yu haolaiwu" 周传基与邵牧君谈中国电影与好莱坞 [Zhou Chuanji and Shao Mujun talk about Chinese cinema and Hollywood], *Dianying yishu* 1 (1989): 43–53.

43. Zhou Chuanji, "*Dianying yu yi dianshi weizhu de qita chuanbo meijie de guanxi*" 电影与电视为主的其它传播媒介的关系 [Cinema's relation to television and other media], *Dangdai dianying* 4 (1989): 41–46.

44. Zhang Wei, "*Dazhongxing dianying de xinli duiying*" 大众型电影的心理对应 [The psychological parallel to popular film], *Dazhong dianying* [Popular film] 6 (1987): 4–5.

45. Li Tuo et al., "*Duihua yulepian*" 对话娱乐片 [Conversations on entertainment films], *Dangdai dianying* 1 (1987): 55–67.

46. Li Tuo et al., "*Duihua yulepian*."

47. Li Tuo et al., "*Duihua yulepian*."

48. Chen Xihe, "*Ren de zhuti, yulepian*" 人的主题，娱乐片 [The theme of the human and entertainment films], *Dazhong dianying* 6 (1987): 6–7.

49. When the "happy alliance" between the CCP and the intellectuals under the shared project of modernization drew near to an end, and the increasingly commercialized cultural production whirled away in a different direction, humanist intellectuals were no longer united around the shared project of

enlightenment and the dream of modernization, but were fractured as market forces increasingly permeated the cultural production of post-Mao China. In this sense, the debates surrounding the issue of an eclipsed "humanist spirit" in the early 1990s became a lament for the lost dream of enlightenment, but they also exposed the contradictions and conflicts dormant in the culture of the 1980s.

Wang Jing made the point that the broken collaboration between the culture elite's making of their own utopian discourse of enlightenment and the state's project of modernization was signaled by the television miniseries *Heshang* [River elegy] and finally came to an inevitable collision on June 4, 1989. See Wang, *High Culture Fever*, 2.

For a detailed and insightful study of the debate on the "humanist spirit," see Jason McGrath, "Ideologies of Popular Culture: The 'Humanist Spirit' Debate," in *Postsocialist Modernity: Chinese Cinema, Literature, and Criticism in the Market Age* (Stanford: Stanford University Press, 2008). McGrath notices that for the human-spirit advocates, the "main culprit" for the loss of the humanist spirit was "the 'vulgarization' (*cubihua*) or 'secularization' (*shisuhua*) brought on by the commodification of culture in the market economy" (32).

50. Jean Baudrillard, "Simulacra and Simulations," in *Jean Baudrillard: Selected Writings*, 2nd ed., ed. and intro. Mark Poster (Stanford: Stanford University Press, 2001).

51. Qian Yunxuan, "Cuo Wei *chuangzuo gouxiang*: *Meishu gousi*"《错位》创作构想：美术构思 [The ideas of producing *Dislocation*: Art designer's notes], *Dangdai dianying* 3 (1987): 116–18.

52. Wang Xinsheng, "Cuo Wei *chuangzuo gouxiang*: *Sheying chanshi*"《错位》创作构想：摄影阐释 [The ideas of producing *Dislocation*: Cinematographer's notes], *Dangdai dianying* 3 (1987): 115 (italics mine).

53. Qian Yunxuan, "Cuo Wei *chuangzuo gouxiang*: *Meishu gousi*," 117.

54. One of the most frequently used terms in film critique and theory of this time is "*goutu* 构图," which I roughly translate as "cinematic composition." However, the emphasis of "*goutu*" on careful arrangements of both visual and sound elements, and the sense of "designedness," should not be missing from the translation.

55. Huang Jianxin, "Cuo Wei *chuangzuo gouxiang*: *Daoyan chanshi*"《错位》创作构想：导演阐释 [The ideas behind the production of *Dislocation*: Statement from the director], *Dangdai dianying* 3 (1987): 113–14.

56. Wang Xinsheng, "*Sheying chanshi*," 115.

57. Gilles Deleuze, *Cinema 2: The Time Image*, trans. Hugh Tomlinson and Robert Galeta (Minneapolis: University of Minnesota Press, 1989), 265.

58. Yao Xiaomeng, "*Dui yizhong xinde dianying xingtai de sikao, shilun dianying yixiang meixue*" 对一种新的电影形态的思考：试论电影意象美学 [Some thoughts on a new cinematic aesthetics: A tentative discussion on the cinematic aesthetics of "thought-image"], *Dangdai dianying* 6 (1986): 44–51.

59. Zongqi Cai, "The Early Philosophical Discourse on Language and Reality and Lu Ji's and Liu Xie's Theories of Literary Creation," *Frontiers of Literary Studies in China* 5, no. 4 (2011): 477–510.
60. Zongqi Cai, "The Early Philosophical Discourse on Language and Reality."
61. The Chinese text is: "情瞳昽而弥鲜, 物昭晰而互进." The translation of the sentence above comes from Zongqi Cai.
62. Zongqi Cai, "The Early Philosophical Discourse on Language and Reality."
63. Yao Xiaomeng, "*Dui yizhong xinde dianying xingtai de sikao, shilun dianying yixiang meixue.*"
64. Qian Xuesen, "*Xitong kexue, siwei kexe yu renti kexue*" 系统科学，思维科学与人体科学 [Systems science, noetic science, and somatic science], *Ziran Zazhi*, no. 1 (1981): 3–9.
65. Qian Xuesen, "*Xitong kexue, siwei kexe yu renti kexue.*"
66. Yang Chunding, *Wenyi siweixue* 文艺思维学 [Studies of artistic thinking] (Nanjing: Dongna daxue chubanshe, 1989).
67. Yao Xiaomeng, "*Dui yizhong xinde dianying xingtai de sikao, shilun dianying yixiang meixue.*"
68. Yao Xiaomeng, "*Dui yizhong xinde dianying xingtai de sikao, shilun dianying yixiang meixue.*"
69. For a compelling investigation into the historical emergence of cinema as an affective medium in Republican China, and especially how the affective power of cinema was understood in terms of "resonance" 共鸣力, see Weihong Bao, *Fiery Cinema: The Emergence of an Affective Medium in China, 1915–1945* (Minneapolis: University of Minnesota Press, 2015).
70. Wang Jixing, "*Wo yu 'xiaoluobotou'*: Mokuzhongde huanxiang *daoyan suoji*" 我与"小萝卜头"：《魔窟中的幻想导演琐记》 ["Little radish head" and me: Director's notes on *Visions from a Jail Cell*], in *Zhongguo dianying nianjian 1987* (Beijing: Zhongguo dianying chubanshe, 1990), 3–40.
71. Chris Berry points out that in Chinese films produced in the Mao era, sequences of shot and reverse shot are often used for social conflict and disharmony, whereas exchanges of dialogue between people in a harmonious relationship are often rendered in medium shots or even long shots so that the characters are always in the same frame. See Berry, *Postsocialist Cinema in Post-Mao China: The Cultural Revolution after the Cultural Revolution* (New York: Routledge, 2004), 51–58.
72. Cheng Youjin, "*Yibu qugaohegua de ertongpian*" 一部曲高和寡的儿童片 [A children's film that is caviar to its audience], *Dianying pingjie* [Film review] 9 (1987): 9.
73. Eugene Thacker, "Dark Media," in *Excommunication: Three Inquiries in Media and Mediation*, ed. Alexander Galloway, Eugene Thacker, and McKenzie Wark (Chicago: University of Chicago Press, 2014), 131.

74. Thacker, "Dark Media," 119.

75. Fredric Jameson, *The Geopolitical Aesthetic: Cinema and Space in the World System* (Bloomington: Indiana University Press, 1992), 20–22.

76. This interrogation of the mechanism of producing "reality" to a certain degree is tied to the film's unconventional narrative about the Cultural Revolution. Since the late 1970s, the CCP had disseminated a discourse about rectifying the past in order to sweep the past behind and create a new order for its Reforms and Opening policy. This generated a pervasive mode of melodramatic representation of the Cultural Revolution in both literature and cinema, a mode that affirms the rectification of the wrongs in the end. As critic Hu Ke pointed out, there are other ways to tell the story of the film: "If the story is told in a direct way, it will fit into the category of Scar literature; it can also be told as a detective story featuring an upright and charismatic official who has determinedly got to the bottom of the case." See Hu Ke 胡克, "Kongbupian yu 'heilou guhun'" 恐怖片与《黑楼孤魂》, *Wenyi bao*, no. 5 (1989). In either case, the melodramatic mode of accusation and the narrative closure of the case function as a cathartic release that affirms the rectification discourse. *The Lonely Spirit* questions this mechanism of rectification by bringing to the center the unrepresentable and the untellable. In the film, Huo tries to stop the ghost's revenge on the director because he believes that the truth has to be clarified, and justice has to be reestablished, but only in a legal and "human" way. The ghost, however, refuses to accept the "human" method of pursuing justice, not only because no "human"-centered medium would be able to provide any evidence of the crime, but more important, the compliance to the "human" mode of justice is a concession of the power to define the very notion of "justice." In other words, the film, by invoking supernatural powers that defy human rationality and control, suggests the existence of the alternative that cannot be assimilated into the current system of justice, nor conform to the existing political economy of visuality and perceptions. Also pertinent here are the power relations involved in any kind of historiographical writings: Who chooses what evidences to produce what kind of "truth"? If historical writing is predicated upon a self-conscious filtering of information and the production of narratives, what are rendered invisible through this process?

77. Eugene Thacker shares a similar view in his description of "dark media."

78. Taojing and Ye Luhe, "Zhongguo diyi er" 中国第一耳 [The first ear of China], *Dianying yishu*, no. 6 (1996): 66–72.

79. For a discussion of *Song at Midnight* and the film's promotion strategy, see Yomi Braester, *Witness Against History: Literature, Film, and Public Discourse in Twentieth-Century China* (Stanford: Stanford University Press, 2003), chap. 3.

Epilogue

1. "Timeline of Chinese Internet," provided by China Internet Network Information Center, http://www.cnnic.net.cn/hlwfzyj/hlwdsj/.

Index

Page numbers in italics refer to illustrations.

advertising, 170, 171, 183–84, 185, 191, 192; aesthetics and, 177; agencies/number of, 168; capitalist, 165, 166; communicative effects of, 164; discourse of, 194; experimental, 194; forms of, 165, 172; impact of, 168, 173; market information and, 165–68; maximizing, 174; mechanism of, 194; socialist, 163, 165, 166, 288n12; stimuli of, 275; studies, 37, 164, 167, 168, 169; subliminal, 175–77; television, 233
aesthetics, 23, 30, 34, 121, 137, 181, 190, 195, 215, 224, 229, 251; advertising and, 177; applied, 185; cinematic, 198, 234–39, 298n58; documentary, 199, 202; information, 164, 183–84, 186–87, 188; modernist, 122; politics and, 37; shadow-play, 136
affect, 28, 103, 177; affectivity, 163, 175–77, 187; flow of, 214–19; market of, 188–94; viral, 177–83
AI. *See* artificial intelligence
Amazon Mechanical Turk, 112, 113, 114, 116, 117

amodal, 44, 65, 66
anime, 164, 208, 259, 260
Apple, 59–60
architecture, 142, 153, 185, 231, 269n13
Arnheim, Rudolf, 187
art, 13, 23, 170, 200; socialist, 24; visual, 37
artificial intelligence (AI), 100, 111, 113, 114, 115, 117, 184, 236; developments in, 116; experts, 86, 90–91, 112; research, 32, 84, 86, 89, 90, 112; systems, 84, 85, 86, 87, 98
Ashby, W. Ross, 122, 123, 140, 141
"Astro Boy," 207–8, 296n21
Atlantic Trans-International Corp., 193
"At Middle Age" (Shen Rong), 95–97, 98–99, 100, 102
Atomu, 208
authenticity, 131, 154, 203, 204, 213, 226, 253, 295n13; cinematic, 251
autonomy, 95, 124, 137, 150, 187, 188, 199; aesthetic, 34, 37; depoliticized, 108, 109
autopoiesis, 14, 140, 141

301

Autopoiesis and Cognition (Matunara and Varela), 140

Bach, Johann Sebastian, 142
backwardness, 134, 140, 145, 259
Baidu, 112–13
"Baomu" (Maidservants), 99
Barbrook, Richard, 29
Bateson, Gregory, 140
Baudrillard, Jean, 195, 212, 226
Bazin, André, 25, 136, 234; on photorealism, 202; realism and, 293n2; theory of, 137; understanding of, 201
Beauty's Head in a Haunted House (film), 226
behavior, 17, 191; consumption, 166; intelligent, 87, 115; love, 228; quantitative analyses of, 47
Beijing Advertising Agency, 167
Beijing Broadcasting Institute, 174
Beijing Film Academy, 251
Belinsky, Vissarion, 200
Bell, Daniel, 29, 30, 69, 70, 87, 88
Beninger, James, 16, 17
Bergson, Henri, 239
Berkeley, George, 65
Berlin Wall, 27
Berry, Chris, 25, 26, 299n71
Bertalanffy, Ludwig von, 68
Bethune, Norman, 96, 103
bioelectricity, 71, 81
biological conditions, 46, 47, 188
Black Cannon Incident (film), 34, 122, 224, 227; generic images of, 157; geometric graphics in, 149; intellectuals in, 146; still from, 148; strange loops and, 144–47, 149; style of, 153; urban modernity and, 152
Blow Out (film), 246, 249
body: cybernetic, 35, 49, 213; digitizing, 75; function of, 63; holistic view of, 48; information environment and, 2, 35, 56; information systems and, 27, 65; laboring, 117; as medium, 7–8; physical, 111; physiological limits of, 55; somatic science and, 43; waveform communication of, 35
boundaries: human–machine, 22; reconfiguration of, 9
brain, 112, 113; activity of, 81; bioelectrical currents of, 62; framework of, 71; research on, 90
Brooks, Peter, 285n37
"Brotherly Love amid the Same Class" (Liang), 96, 97, 105, 107
Brown, Nick, 238
Building Expert Systems, 93
bureaucracy, 16, 17, 98, 144, 145–46, 227, 259
Burroughs, William S., 180
butterfly effect, 240
Button, Peter, 24, 199

Cai, Zongqi, 235, 295n13, 299n61
Cai Shiyong, 202, 203
Cai Xiang, 80, 106, 235
Cai Yi, 199
capitalism, 7, 28, 37, 78, 116, 167, 246; development of, 9, 30, 88, 125; employment system of, 31; global, 21, 23, 34, 44, 52, 78, 122, 151, 152, 157; hegemonic, 32; ideology of, 110; industrial, 88, 117; information, 11, 21, 33, 44, 75, 78, 82, 114, 261; socialism and, 26; systemic problem of, 165; universalizing/homogenizing power of, 8; Weberian thesis of, 126
Casio, 164
CASNET, 87
Cassandra Crossing, The (film), 222

Index

cause-and-effect relation, 142, 143, 144, 145, 160, 214
CCTV. *See* China Central Television
Center for Electrified Education, 62
central planning, 69, 192, 275n53
Central Propaganda Department, 167
Chang'an school, 139
Changchun Film Studio, 225
Chari, Sharad, 27
Chen Cun, 192, 293n82
Chen Kaige, 131, 133, 195, 251
Chen Lai, 131, 133
Chen Xihe, 135, 136, 138, 223, 285n37
Chen Xin, 46, 47, 66, 68
China Academy of Sciences, 89
China Advertising, 167, 168, 169, 170, 176
China Association for Artificial Intelligence, 89
China Central Television (CCTV), 61, 117, 119, 120, 164, 173, 174, 208
China Research Net (CRN), 255
Chinese Academy of Social Sciences, 131
Chinese Association for Somatic Science, 66
Chinese Culture Academy, 130, 131
Chinese Institute of Electronics, 3
Chinese Journal of Nature, 40, 50, 63, 66; cover of, *41*
Chinese medicine, 49, 89, 92, 106; *qigong* and, 48
Chinese Odysseus (film), 256, 260
Chow, Stephen, 256, 260
cinema, 35, 137, 138, 156, 204, 207, 231; affective power of, 197, 239, 244; authenticity/suppositionality and, 203; communicative efficacy of, 244–45; critique of, 238–39; didactic rule of, 136; digital, 212; domestic, 219–24; experiments in, 25–26; as haunted medium, 244–51, 253–54; holographic, 212; hybridity of, 214; liminality of, 197, 198; mediating role of, 229; as medium, 199, 245; new-wave, 37; panorama, 221; pan-sensory, 207; reinvention of, 197, 199; representational capacity of, 248; social functions of, 136; theory of, 38, 122, 137; transformations of, 11, 38, 224; understanding of, 25, 236, 238
cinema of attractions, 216
civilization, 119, 120, 134, 145, 146, 190, 222; industrial, 69, 88
cloudsourcing, 84, 112
Clough, Patricia Ticineto, 217
Club of Rome, 130
coding, 67, 87, 89, 90, 91, 146, 248; binary, 36, 59
Cold War, 6, 10, 11, 27, 28, 29, 32, 37, 45, 117, 121, 122, 124
Cold War Left, 28, 29, 30
Coming of Post-Industrial Society, The (Bell), 30, 69, 88
commerce, 129, 170, 172
commercialization, 26, 37, 38, 164, 194, 222, 224, 254
commercials. *See* advertising
Commission on the Year, The (American Academy of Arts and Sciences), 29
commodities, 166, 167, 170, 176
communication, 3, 13, 15, 20, 43, 68, 112, 146, 159, 170, 238; advertising and, 164; aesthetic, 185; cooking pots and, 9; diagram for, 74; effective, 169, 174, 237, 245; failure of, 244; high-speed, 30; informational mode of, 75; medium of, 12, 230; mode of, 163; networks, 16, 31, 75; studies, 13, 169, 184–85; system, 73, 159;

technical, 16; threshold of, 246–47; voice, 57; waveform, 35; wireless, 6, 267n2
Communications Studies Department, 169
communism, 28, 29, 43, 44, 82, 126
computation, 8, 19, 257; algorithmic, 259; rhythmic, 144
computer displays, abstract patterns on, 233
computer programs, 91, 92, 107, 242
computers, 15, 215, 225, 232; high-speed, 83; home/personal, 59–60; intelligent, 88; knowledge/experiences and, 85
computing, 16, 18, 29, 30
Confucianism, 126, 133, 136, 234
connectivity, 3, 6, 7, 21, 228, 255; ineluctable, 159–65; language and, 161
consciousness, 100, 151, 163; Confucian, 146; feudalist, 146; human, 68, 71, 168; revolutionary, 43; stream of, 178, 179–80, 183; traditional, 146; understanding, 204
consumerism, 3, 6, 8, 130, 163, 165, 254
Contemporary Cinema (journal), 201, 223
Control Revolution, 16, 17
Conversation, The (film), 246
coolness, professional, 100–103, 104, 107, 108
Coppola, Francis Ford, 246
Correspondence on Somatic Science, 66
crowded bus, metamorphosis in, 209
crowdsourcing, 33, 36, 84, 112
Cuiqiao, 119, 134, 138, 139
cultural production, 23, 255, 298n49; commercialization of, 164, 222, 224; marketization of, 197, 244; socialist, 37, 151
Cultural Revolution, 2, 24, 37, 45, 57, 79, 81, 98, 105, 110, 127, 128, 129, 130, 163, 179, 189, 196, 200, 219, 246, 251; advertising and, 166; Mao and, 43; violence of, 82
cultural structure, 129, 190, 191
cultural system, socialist, 192, 193
culture, 125, 170, 190; backwardness of, 258; capitalist, 28; Chinese, 129, 133, 188, 190; commercial, 244, 268n7; Confucian, 126; consumer, 254; contemporary, 19; humanistic, 124; ideology and, 138; literary, 70; material, 153; media, 208, 213, 260, 289n28; politics and, 138; popular, 49, 175, 220, 260–61; print, 51, 52; traditional, 144; visual, 70; Weberian thesis of, 126; Western, 133
"Culture: China and the World" series, 130, 131
"Curious Case, The," 85, 93, 95, 102, 109, 110, 111
cybernetic logic, 20, 30, 75
cybernetic loops, 26, 173, 176, 180, 232
cybernetics, 7, 11, 29, 36, 47, 68, 72, 75, 84, 110, 121, 123, 127, 128, 140, 141, 184, 186, 204, 245, 259; affect and, 103; analytics of, 124; biological models of, 86; critique of, 10; developments in, 18; disseminating, 129; imagination and, 19; interconnections of, 269n13; theory, 71
Cybernetics (Wiener), 276n61

Dai Ruwei, 83, 84
data: biological, 47; collection, 17, 35, 123; digital, 8, 78; extrasensory,

Index

66–67; inter-conversion of, 64; physiological, 47; process, 59, 87; sensory, 67; visible, 59
Dawnlight One (satellite), 46
defamiliarization, 138, 177–80, 181, 183, 184, 185
Deleuze, Gilles, 84, 232
Delluc, Louis, 135
Deng Lijun (Teresa Teng), 80
Deng Xiaoping, 44, 51, 98, 166; developmentalist policies of, 2, 30, 70; futuristic discourse and, 28; market reforms and, 11, 82; Opening and Reforms and, 32; science/technology and, 79; social changes by, 10
De Palma, Brian, 246, 249
depoliticization, 36, 84, 103, 104; politics of, 70, 109, 261
Descartes, René, 115
Design for a Brain (Ashby), 122
Destiny Club, 80, 81
development: arrested, 157; economic, 21, 30, 79, 149, 150, 151; scientific, 107; temporality of, 152
developmentalism, 30, 34, 70, 125, 128, 259; ideology of, 28; linearity of, 32
Dialectics of Nature (Engel), 130
dianxing, 23, 24
Diderot, Denis, 65
Dienst, Richard, 216, 217
digital, 8, 11, 16, 36, 64, 65, 67, 82; convertibility of, 78; flexibility of, 67; newness of, 59; ur-history of, 35
digital devices, 19, 168, 259, 272n3
"Director's Notes" (Huang), 145
Dirlik, Arif, 26, 27, 30, 32
discourse, 146, 150, 151, 181, 194; aesthetic, 164; cinematic, 121; critical, 164, 198; cultural, 239; developmental, 79; futuristic, 7,

28; humanist, 117, 196–97, 224, 228; intellectual, 224, 245; literary, 183; modernization, 152; official, 55; popular, 55; scientific, 32, 35, 44; socialist, 25
"Discussion on the Essential Nature of Cinema" (Kong), 201–2
Dislocation (film), 23; nightmare of, 224–29; still from, *225, 227, 228, 230, 232, 233, 234*
Dneprov, Anatoly, 110
doctors: barefoot, 106, 107; human/fallible, 95–100; robot, 85–90, 99, 100, 109, 117
Donald, Stephanie, 139–40
"Dreams" (story), 54, 78, 79
Dreyfus, Hubert L., 86, 90, 114–17
Dreyfus, Stuart, 115
Drucker, Johanna, 19, 109
Dunn, Elizabeth, 275n53, 296n35
Dushu (journal), 52
Dushu zazhi (journal), 105
Dyer-Witheford, Nick, 111

"East is Red" (satellite), 46
Economic and Philosophic Manuscripts of 1844 (Marx), 98
economic life, 28, 46, 146, 165, 218
economy, 7, 108, 114, 297n36; commercial, 129; commodity, 34; cultural, 255; digital, 260; information, 33, 60, 194, 224, 260; knowledge-based, 69. *See also* market economy
education, 43, 70, 241; computer-aided, 61, 62; television and, 60, 274n36
Edwards, Paul, 86, 117
"EIDAK" system, 59
Eisenstein, Sergei, 135, 296n27
electrocardiogram (EKG), 47
electroencephalogram (EEG), 47, 161
electromyogram (EMG), 47

electronics: audio, 248, 251; consumer, 57, 60, 75, 226, 232; production of, 107
Electronics World, 52, 57, 62; cover of, 53, 58; illustration from, 63
Elementary Explorations on the Techniques of Modern Fiction (Gao), 150
Engels, Friedrich, 43, 130
engineering: computer, 92; metasynthetic, 83, 84, 117; social, 123; systems, 123
Engineering Cybernetics (Qian Xuesen), 35
enlightenment, 23, 65, 298n49
entertainment films, 23, 26, 196, 197, 222, 223–24; aesthetic effects of, 224; development of, 223
environment, 46, 122, 143; computational, 8; cultural, 37; hypermediated, 212; information, 167, 180; interior, 121; media, 6, 11, 36, 163, 164, 191, 203–7, 259; social, 138; urban, 145
epistemologies, 8, 140, 241, 245, 248, 251
Escher, M. C., 142, 154, 156; print by, 143
ethics, 136, 198, 223, 251; promulgation of, 285n37; socialist, 24, 85, 103, 166
"Even Telegrams Are Not Fast Enough," 55–56
expert systems, 21, 84, 95, 112, 115; development of, 89–90, 109, 111; goal of, 85–86; second-generation, 92, 93
Exposition on Literature, An (Lu Ji), 235
extrasensory powers, 39, 55, 56, 66, 74, 248; advocates of, 40, 43; children with, 41, 42; communism and, 44; interest in, 50, 67; magic waves and, 65; mechanisms of, 54; medium for, 40; scientific discourses on, 44; as waveform, 62–63

Fan, Fa-ti, 107
Fangfang, 93, 94, 102, 109, 117; behavior of, 90; as human agent, 111; labor/life and, 111; robot doctors and, 99
feedback, 67, 123, 142, 180
feedback loops, 7, 109, 141, 167
Feigenbaum, Edward, 90, 91; expert system and, 85–86, 92, 112; knowledge engineering and, 86–87
feudalism, 28, 36, 49, 120, 121, 128, 129, 146, 258
Fifth Generation, 34, 87, 88
Film (Wead and Lellis), 201
Film Art (journal), 202
film industry, 219, 220–21, 222
filmmaking, 25, 136, 199, 220–21, 248; process of, 245; science and, 137
films, 24, 25, 136, 137, 204; categories of, 253; counterespionage, 156, 157; distribution of, 220–21; entertainment, 23, 26, 196, 197, 222, 223–24; experimental, 197, 222, 223; exploratory, 248, 253; holographic, 205; interpretive, 239; martial art, 208, 210; postcard, 216; post-Cultural Revolution, 146; science fiction, 215; scientific understanding of, 136; Soviet, 23; television and, 221–22
film theory, 23; Chinese, 135, 136; ultrastable system of, 133–40; Western, 135, 238
fishbone antennas, 3, 6, 267n4; photo of, 6
flashing, high-speed, 175

Index

Flights of Fantasy (film), 214–15, 216, 217, 228, 241; cinema/television and, 219; metamorphosis in, 207–8, 210, 212–14; stills from, 209, 211
fluidity, images of, 229–32
Ford, Henry, 275n53
Fordism, 69, 296n35
form, politics of, 188–94
formalism, 137, 162, 184, 188, 189
Foxconn, 7
Future of Intellectuals and the Rise of the New Class (Gouldner), 104
Future Shock (Toffler), 52

Gabor, Denis, 204–5, 295n15
Galleries (Yao), 154, 155
Galloway, Alexander, 9, 12, 13, 19, 84, 270n39
Gan Yang, 130, 131
Gao Xingjian, 150
Ge Fei, 183, 191, 292n79
general intellect, 111, 112, 113, 114, 126, 133, 282n60
General Problem Solver, 86
geopolitics, Cold War, 10, 28, 86, 121, 122, 124, 157
Gestalt, 177, 184, 202
ghosts, 116, 246, 247, 248, 250, 300n76
Giddens, Anthony, 95, 100, 103
Global South, 31, 151
Gödel, Escher, Bach (Hofstadter), 141
Gödel's Theorem, 142
Gold Star TV, 170
Goodman, Steve, 277n68
Google, 84, 112, 113
Gorky, Maxim, 24, 200
Gouldner, Alvin W., 104–5, 124, 125
Grand Theater, 253
Graphical User Interface (GUI), 18
graphics, 147, 149
Grundrisse (Marx), 111, 114

Guangzhou Academy of Fine Arts, 169
Guan Zhaozhi, 45
Guillory, John, 12, 13, 16
Gunning, Tom, 214, 215, 216
Guowai shehui kexue wenzhai (journal), 105, 124
Gu Qing, 139, 140
Gu Xin, 105

Haken, Hermann, 68
Halas, John, 205
HAL 9000, 112
Hansen, Mark B. N., 8, 36, 64
Hansen, Miriam, 151
Han Shaogong, 78
Hardt, Michael, 103, 268n10
Hayles, N. Katherine, 9, 18, 20, 68, 71, 140, 141, 164
He Chongyin, 40, 43, 63, 66
Hegel, G. W. F., 12, 121, 127, 283n3
Hegelianism, 24
He Guimei, 125, 126
He Weiling, 130, 131, 132
history, 120, 121, 131, 134, 135, 254; complexity/contingency of, 82; media, 11; revolutionary, 25; ultrastable structure of, 22; unreadable, 78–82
Hofstadter, Douglas R., 141, 142, 144, 154
Hollywood, 23, 215, 220, 222
"Holographic Motion Pictures and Holographic TV of the Future," 206
holography, 196, 197, 198, 204, 207, 212; capacity of, 206; using, 205
homeostasis, 121, 126, 140, 141
Hong Kong, 2, 3, 6, 50, 219–20, 223
Horn, Eva, 14, 15
Hou Yao, 135–36
Huang Jianxin, 34, 122, 144, 145, 154, 156, 157, 230; *Black Cannon*

308 Index

Incident and, 153; discrete spaces and, 231; *Dislocation* and, 224; urban modernity and, 152
Huang Ziping, 150–52
Huashi, photo report from, 42
human agency, 23, 109, 122, 143, 180
humanism, 68, 98, 110, 111, 197
humans: boundaries of, 109; complete, 224; environment and, 152; ghosts and, 247; heaven and, 1–2, 68; lifeless sculptures of, 226; machines and, 20, 22, 45–47, 62, 83, 84, 93, 109, 110, 111, 114, 116, 117, 119; mannequins and, 226; nonhumans and, 227; technology and, 55, 262; things and, 110; transformation of, 111
hyperreality, 195, 196, 212
hypnotism, 47, 80, 175

idea-image *(yixiang)*, 23, 197, 198; ambiguity/polysemousness of, 238; cinematic aesthetic and, 113, 234–39; understanding of, 236
identity, 101, 108, 123, 210; human, 23; national, 79
ideology, 16, 27, 32, 128, 137; Cold War, 86; culture and, 138; Maoist, 190; official, 79, 258; social, 3; socialist, 26, 105
image-recognition, nonvisual organs and, 40
images, 180, 230, 234, 235; advertising, 174, 177; character and, 200; cinematic, 64, 121–22, 197, 202, 213, 216, 236, 239, 244, 248; concepts and, 201; digital, 8; enframing, 38; enigmatic, 244; frameless, 203–7; generic, 157; holographic, 206; immobile, 135; media, 217; memory, 170, 238; object, 236; phantasmagoric, 154; sound, 230; thoughts and, 195, 198; three-dimensional, 205; two-dimensional, 238; understanding of, 25; visual, 230
image-thinking, 116, 200, 236
imagination, 9, 19, 31, 85, 177; popular, 6, 32, 35; social, 33
industrialization, 17, 31, 88, 125, 144, 152
information, 18, 23, 35, 69, 70, 89, 90, 103, 123, 164, 177, 181, 228, 249; abstract, 75; advertised, 169; amodal, 44, 66; bombs, 9, 37; circuits, 22, 44, 67; collecting, 3, 61, 71, 173; commodity, 167; control and, 31; as corporeal experience, 74; depoliticized, 36, 45, 82; dualism of, 75; enframing, 213; extrasensory, 63, 64, 66–67, 74; market, 37, 165–68; mixed, 191; noises and, 170–75; nonvisual, 66; pictorial, 64; postsocialism and, 37; processing, 63, 64, 186; production and, 88; proliferation of, 34; *qi* and, 50; semantic, 187; sensory, 65; song of, 51; waves of, 204
information body, 8; discontent with, 69–71, 74–75, 78
information environment, 7, 19, 25, 36; enveloping, 6; human body and, 2, 35, 56; waves and, 61
information explosion, 44, 65; magic waves and, 51–52, 54–56
information fantasies, 2–3, 7, 10, 22, 28, 33, 38, 44, 45, 259
information flows, 9–10, 48, 65, 216–17, 261; liberal politics of, 23; network of, 75
information platform, 44, 57, 64
"Information Pot," photo of, 2
information pots, 1, 3, 6, 7, 9, 10; photo of, 2

Index

information processing, 8, 9, 16, 27, 47, 69
information society, 2, 16, 20, 30, 31, 35, 69, 88; futuristic discourses of, 7; postsocialism and, 32
information systems, 64, 75; body and, 65; digital, 60
information technology, 10, 16, 19, 25, 26, 29, 30, 31, 35, 60, 83, 88, 195, 226, 259, 261; Chinese participation in, 11; emergence of, 33; newness of, 32; waveform-based, 52, 67
information theory, 13, 37, 78, 188, 245; applied, 184; influence of, 162
Information Theory and Esthetic Perception (Moles), 185
information transmission, 46, 49, 52, 61, 62, 64, 67, 70, 71, 74, 81, 82, 83, 170, 175, 205, 216; high-speed, 56; instantaneous, 69; mechanisms of, 43; nonstop, 68
information work, 8, 17, 33, 69, 70, 88, 214
Institute of Research and Modern Education Technology, 61
Institute of Space Medico-Engineering, 46
intelligence, 100, 115–16; cloudsourcing/crowdsourcing of, 84. *See also* artificial intelligence
intelligentsia, 65, 95, 98, 104, 105
interface, 17–22, 109; design of, 92; dissolution of, 18, 19; friction, 90–95; human–machine, 17, 111, 114; objectification/fixation of, 19–20; politics of, 85; revisiting, 109–14; user-friendly, 19, 20, 21, 92, 270n39
internet, 10, 15, 35, 84, 259, 262
Irani, Lilly, 113, 114, 116–17
iron wo/man, 55

Jakobson, Roman, 161, 188
Jameson, Fredric, 246
Jet Propulsion Laboratory, 45
Jin Guantao, 36, 120–21, 122, 123, 124, 125, 126–27, 130; dialectics and, 128; homeostasis and, 141; journal by, 129; modern science and, 136; repetitive cycles and, 144; scientism and, 127; "Toward the Future" and, 131, 142; ultrastable system and, 135, 136, 141
Jin Hezai, 255, 256, 259, 260
Jin Kemu, 52, 184–85, 186
Jin Yong, 220
jishi meixue, 199, 201
Jiuzhou Fantasy Media and Culture Company, 256
Jobs, Steve, 15
Johnston, John, 282n70
Joseph, Branden, 277n68
Journal of Dialectics of Nature, The, 129–30
journals, 52, 121, 129–30; literary, 78, 192; science fiction, 55
Joyce, James, 179, 188

Kaige, Chen, 34, 253
Kehuan haiyang (journal), 55
Kehuan shijie (journal), 55
Kelly, Kevin, 100, 112
Kexue huabao (journal), 110
Kexue wenyi (journal), 55; illustration from, 50
King of the Children (film), 251
Kittler, Friedrich A., 12, 64, 67
knowledge: computing, 92; depoliticized, 103–9; dissemination of, 21, 106; engineering of, 86–87, 89; expert, 90–95, 108, 109; individuality and, 74; level of, 78; mining, 92–93; neutralization of, 36, 103; obtaining, 54;

politicalized, 108; scientific, 32, 52, 101–2, 111, 128; transmission of, 74, 85
knowledge production, 21, 32, 87; mass line of, 103–9
Kong Du, 202, 212
Kubrick, Stanley, 112, 251
Kyōryū Sentai Koseidon (film), 260

labor, 114, 259; affective, 36, 100–103, 104, 218, 228, 268n10; collective, 113; communicative, 36; conditions of, 7; division of, 21, 70, 99; fan, 33; forms of, 26; hierarchies of, 21, 117; individual, 111; industrial mode of, 103; manual, 89; manufacturing, 31; mental, 70, 268n7; physical, 69, 70, 88, 268n7; products of, 110; redistribution of, 99; subjectivity and, 111; visibility/invisibility of, 117; wage, 103, 113
labor relations, reorganization of, 84–85
landscape, 144, 159; Chinese history and, 120; natural, 135; politics of, 139; rural, 37, 152; symbolic, 135; urban, 210
language, 94, 146, 174, 234; cinematic, 122, 137, 151; computer, 91; connectivity and, 161; Freudian, 222; general, 92, 93; international, 151; poetic function of, 161; political, 146; symbolic, 134; technical, 146
Language of New Media, The (Manovich), 212
large-scale integration (LSI), 59
Latham, Michael, 27–28
Lazzarto, Maurizio, 114
Legend of Condor Heroes, The (TV series), 220

Lei Feng, 279n30
Lellis, George, 201, 202, 212, 237
life: politics of, 109–14; urban, 153
Life (film), marriage scene in, 138
liminality, 18, 35, 38, 45, 71, 197, 198, 244–51, 253, 254; cinema of, 22–27; edge of, 78–82
Limits to Growth, The (Club of Rome), 130
Lin Biao, 289n28
Lin Caihong, 90, 99
literature, 23, 33, 150, 164, 165, 183, 184, 188, 200, 201, 237; advertising, 191, 192; experimental, 194; Mao-era, 106; popular, 192; pure, 78, 192; roots-seeking, 78, 189; Western modernist, 149
"Little Red Book" (Mao), 289n28
Li Tuo, 24–25, 144, 150, 223, 224; Chinese cinema and, 136–37
Liu, Lydia, 110, 162, 188
Liu Qingfeng, 36, 120–21, 122, 123, 124, 125, 126, 128, 130, 131, 235; homeostasis and, 141; journal by, 129; love letters and, 127; modern science and, 136; ultrastable system and, 135, 136, 141
Liu Xie, 234, 237, 238
Li Zehou, 130, 131, 136
Locke, John, 65
Lonely Spirit in a Dark Building, The (film), 38, 245, 249, 251, 300; still from, 247, 250, 252, 254
"long-take" theory, 137
Lu Ji, 23, 235, 237, 238
Lu Wenting, 95–101, 102, 103, 104, 107, 108–9, 235
Lyotard, Jean-François, 101–2, 103

machines, 146–47; automatic, 83; cybernetic, 116, 117; humans and, 20, 22, 45–47, 62, 83, 84, 93, 109, 110, 111, 114, 116, 117, 119;

information-processing, 67; intelligent, 111, 115; thinking, 86
Mackay, Donald, 295n15
magic waves, 7, 36, 61, 62; digital, 43–44; extrasensory powers and, 65; information explosion and, 51–52, 54–56; popular imaginations of, 35. *See also* waves
Mang Ke, 131
Manovich, Lev, 212, 213
Mao Zedong, 23, 24, 31, 51, 69, 70, 81, 96, 97, 98, 139–40, 270n43, 279n30, 285n37, 289n28; class politics and, 275n55; Cultural Revolution and, 43; discourse of, 146; intellectual policy of, 79; mass line and, 106; mass science and, 107
market economy, 11, 23, 108, 164, 167, 170, 171, 186, 191, 296n35, 298n49; information and, 37; pragmatics of, 177; transnational, 297n35
"Market Information" (program), 171
marketization, 22, 23, 149, 164, 197, 224, 228, 245, 260, 268n7, 296n35; post-Mao, 69; process of, 38; reforms of, 30
martial arts, 208, 210, 213, 215, 219, 220, 223
Marx, Karl, 29, 43, 127; on general intellect, 114, 282n60; on knowledge/scientific power, 111; polarized society and, 88; social development and, 29; wage labor and, 113
Marxism, 28, 68, 98, 128, 166, 184, 188, 200, 236; classic, 124, 125; knowledge of, 29
Marxism-Leninism, Scientism and, 126–27
mass line, 103–9

Mass Movement, 45–46
Matunara, Humberto R., 140, 141
Ma-Xu Weibang, 253
Ma Yuan, 182–83
McCarthyism, 45
McCorduck, Pamela, 87
McGrath, Jason, 24, 28, 270n43, 295n13
McLuhan, Marshall, 12, 29
media, 18, 22, 29, 33, 34, 163, 197, 208, 221, 222, 260; advertising and, 172; archaic, 262; cinematic, 25, 38; communication, 13, 68; cybernetic environments and, 33; digital, 11, 16, 35, 44, 64, 66, 82, 111, 116; electronic, 25, 191, 195, 215, 216; emergence of, 11, 12, 220; flexibility/convertibility between, 64; home, 219–24; imagination and, 19; information, 43, 44, 204; materiality of, 15, 34; mediation and, 3, 12–17; new, 59, 262; old, 59, 70; Party, 171–72; performance and, 214; popular, 208; psychic, 40, 57; role of, 206, 244; state-owned/operated, 170–71; systems, 165, 172, 191; technical, 12, 16, 186, 274n36; understanding of, 14, 15, 23
media studies, 8, 13, 14, 15, 35, 164, 268n10, 288n22
media theory, 11, 14, 35, 221
mediation, 84, 165, 198, 199, 245; ethics of, 38; media and, 3, 12–17; modes of, 9, 12; postsocialist, 32; precarious, 22–27; process of, 9, 13, 17–18; theory of, 14
medium: concept of, 13; liminal, 198; message and, 161; notion of, 15
memories, 114, 169; cultural, 239, 241; historical, 198; visions without, 239–41, 244
Meng Yue, 189–90

Merleau-Ponty, Maurice, 115
metamorphosis, 196, 204, 208, 213, 296n27
metaphysics, 115, 196, 226
Metz, Christian, 238
Michelangelo, 187
microcomputers, 18, 59, 89
microprocessors, 16, 59, 60, 163
"Mighty Atom," 207–8
Mind Over Machine (Dreyfus and Dreyfus), 115
Ministry of Culture, 220
Ministry of Education, 61
Mistaken Identity (film), 225–26
Misty Poems, 189
modern, 34, 147; depoliticization of, 30; design, 185; notion of, 30; temporalities of, 149–52
modernism, 28, 34, 149–52; aesthetics of, 122, 186; Chinese, 150, 151, 152; literary, 188; restless/perplex and, 151–52; techniques/forms of, 151; Western, 149, 150
modernity, 79, 95; anxiety of, 36, 144; capitalist, 34, 37; embrace of, 44; fantasies/dreams of, 151; high, 153; political, 107; postsocialist, 28; scientific, 107; urban, 152
modernization, 29, 121, 131, 133, 149–52, 259; absence of, 126; anxieties about, 119, 144; arrested development of, 157; Cold War, 122; discourse of, 150, 151; embrace of, 28, 44; forerunners of, 146; ideology of, 126; industrial, 145; strange loops and, 147–48, 149; theory of, 27, 122–26
"Modernization and Modernism" (Xu), 149
"Modernization of Film Language, The" (Zhang), 25
Moles, Abraham, 185, 186, 187, 189

Morgan, Daniel, 201, 293n2, 294n9
Mosco, Vincent, 15
Mu Deyuan, 245
Munsterberg, Hugo, 202
Musical Offering (Bach), 142
MYCIN, 85, 87
"Mysterious Waves," 203

Nagra IV-S recorder, 248, 250, 253; photo of, 252
narratives, 135, 191; revolutionary, 240; science fiction, 261
National Conference of Science, 2, 79
Neo-Confucianists, 133
Neorealism, 25, 37
neuroscience, 90, 110
New Cinema, aesthetic of, 133–40
New Era, 31, 32, 292n79
New Philosophy for New Media (Hansen), 8
Newsletter of Research in the Dialectics of Nature, 130
New Wave, 25, 37, 189
Ni Zhen, 134
noises, 181; information and, 170–75
nonvisual organs, image-recognition through, 52, 54, 63, 66
nostalgia, 31, 52, 80, 261

observer/system dichotomy, polemic of, 140–44
On Shadow Play Writings, 135
Opening and Reforms, 32
"Open Love Letters" (Liu), 127
Open-up, 149
Operations Research, 123–24

Pan Xiao, 98, 279n30
Parapsychological Association, 66
Parsons, Talcott, 124, 125
patterns, formation/self-organization of, 68

Peirce, Charles Sanders, 13
Peking University, 52, 89, 110, 115, 125, 127
People's Daily, 69, 88, 98, 163
perception, 8, 34, 52, 175, 182, 185, 187, 205, 213, 235; aesthetic, 190; extrasensory, 44; multisensory, 25; sensory, 65, 66, 71, 74, 151; understanding, 204; visual, 241
performance, 86, 91, 147, 149, 167, 215, 218, 227, 228; front stage/back stage, 95; media and, 214
Perils of a Rich Boy, The (film), 216
Peters, Benjamin, 269n13
Peters, John, 267n2
Philosophy of the Human, The (Jin), 141
photorealism, 152, 202, 212
physiological conditions, 46, 47, 48, 52, 62, 176, 180
plasticity, 67, 212, 213
poetics, Chinese, 197, 234, 236, 237, 238, 239
politics, 28, 30, 85, 146, 208, 237, 261, 290; aesthetics and, 37; class, 275n55; class-struggle, 79; Cold War, 31, 45; consensual, 29; culture and, 138, 194; depoliticized, 108; intellectual, 164; metatheory of, 26, 27; post-Mao, 126–31, 133; postsocialist, 23, 122, 194
Popular Cinema (journal), 222
postsocialism, 8, 26, 38, 45, 193, 198, 199, 217; as analytic, 27–32; global conditions of, 11; information and, 32, 37; prognostication of, 82
pots. *See* information pots
power: affective, 186–87, 237; authority from, 105; ideological, 197; redistribution of, 10; relations, 22; scientific, 111; social interests and, 75; state, 165, 218, 245; supernatural, 210, 300n76

Prague linguistic circle, 184
Print Gallery (Escher), 142, *143*
production, 21, 111, 174; capitalist, 116, 165; cultural/literary, 164, 172; farm, 284n22; information and, 88; socialist, 31, 275n53; supplies/shortages of, 69. *See also* cultural production
professionalism, 95, 102, 105, 107; depoliticized, 109; neutral, 108
propaganda, 28, 138; political, 170, 201
Prosperity and Crisis (Jin and Liu), 121, 130
Protestant Ethic and the Spirit of Capitalism (Weber), 125, 133
psychoanalysis, 175, 195, 197, 238
psychology, 146, 169, 175, 176, 179, 190, 231
PUFF, 93; dialogue record of, 94
pulse-code modulation (PCM), 57

qi: ancient notion of, 49; black, 51; as waveform information, 48–51
Qian Xuesen, 1, 2, 7, 35, 46, 52, 56, 68, 79, 83–84, 206, 236; Dreyfus and, 114–17; extrasensory powers and, 40–41, 66, 67, 74; metasynthetic engineering and, 84; *qigong* and, 48, 49; somatic science and, 43, 45, 47; systems theory and, 123
Qian Yunxuan, 229
qigong, 35, 47, 55; Chinese medicine and, 48; denunciation of, 10, 49; integration of, 48–49; study of, 2, 49, 51
qigong fever, 1, 10, 48
qigong masters, 1, 47, 48, 50, 55
qigong therapy, *qi* and, 51

radio, 12, 14, 16, 37, 56, 61, 62, 64, 82, 163, 165, 171, 173, 186, 261

rationality, 64, 105, 248; communicative/scientific, 194; cultural, 190; defying, 300n76; scientific, 108, 122; technological, 149
realism, 26, 156, 204, 224, 234, 293n2, 294n4, 295n13; away from, 199–203; Bazinian, 23, 196, 198, 199, 201, 236; cinematic, 38; clichéd, 25; critical, 24; perceptual, 201, 294n9; true, 152; understanding of, 196. *See also* socialist realism
reality, 23, 212, 234, 248; absence of, 241; absolute, 141; distortion of, 137; economic, 165; higher, 196; multiplication of, 25; murkiness of, 26; social, 13, 14; virtual, 83
real world, cinematic world and, 212
"'Rectifying the Name' of Advertising" (Ding), 167
Red Cliff, 240
Red Detachment of Women, The (film), 139
Red Flag (journal), 200
Reforms and Opening, 55, 287n9, 300n76
representation, 26, 154, 216; realistic, 134, 198
research, 186; archaeological, 135; information, 32, 35; interdisciplinary, 66; parapsychological, 66; *qigong*, 49; scientific, 7, 33, 46, 167; technology, 33, 35
River Elegy, 119, 120, 131
robot doctors, 100, 109, 117; advantageousness of, 99; inside/outside text, 85–90
robots, 62, 99, 100, 226, 228, 256; double, 227, *227*; Freudian, 110
Rodowick, D. N., 198
Rofel, Lisa, 268n7

Rostow, Walt, 29
Rural Development Group, 131

Saussure, Ferdinand de, 238
Schiller, Dan, 11
Schmalzer, Sigrid, 107
science, 35, 79, 106, 149, 170; applied, 186; class character of, 107, 108; cognitive, 116; elite, 105, 107; filmmaking and, 137; indigenous, 107; information, 10, 28, 122, 237; management, 123; natural, 127; noetic, 116, 237; optical, 213; philosophical thought and, 127–28; purposeless purpose of, 136; technology and, 32, 153
science fiction, 3, 32, 33, 44, 54, 71, 78, 215, 253, 261; -cum-horror, 225; science popularization and, 79; venues for, 55–56; wave of, 79
Science for the People, 107
Scientific Study Group of *Qigong* (Tsinghua University), 50
scientism, 125, 126–27, 129
screen, 38, 39, 52, 63, 135, 147, 174, 175, 195, 196, 204, 208, 210, 212, 218, 220, 221, 225, 231; cinematic, 215, 216, 221; dissolution of, 27; effects, 63, 64; holographic, 206, 207; television, 57, 59, 60, 63, 64, 232; theatrical, 221
self-consciousness, 52, 100, 195
self-marketing, 220
self-producing system, 143, 144, 146
self-production, 220
self-references, 142, 182; reflexive, 152–54, 156–57
self-reflexivity, 114, 141
self-sacrifice, 96, 98
Shanghai, 40, 61, 130, 167, 219, 222, 253, 255
Shannon, Claude E., 74, 75, 81, 140, 184, 186, 295n15; economic

principles of, 185; general communication system by, 72–73; information theory and, 37
Shao Yanjun, 192, 293n85
Shaviro, Steven, 33, 268n10
shotgun microphone, photo of, 247
shuguang hao (spacecraft), 46
Shu Ting, 3
Sianne Ngai, 217
Sichuan Daily, 39, 40
"Siema" (Dneprov), 110
Siema (robot), 110
signals: processing, 67; selection of, 161; from unknown sources, 233
signifiers: floating, 182; flows of, 163; mystical, 51; verbal/semiotic, 164; words and, 162
signs, 184; conventionality of, 238
Simon, Herbert, 86, 89
simulacra, 196, 198, 203–7, 226, 239, 241, 244
Sinclair ZX81 computer, 59
Sino-Japanese war, 96, 133, 134
"Sleepless Son-in-Law, The" (story), 54–55
sleep time, making use of, 54, 68
Smith, Adam, 29, 88
Sobchack, Vivian, 215
social activities, 123, 170
social agents, 22, 222
social analysis, systems-theory based, 122
social arenas, 10, 25
social changes, 10, 198
social forces, 3, 15, 26, 27, 68, 165
socialism, 7, 9, 24, 31, 32, 192; actually existing, 26; capitalism and, 26; inefficiencies of, 28; information economy and, 33; reality of, 23; state, 98, 126
Socialist Bloc, 124
socialist realism, 23, 135, 137, 178, 179, 192, 196, 198, 199, 200, 201, 223, 224; acknowledging, 26; aim of socialism and, 24; disintegration of, 25; narratives of, 139; revolt against, 191. *See also* realism
social life, 14, 27, 95, 103, 114, 152
social organization, 144, 192, 259
social phenomena, 32, 186
social practices, 22, 43
social relations, 16, 22, 23, 101, 117, 219
Social Science Research Council (SSRC), 27
social system, 30, 125
social theory, 13, 127
social values, 10, 28, 70, 198
society, 7, 129, 135; industrial, 124; modern, 27, 95; oneness of, 124; polarized, 88; Parsonianist conception of, 124; transformation of, 297n36. *See also* information society
Society for China Advertising Studies, 167–68
Society for Psychical Research, 66
socioeconomic changes, 10, 255
socioeconomic conditions, 117, 188
somatic science, 43, 45, 47, 66
Song at Midnight (film), 253
sound, 180; revenge through, 250
space, 176, 204; advertising and, 177; asynchronous, 231; cinematic, 207; discrete, 229–32; domestic, 96; extradiegetic/diegetic, 208; homogenous, 75; living, 196, 212; media, 212; physical, 207; post-socialist, 219; representational, 196; urban, 155
spaceflight, environmental control for, 46
spatiality, 238, 241, 251; temporality and, 135
Spies in the East Harbor (film), 157

"Spiritual-Pollution," campaign against, 79
Stages of Economic Growth (Rostow), 29
State Council, 218
sticky fractions, 168–70
stimuli, 244; suicidal consumption of, 82
Story of the West Wing, The (film), 135
strange loops, 122, 142, *148*, 256, 257, 258, 259; displaced, 144–47, 149; modernization and, 147, 149
"Strange Loops," staging, *148*
structuralism, 13, 124, 162, 188, 189, 190, 195, 238
structure, 15, 47, 184; deep cultural, 126; formation/self-organization of, 68
structure of feeling, 44, 79, 80, 272n6
"Studies on Dialectics of Nature," 276n61
subjectivity, 141; labor and, 111; mobilization of, 56; postsocialist, 22, 25, 32, 197, 198, 219
Sun Ganlu, 183
Sunshine and Showers (film), 218
Superman III (film), 253
systems theory, 48, 68, 121, 128, 141, 144, 184; analytics of, 124; applying, 123

Tang Yijie, 130, 131
Tang Yu, 39
Tao Jing, 251
technology, 8, 28, 34, 55, 79, 89, 102, 106, 111, 149, 170, 198, 212, 251, 254, 262; advances in, 15, 17; audiovisual, 57; biocybernetic, 35; communication, 15, 16, 17, 20, 67, 186; computer, 16, 91, 107; cybernetic, 258; digital, 15; electronic, 180, 226; GPS, 18; holographic, 204, 206; information, 10, 11, 16, 19, 25, 26, 29, 30, 31, 32, 33, 35, 60, 195, 226, 259, 261; intellectual, 69; laser, 206; media, 3, 12, 32, 36, 57, 62, 191, 259; neutralization of, 36, 103; optoelectronic, 206; satellite, 3, 45; science and, 32, 153; social imaginations of, 33; sound, 253; space, 45
telecommunications, 16, 29, 30
telegraphs, 12, 55–56, 145, 267n2
telephones, 16, 59, 64, 67, 159, 160, 162, 163, 175, 225
television, 3, 30, 56–57, 82, 174, 197, 219–24, 232; advertising on, 173; cable, 59, 222; in desert, *232*; development of, 64, 220; digital, 57, 59, 272n3; disk, 60; education and, 274n36; films and, 221–22; holographic, 204; images of, 217; information transmission of, 64; satellite, 61
Television Electronic Disc, 60
television stations, 56, 163, 267n2
temporality, 135, 217, 241, 249, 258; cause-and-effect, 216; regulation of, 69; spatiality and, 135
Terminator (film), 256, 260
Tetsuwan Atomu (anime series), 164
Thacker, Eugene, 9, 12, 245
theaters, 207, 239; attendance at, 219
theory, 12, 198, 295n15; practices of theorization, 199
thinking, 86; associative, 179, 180; image, 200, 201; logical, 236
Third Wave, The (Toffler), 2, 16, 28, 30, 69, 88; book cover of, *4, 5*
thoughts, 234, 236; communication of, 230; images and, 195, 198
"Three For" company, 218–19
Three Spheres II (Yao), 154

Toffler, Alvin, 2, 28, 52, 69, 130, 257, 258; information technology and, 31; on production, 88
"Toward the Future" series, 30, 130, 131, 141–42
transformation, 8, 9, 11, 38, 108, 111, 126, 208, 210, 212, 224, 297n36; generic, 213; political, 31; postsocialist, 35, 85; social, 16, 23, 31, 44, 79, 165, 197
Troubleshooters (film), 218
truth, 102; objective, 104; promulgation of, 285n37; socialist, 24, 25
"Turk, The," 113, 116
2001: A Space Odyssey (Kubrick), 112, 251

ultrastable system, 36, 120, 121, 122–26, 131, 133–40, 141, 149, 157, 190, 259
uncanny double, 227
Understanding Media (McLuhan), 29
universalism, 24, 104, 105
urban areas, industrial, 145
urbanization, 145, 245
urban life, eulogy to, 153
utopia, 23, 31, 33, 34, 79

value, 250; aesthetic, 187; Marxist theorization of, 166–67
Varela, Francisco J., 140, 141
Vercellone, Carlo, 114
Verdery, Katherine, 27, 275n53
videocassettes, 220, 221, 232
Videotext, 59
Virno, Paolo, 113, 114
virtual, 3, 18, 33, 83, 116, 197, 203, 206, 235, 236, 237, 244, 262; actual and, 238
virus-words, intimacy of, 180–81
vision: without memories, 239–41, 244; political, 261; power of, 51; socialist, 26

Visions from a Jail Cell (film), 239; stills from, 240–43
Von Foerster, Heinz, 140, 141

Wang Hui, 108, 297n36
Wang Jing, 125, 287n9, 289n26, 298n49
Wang Meng, 37, 159, 164, 172, 173, 179, 182–83, 189, 191, 193, 287n1, 289n28; "The Blinking of the Bell," 159, 177–78, 180, 181; "Fine Tuning," 173; formalism/structuralism and, 162; "Green Sun," 182, 183, 190; human mind and, 180; "A Lost Dream," 70, 76, 77, 78; "Thrilling," 189, 190; "To Alice," 181, 183, 189
Wang Ruoshui, 98
Wang Shouzhi, 169
Wang Weiyi, 207
Wark, McKenzie, 9, 12
waveforms, 35, 70; abstract, 74; extrasensory powers as, 62–63; information technology and, 67; *qi* as, 48–51; sensory data and, 67; universal power of, 74
waves, 196, 198; as digital, 64–69; electromagnetic, 52, 54, 221; frequency of, 81; information, 40, 56–57, 59–64; mysterious, 6; nonsensical, 78–82; optical, 213; random, 81; theory of, 203; ultrasonic, 81. *See also* magic waves
Wead, George, 201, 202, 212, 237
Wealth of Nations (Smith), 88
Weber, Max, 122, 125, 126, 133
Web Services, 112
Weeks, Kathy, 268n10
Wei Yahua, 85, 280n37
Wiener, Norbert, 47, 68, 276n61
Wild Mountain (film), 251, 253
Williams, Raymond, 14, 216, 272n6

Wired, 100
Woolf, Virginia, 179
Working Man II (Yao), 154, 155
"Worldwide New Technology Revolution and Our Strategies, A," 88–89
World Wide Web, 10, 83, 255
writing: avant-garde, 293n85; experimental, 181, 182; fiction, 190; Mao-style, 188; modernist, 22
Wu Liang, 172, 176, 177, 183, 184
Wu Tianming, 138

Xiaoshuo Lin (journal), 78; illustrations from, 76, 77
Xu Chi, modernism and, 149–50

Yamaha Fish Stall (film), 218
Yang Chunding, 237
Yan Hairong, 98
Yao, C. J. (Yao Qingxhang), 152, 154; constructivist method of, 153; drawing by, 155; material culture and, 153; painting by, 155; self-referential play by, 156
Yao Xiaomeng, 113, 212, 234, 236, 244; cinematic effects and, 237–38, 239; idea-image and, 238; psychoanalytic terms and, 197; signs and, 238; work of, 195, 196; *yixu* and, 238

yellow earth, 119–20, 134, 144; rural landscapes and, 152; transhistorical image of, *143*
Yellow Earth (film), 34, 37, 119, 134, 136, 138, 140, 144; cinematic images from, 121–22; cinematography of, 133; landscape of, 139, 159; realism and, 234; rural areas and, 145; still from, *120*; ultrastable system and, 141
Yellow River, 119, 120, 134, 139
Ye Yonglie, 260
yixiang. *See* idea-image
Yuan Ying, 199, 201
Yu Guangyuan, 130

Zhang Nuanxin, 25, 137
Zhang Xianliang, 207
Zhang Xudong, 30, 34, 137, 139, 151, 191, 292n79
Zhang Yimou, 34, 133, 134, 195
Zhang Zeming, 218
Zhao Yuezhi, 11
Zhao Ziyang, 88–89
Zheng Dongtian, 134
Zheng Jiqiao, 200, 201
Zheng Wenguang, 260
Zhihui shu (journal), 55
Zhongguo Qingnian, 279n30
Zhongguo Wenhua shuyuan, 130
Zhou Chuanji, 221–22
Zhou Yang, 24, 200, 270n43

XIAO LIU is assistant professor in the Department of East Asian Studies at McGill University.